12/81

Barbara,

Thought you'd enjoy some old recipes from Good Old New England. Enjoy

Love,
Jack

The Mystic Seaport Cookbook

THE
Mystic Seaport
COOKBOOK

❧ 350 YEARS ❧
OF NEW ENGLAND COOKING

By Lillian Langseth-Christensen

WITH THE COOPERATION OF

The Marine Historical Association, Incorporated

GALAHAD BOOKS · NEW YORK

Contents

An Introduction to Mystic Cookery

In the town of Mystic, Connecticut, the cookery grew out of an exciting combination of circumstances. It evolved out of parent recipes brought over by the early English settlers, out of the natural foods they found here, out of Indian cooking, and out of necessity; but above all it grew out of the sea.

The sea, which many of the settlers had never seen before they crossed it, became their mainstay. It produced the fish for their nets, the oil for their lamps, and the trade that was ultimately to make the region a strong maritime colony.

The climate and location of Mystic isolated it in a way that also strongly influenced its cooking. The soil was rocky, the growing season short, and the natural resources few. The settlers had to be provident. They had to dry their vegetables and salt their cod for the winter. It is no wonder that baked beans and fish chowders developed as naturally as the wonderful uses for maple syrup and cranberries.

Mystic grew and prospered from the sea. Her cookery became a combination of seafarers' needs and the treasures they brought back from their voyages. It grew out of cooking on new soil and under new conditions such as cooking afloat. Mystic vessels sailed farther and farther afield; in time, they sailed to the Mediterranean, the Indian Ocean and the Orient. Whale oil from every sea was brought to New

London, New Bedford and Nantucket. Spices came as well—jars of ginger and dried cinnamon bark. The characteristic cooking of Mystic took on lovely nuances, new scents and seasonings.

~~~

In gathering authentic recipes for this collection, I have been privileged to use three out-of-print cookbooks. Mrs. Mary Greenman Davis gave me her copy of *Stonington Cooks and Cookery*, Miss Margaret Mallory let me have her annotated copy of *The Old Gem Cookbook*, and Mrs. Lydia G. Andrews allowed me to use her old copy of *The Food Log*. The recipes I borrowed are identified in the book, but I would like to thank them especially for sharing valuable possessions with me. As an ardent collector, I know how hard it is to hand over a treasured cookbook to anyone, let alone drop it into an unresponsive mailbox. *The Food Log* is attractively bound in two hard covers connected with thin leather thongs tied with square knots. Mrs. Andrews, who edited the book, writes, "We had a committee tie those square knots."

While I have not had a committee to tie knots, I have had friends, digging friends, who found rare recipes for everything I asked for and more than I had ever hoped for. Mrs. Alma Eshenfelder started a movement for Portuguese bread baking, and Mr. Critchell Rimington, the publisher of *Yachting*, stirred up swarms of recipes from his amphibious world. Friends discovered recipes that are as much a record of the past as they are a guide to future cooking. They were tested and adapted, and in many cases they were left just exactly as they were found. Every recipe is part of the history of Mystic, the story of its growth from a few huddled houses to its present commemorative role in the history of America.

Mystic cooking today is still a combination of pioneer, Indian and English cookery. Here you will find the dishes that made New England famous—corn and cornmeal dishes, baked beans, and best of all, the clambake. And yet, after 350 years, this cookery is still individual; you will find many recipes for the basic dishes, but no two are the same. Influencing everything is the sea, which provided the livelihood of Mystic and offered it treasures of food.

My publishers and I wish to thank the members of the Marine Historical Association and friends of Mystic Seaport for their enthusiastic response. Interest in the history of the sea and food seem to go happily hand in hand. We are grateful for the recipes which were contributed as well as for the extra thoughtfulness and effort that brought them in promptly, with the personal touch which goes only with recipes that are really used and enjoyed at home.

~~~~~

Around the year A.D. 1000 the Vikings spent several seasons on the North Atlantic coast of America, but as far as we know they never attempted a permanent settlement. The Dutch explored the coast of New England in the seventeenth century, and one of them drew a map dated 1616 which included the Siccanemos River, now the Mystic River. After 1620 there were no more false starts. The Puritans were here to stay.

By 1630, one of the small groups that broke away to develop a new area had selected the mouth of the Siccanemos and started the settlement that is now Mystic. These were people who were searching for freedom to practice the principles of their religion. We who are concerned with what they cooked and ate can only describe them as serious and upstanding.

Inevitably, the Puritans came upon American Indians of the coastal tribes. Many of the Indians were knowledgeable in growing and preparing food, and generous in their readiness to teach the settlers all they knew. Nevertheless, there were constant hazards. The Mystic men, however, were a steadfast people with a purpose. Undaunted, they faced the hardships and labors of establishing themselves in what one of them described as "a howling wilderness."

Mystic men worked, and Mystic wives made it possible for men to work—an equally important job. The wives turned primitive little houses into homes and hand-to-mouth eating into nourishing meals. Besides spinning and weaving, sewing and knitting, Mystic wives made soap, candles and emulsions. They grew and dried herbs; they planted and tended the vegetable garden and stocked the root cellar. They dried the pod vegetables, made jams, conserves and preserves, pickles and relishes. They sometimes milked the cow, always churned the butter, and made cheese and sausages. They also cleaned house, washed and ironed, cared for the children, and nursed the sick. They salted and corned and smoked the meats and baked the bread; they cooked the meals. And besides all that—they watched for the ships.

After the first severe winters, or because of the memory of those hungry times, the settlers lived with the utmost providence. Their larders, root cellars, pork barrels, canisters—right down to their neatly bunched dried herbs—were as reliable as our best-stocked pantry shelves and freezers. The meals changed in character with the seasons, but rarely did they lack wholesomeness. Dried vegetables gave way to fresh in summer; fresh cod was replaced by salt cod in winter; bacon and salt pork were eaten all year round.

One of the first things that had to be done after the establishment of a new settlement was clearing the land for pasturage. The north-eastern woodlands of America offered the Indians all they needed: game in the forests; fish in the lakes and streams; shellfish, seafish and salt along the ocean; wild grapes, berries and apples; and adequate soil for their corn and beans. That was all very well for the Indian way of diet, but the settlers wanted their milk, butter, cheese and eggs. Every vessel that crossed the Atlantic brought its share of cows and fowls, pigs and sheep. The custom of carrying a fresh cow to supply milk for children continued for more than 250 years.

Trees were felled to build houses and ships, rocks and stones were dragged aside and, for lack of other purposes, used to build New England's endless miles of stone walls. As soon as there were green pastures, milk and butter were available. Butter was stored and traded to New London, Boston or even the West Indies. Milk went into cheeses, and almost every home had a churn and a cheese press. In an age when waste was unthinkable, all the milk that was not consumed went into cheeses that could be stored for long periods. The skimmed milk left from butter and cheese making was fed to the hogs.

English mothers taught their daughters the skills of cookery, and many a young bride came to New England knowing how to boil a pudding, bake a tart, and roast a joint. The application of this basic knowledge to the materials on hand was the basis of Colonial cookery.

England's thin pancakes, requiring a special pan, became New England's thick, nourishing griddle cakes, slapjacks and flapjacks. Soups became chowders, and tarts of complicated puff pastry became pies. Piecrust was made with lard and water and pancakes from cornmeal.

~~~

The great whaling ports along the New England coast have given way to teeming modern cities. Many of the memorable landmarks have been destroyed and, except in name, forgotten. Very little would remain if the flavor of the times had not been preserved at Mystic Seaport, and if the *Charles W. Morgan,* last of the great whaling ships, had not come to rest there. Mystic Seaport shows us what has not survived elsewhere: a picture of an era and an industry, a picture of vitality, courage, stamina, generosity. Our contemporary visions have widened so rapidly that today, if it were not for Mystic Seaport, we would find it difficult to bring into focus the life of the New England farmers and whalemen.

Elsewhere we are surprised by museum collections of armor, costumes and beds, which show us how small everything was. The bunks in the forecastle of the *Charles W. Morgan,* where the whalemen slept, will come as a shock. There have been visitors to Mystic Seaport who saw the bunks on the *Charles W. Morgan* and simply assumed that whalemen were small. Actually, they were big and strong, but their bunks were short so that they could wedge themselves in and be braced against the motion of the ship.

The surprise at those sleeping arrangements is mild compared to the reaction to a visit to the galley—the cookroom or kitchen of a sailing vessel—a few square feet and a small iron stove, no larger than the bo's'n's locker, from which to feed a crew of strong, hardworking men for voyages that lasted for years. The galley and utensils make us aware of the constant difficulties, the almost unsurmountable obstacles and handicaps that had to be overcome to produce a single meal. The galley was often a small house on deck, usually forward, so that the smoke and smells of cooking would go forward with the wind. In severe storms the entire galley was sometimes carried away and the ship was left as destitute as a house without a kitchen. On the *Charles*

W. Morgan at Mystic Seaport the galley is below, next to the bo's'n's locker, and the average housewife would not be able to get a family dinner in it, let alone feed captain and crew. The fact remains that the cook did feed large strong men from a galley he could just turn around in.

As we adjust to the size of everything and consider what was accomplished by these whalers and what they contributed to the history of America, we recognize that the size of these seaports and ships was not in scale with the great individuals who built the seaports and manned the ships.

In the life of an average Mystic seaman, he ate as many meals on land as afloat. It stands to reason that he longed constantly for the land meals when he was at sea and expected homecoming to be all he had been dreaming about. There were no Mystic wives who were indifferent cooks. They had to give their husbands meals to remember and to return to. However, we hear that after 1650 Mystic settlers did not depend entirely on their wives for their food. Many sea captains were excellent cooks and took pleasure in reproducing dishes they had tasted on their voyages.

Although whaleships did not carry butter for the crew, the captain had butter and there were methods for keeping it reasonably fresh. The Vikings and later the Norwegian seamen practically sailed on the sturdy cheeses of Scandinavia. New England's cheeses were never as dense, but they combined the same virtues of being nourishing and imperishable. Other foods carried to sea were pies and gingerbreads. You will find among the recipes foods that make good galley fare today.

Life at sea and life on shore were closely involved. For instance, for every sea term that came to be used on land, there is a land term that has gone to sea. In Mystic the men that went to sea tended the farm between voyages and many of their expressions originated in the farmyard. *Gear*, *rig* and *tack* are harness words that went to sea. On the other hand, *to broach a subject, set out on a different tack* and *mug up* are sea terms that have come on land. The word *galley*, which has been mentioned as the cookhouse of a ship, is also practically everything else. It is an oar-propelled vessel with or without sails, or a small boat carried by a man-of-war. In the printing trade it is a boat-shaped tray of type and also the proof sheet taken from the type.

~~~

Much of our present-day cookery, which is supposed to be full of new departures and imagination, is simply a rediscovery of what our great-grandmothers knew perfectly well. However, these revivals often lack the delicate touches that made them great.

Who today puts three or four leaves from a peach tree into an apple pie? or snips off the little white ends of some rose petals and sticks the petals under the top crust of a pie? Who grinds up a few pine needles for the goose or pheasant stuffing? or goes to the trouble of crushing a few juniper berries for the sauce?

We have lost much variety and flavor in our constant short-cutting, and we have arrived at a banality that a smart pepper mill and some frozen chives won't cure. It is true times have changed and we would be foolish if we did not accept the great advances made in the food industry. All we urge you to do is to reject the *poor* changes. For the purpose of these recipes, whip fresh cream, use fresh fruits and vegetables when possible, but you need not go back to baking bread for the bread pudding.

While I have not specifically suggested using packaged pie crust or canned bouillon, there is no reason why today's cooks should not avail themselves of these excellent convenience products. When time is short do, indeed, use canned products, concentrates, and other prepared basic foods. Do not, however, combine a can of cream soup with a can of fish in a casserole and think for one moment that you are reproducing Great-great Aunt Abigail's fish pudding.

~~~

It was possible to write this book because of the invaluable sources of historical research material that were made available to me by The Marine Historical Association and Mystic Seaport of Mystic, Connecticut. Many of the members of the Association, now internationally situated, descend from old New England families who have collected and treasured inherited recipes. Their recipes have added to the rich materials which were already collected. It is my hope that this book will illustrate the link between the cookery of the family at home and the cookery of the seafaring members of the Mystic community.

LILLIAN LANGSETH-CHRISTENSEN

I do not know the difference
between the bow and the stern of a ship,
but there is one expression which
I do know and everyone who has ever
been near the sea knows, and
I say it here with feeling:
CHOW DOWN!

PUBLISHER'S NOTE

RELIVING history presents many problems in time—and space. One solution to experiencing past events vicariously is to immerse oneself in the physical setting of a bygone era. Surrounded by homes, furniture, and equipment that were part of the everyday life of another age, the imagination takes over and the clock is turned back.

That is the philosophy on which The Marine Historical Association at Mystic Seaport at Mystic, Connecticut, was founded. It is also the "why" of *The Mystic Seaport Cookbook*.

Mystic Seaport recreates the atmosphere of a nineteenth-century New England shipyard and waterfront village. *The Mystic Seaport Cookbook* is a re-creation of three hundred and fifty years of cooking in New England, a composite of the recipes that were exchanged by our ancestors along the seacoast.

As the visitor walks along the main streets of Mystic Seaport he steps back in time when he passes the tavern, the cooperage, the hoop-maker's shop, the firehouse, the apothecary, the general store—in short, the pieces that made the patchwork quilt that was life in the American whaling days of the 1800s.

The refurbished buildings and the ships at the wharves cannot be brought home as souvenirs, but the recipes used by the early inhabitants are easily carried away. What could be a more enjoyable way of re-capturing the feelings of a tired seafarer returning home than sitting down to the sort of feast that may have been waiting for him? Wives of Mystic sailors spent months, even years waiting for their ships to come home—ample time in which to plan meals that must have verged on the sumptuous.

Funk & Wagnalls is proud to publish the product of Lillian Langseth-Christensen's study of eating habits on the shores of the Mystic River and in the ships that set sail from its port. Many of the dishes are taken from old Mystic family recipe books, treasured heirlooms now but day-to-day cookbooks in the past. All have been made practical for use in twentieth-century kitchens. And while we do not expect readers to rise from a Mystic meal ready to set sail on the nearest whaling ship, you may wish you could.

CHAPTER I

~~~

Appetizers, Salads and Dressings

WHEN Mystic Seaport was a small settlement, soups, stews, chowders and bread were usually the entire meal. As the village grew, meals grew and soups dwindled down to being the first course. Anything served before the soup was unheard of, and the word "appetizer" would have offended the generations which worked up their good healthy appetites with good healthy work.

When Mystic started to eat a little something before the soup it came, quite naturally, out of the sea. Later fruits and spiced cranberry juice were added, and finally Mystic got down to enjoying the hour before dinner and made some excellent contributions to it.

ℰ𝒳 Clam Meringues

Excellent with cocktails, or as a light luncheon dish served with a salad.

1 can (7½ ounces) minced clams	Salt
Grated rind of 1 lemon	Paprika
1 teaspoon lemon juice	8 thin slices of white bread
⅓ cup stiff mayonnaise	3 egg whites

Combine well-drained clams, lemon rind, juice, mayonnaise, salt to taste and a dash of paprika. Set in refrigerator while preparing bread rounds. With a 2-inch cookie cutter, cut 3 rounds from each slice of bread. Arrange the 24 rounds on a cookie sheet. Put it under a hot broiler. Leave broiler door open and watch carefully until rounds are toasted, less than 1 minute. Take rounds out with a pancake turner as they brown. Toast only one side.

Beat egg whites stiff, fold them into the clam mixture, and mound it high on the untoasted sides of the rounds. Put them back on the cookie sheet and sprinkle lightly with paprika. Put them back under the broiler. Again leave broiler door open and stand by with the pancake turner. The meringues will puff and brown in ½ minute. Serve at once. Makes 24 rounds, 8 servings.

Clams on the Half Shell

6 to 12 clams	⅓ to ½ cup cocktail sauce
1 lemon wedge	1 parsley sprig

Wash clams well and chill them for 2 to 3 hours. Open clams with a dull paring knife and discard the top shell. Arrange clams on half shells in circles on large, deep plates filled with crushed ice. Garnish each plate with lemon and parsley. Push a small cocktail-sauce glass down into the ice in the center of each plate and fill with Cocktail Sauce (below).

Accompany the clams with oyster crackers, freshly grated or well-drained bottled horseradish, and Tabasco.
Makes 1 serving.

COCKTAIL SAUCE I

- 1 teaspoon dry mustard
- 2 teaspoons lemon juice
- 1 cup chili sauce
- 1 cup tomato ketchup
- 2 teaspoons Worcestershire sauce
- ½ teaspoon salt
- 1 teaspoon freshly ground black pepper

Stir mustard into lemon juice. Add other ingredients, stir well, and chill until needed.
Makes 2 cups.

Oysters on the Half Shell

- 6 to 8 oysters per person
- Shaved ice
- Lemon wedges
- Freshly ground black pepper
- Oyster crackers
- Thinly-sliced buttered dark bread
- ⅓ cup Cocktail Sauce (below)
- Freshly grated horseradish
- Tabasco

Prepare as for Clams on the Half Shell (above).

COCKTAIL SAUCE II

From New London. An early twentieth-century recipe
Contributed by Miss Hyla Snider

- 1 tablespoon vinegar
- 1 tablespoon Worcestershire sauce
- 2 tablespoons lemon juice
- 1 tablespoon grated horseradish
- 3 tablespoons tomato ketchup
- ½ teaspoon Tabasco
- ½ teaspoon salt

Mix together and serve in small glasses as cocktail sauce.
Makes ½ cup.

ᴄᵛ⅄ Marinated Shrimps I

A present-day Connecticut host serves marinated shrimps with Bloody Marys at noon on Sundays. You can hardly see the house for all the cars parked out in front.

Prepare these the day before they will be served.

3 teaspoons salt	2 dashes of Tabasco
2½ pounds frozen shelled shrimps, thawed	3 generous grinds of Tellicherry pepper
3 large yellow onions, sliced paper-thin	3 tablespoons smallest capers
1 cup oil	3 tomatoes, peeled, seeded and chopped
½ cup tarragon vinegar	¼ cup finely chopped parsley
½ cup white vinegar	1 small avocado, peeled, pitted and diced
3 teaspoons celery seeds	

Bring a quart of water to a rolling boil in a large kettle. Add 1 teaspoon of the salt and drop in about one third of the shrimps. Stand by with a slotted spoon. As soon as the water returns to a boil, time the shrimps and boil them for just 2½ minutes. Take them out with the slotted spoon. Continue until all the shrimps are boiled and well drained. If the water in the kettle starts to boil over, take the kettle off the heat for a moment until it subsides. Drop the onion slices into rapidly boiling water with ½ teaspoon of the salt and boil for 1 minute, just long enough to wilt them and separate the slices into rings. Combine oil, vinegars, celery seeds, Tabasco, remaining 1½ teaspoons salt, the pepper, and capers. Add warm shrimps and onions and stir to mix well. Refrigerate for 24 hours.

Just before serving, stir in tomatoes and half of the parsley. Pour into a chilled bowl and sprinkle remaining parsley and avocado dice over the top.

Makes 8 servings.

ℰ✗ Marinated Shrimps II

Prepare shrimps exactly as in the foregoing recipe, substituting lemon and lime juice for the oil and vinegar and omitting the celery seeds. Use 4 lemons, juice and grated rind, and 4 limes, juice only.

ℰ✗ Garlic-Broiled Shrimps

2 pounds shrimps, about 15 to a pound
4 garlic cloves, crushed
½ onion, chopped fine
¼ cup chopped parsley
⅔ cup butter
Salt and freshly ground black pepper

Shell shrimps, but leave tails on. Cut down the back with a sharp knife, rinse out sand vein, and flatten out. Pat dry with a kitchen towel. Stir garlic, onion and parsley into butter over low heat. Add salt and pepper to taste. Dip shrimps into the butter and arrange them on a shallow heatproof dish or on a foil-lined broiler rack. Broil on top broiler shelf for about 7 minutes, or until sizzling. Serve from platter with remaining garlic butter poured over.
Makes 6 servings.

ℰ✗ Shrimps in Sauce

2 pounds shrimps, about 15 to a pound
3 tablespoons tarragon vinegar
¼ onion, minced
¾ cup mayonnaise, well beaten
¾ cup chili sauce
¼ cup sweet pickle relish, well drained
3 tablespoons freshly grated horseradish, or 1 tablespoon bottled horseradish, all moisture pressed out
2 tablespoons chopped parsley

Shell and devein shrimps. Boil a few at a time in salted water for just 4 minutes. Drain and sprinkle with vinegar. Beat onion into mayonnaise and chili sauce. Add relish and horseradish. Pour sauce over shrimps just before serving. Sprinkle with parsley.

Serve as a cocktail-party appetizer with a cocktail pick in each shrimp. Serve as a first-course shrimp cocktail by dividing over 6 lettuce leaves in 6 stemmed cocktail glasses.

Shrimp Rounds

12 slices of thin white bread	½ of 3-ounce package of cream cheese
1½ pounds cold cooked shrimps, about 24, peeled and deveined	2 tablespoons sour cream or sweet cream
4-ounce wedge of Roquefort cheese, at room temperature	½ tablespoon sherry
	1 teaspoon minced onion
	3 tablespoons minced parsley

Cut two 1¾-inch bread rounds from each slice. Peel, devein, and cook shrimps (see above). Crush cheeses and whip them into a soft spread with sour cream, sherry and onion. Spread cheese generously on bread rounds. Press a shrimp down on each, leaving a border of cheese. Roll the border lightly in parsley. Enough should adhere to make it look green. Serve as an appetizer with cocktails.

Makes 24 rounds, 12 servings.

Broiled Lobster in Clam Shells

36 clam shells	¼ cup chili sauce
2 teaspoons soft butter	2 tablespoons tarragon vinegar
1 pound cooked lobster meat, diced	2 teaspoons dry mustard
12 slices of bacon, each cut into 3 pieces	1 teaspoon celery salt
1 cup mayonnaise	1 teaspoon paprika
	¼ teaspoon sugar
	Salt, if needed

Lightly butter the clam shells and divide the lobster meat among them. Fry bacon until just crisp, drain, and place 1 piece over the lobster in each clam shell. Stir remaining ingredients into a smooth sauce and pour a heavy layer over each piece of bacon. Put shells under a hot broiler and brown lightly with the broiler door open. Broil for 3 minutes, just long enough to heat the lobster through.
Makes 6 servings.

ℰ✗ Crabmeat-Stuffed Eggs

In Mystic Seaport, they say eggs should be stuffed with fish or shellfish.

8 hard-cooked eggs, cut lengthwise into halves
1 cup well-drained crabmeat,*
   flaked

½ cup mayonnaise
1 teaspoon minced onion
½ teaspoon paprika
16 little parsley sprigs

Take yolks out of eggs. Rice the yolks through a coarse sieve and set aside. Fill whites with crabmeat stirred with mayonnaise, onion and paprika. Sprinkle riced egg yolk over each egg and garnish each top with a parsley sprig.
Makes 8 servings.

ℰ✗ Crabmeat Cocktail

2 pounds fresh or frozen crabmeat, well drained
1 tablespoon minced onion
3 tablespoons sweet green
   pickle relish, all moisture
   pressed out
½ cup chili sauce

½ to ⅔ cup mayonnaise
Salt
6 lettuce leaves
3 hard-cooked eggs, separated
   and riced
3 tablespoons minced parsley

* Use fresh lump crabmeat, frozen, thawed or canned.

Pick over crabmeat. Combine onion, relish, chili sauce, mayonnaise and salt to taste. Fold in the crabmeat and add a little more mayonnaise to taste. Divide over 6 lettuce-leaf-lined cocktail glasses and sprinkle with riced egg white, riced egg yolk and parsley.
Makes 6 servings.

⚔ Miniature Crabmeat Soufflés

12 slices of white bread	½ teaspoon dry mustard
½ pound flaked crabmeat, or 1 package frozen crabmeat, thawed and drained	¼ cup Thick White Sauce (page 83)
¾ cup homemade lemon mayonnaise	1 teaspoon grated onion
	3 egg whites, beaten very stiff
	Paprika

Cut twelve 2¼-inch rounds from each slice of bread. Toast under broiler 4 inches from the source of heat on one side only for about 1 minute, until pale golden. Combine crabmeat with mayonnaise, mustard, white sauce and onion, and fold in stiffly beaten egg whites. Pile the mixture high on toast rounds, using all of it for the 24 rounds. Arrange on a baking sheet. Sprinkle generously with an even dusting of paprika. Bake under the same hot broiler until puffed and golden, 4 to 5 minutes. Watch them carefully, because they burn very quickly.

For a luncheon dish or first course, cut 8 rounds as large as the bread will allow. Prepare in the same way as the small ones. Garnish with parsley and serve one to a person.
Makes 12 cocktail servings or 8 luncheon servings.

⚔ Hot Ripe Olives

From Quisset Harbor

Heat super-colossal ripe olives in their own liquor until they are heated through but not boiling. Drain. Stick a cocktail pick into each olive. Serve in a covered dish. If these are served at a large party, serve in fresh batches as they are not good after they are cold.

Cheese and Onion Dip

1 package (8 ounces) cream cheese
½ small onion, grated
3 to 4 tablespoons mayonnaise
Salt

4 carrots, scraped and cut into quarters, then cut into thin slivers, or 1 head of celery, scraped and divided into short stalks

Let cheese come to room temperature. Beat it with onion and mayonnaise. Add more mayonnaise if necessary to bring to dip consistency. Transfer to a small bowl and stick carrot or celery stalks into it, porcupine fashion.
Makes about 12 servings.

Cold Cauliflower with Curried Mayonnaise

In an emergency, when there is little time to prepare for unexpected guests, divide a raw cauliflower into small, bite-sized flowerets and serve them around a bowl of curried mayonnaise.

Beat 1 cup mayonnaise until light. Place 2 tablespoons mayonnaise with 1 tablespoon curry powder in a small cup and stir until smooth and until all lumps have been crushed. Stir mixture back into the beaten mayonnaise. Repeat this process until the desired curry flavor has been reached. The curried mayonnaise will become a little hotter as it ripens.

Other crisp, iced, raw vegetables such as cucumber and zucchini slices may be added to the cauliflower to make a greater variety.

Raw Cucumber Slices

4 medium-sized cucumbers, as straight as possible

Seasoning salt or roughly ground black pepper

Score cucumbers with a fluted knife or a fork. Dry and cut lengthwise into halves. Cut each half into 4 or more lengthwise wedges. Pat them dry with a kitchen towel. Arrange the long cucumber wedges on a bed of shaved ice in a serving platter and sprinkle generously with seasoning salt or fresh roughly ground black pepper. Chill for a few minutes and serve, or serve at once. These are crisp and appetizing and very welcome to weight watchers.

Makes 12 to 16 servings.

Stuffed Endive

1 package (8 ounces) Roquefort cheese

½ of 3-ounce package cream cheese

1 tablespoon sherry

3 to 4 stalks of endive, trimmed and separated into leaves

Crush cheeses with sherry and stir into a smooth paste. Fill into crisp endive leaves. Arrange on a platter and serve.

Makes about 12 servings.

Roquefort Hamburgers

From *The Log* of Mystic Seaport, 1967

1½ pounds beef chuck, ground

3 ounces Roquefort cheese

6 to 8 tablespoons paprika

Divide meat into about 24 even parts. Shape each part around a small cube of Roquefort cheese. If cheese crumbles, press it into a compact cube before rolling the meat around it. Sprinkle palms with paprika and

roll the little hamburgers into even rounds. Roll them in additional paprika until heavily coated and arrange on rack over a foil-lined broiler pan. Broil in infra-red broiler or in oven broiler, set as hot as it will go, until the hamburgers are browned, 3 to 4 minutes on each side.
Makes 8 servings.

HOT HOT SAUCE

1 cup tomato ketchup	1 cup freshly grated horserad-
½ cup Dijon mustard	ish or well-drained bottled
½ teaspoon Maggi seasoning	horseradish

Stir ketchup, mustard and seasoning together until smooth; fold in horseradish. Store in a covered container in refrigerator until needed. Serve with hot Roquefort Hamburgers.

☙ Cheese Pigs

From *The Log* of Mystic Seaport, 1967

8 ounces sharp Cheddar cheese	1 egg, beaten with 1 tablespoon
½ pound butter	water
2 cups flour	Salt
½ teaspoon salt	Shaved almonds, or poppy, car-
	away, or sesame seeds

Put cheese through meat grinder. Work into a smooth dough with butter, flour and ½ teaspoon salt. Chill until needed. Roll out thin on a lightly floured pastry canvas with a stockinette-covered rolling pin. Cut out dough with a little "pig" cookie cutter and place pigs on unbuttered baking sheets. Brush tops with egg, then sprinkle with salt and almonds, or with poppy, caraway, or sesame seeds and salt. Bake in a preheated 325° F. oven until just golden, 10 to 12 minutes. Unless you are certain of the accuracy of your oven, check after 8 minutes. Take from baking sheets with a pancake turner, cool, and store in a covered container until needed.
Makes about 2 dozen pigs.

ꭾ Cheese Ball

1 cup walnut meats, chopped fine	8 ounces cream cheese
2 tablespoons butter	8 ounces Roquefort cheese
1 pound yellow sharp Cheddar cheese	3 tablespoons sherry (optional)
	Salt
	1 parsley sprig

Put walnuts and butter in a 200° F. oven while preparing the cheese. Bring all cheeses to room temperature. Put through food grinder and work into a smooth ball with or without sherry. Add salt to taste if desired. Chill for 20 minutes if the ball becomes too soft to handle.

Transfer walnuts to stove top and fry, stirring until golden. Drain on paper towels. Roll cheese ball in the nuts to coat it completely. Press them down slightly. Garnish top with parsley and serve with crackers. Makes 16 to 20 servings.

ꭾ Spiced Cranberry Juice

½ cup dark brown sugar	2 cans cranberry jelly
3 cups cranberry juice	2 cups pineapple juice
Pinch of grated nutmeg	12 whole cloves
½ teaspoon ground cinnamon	3 tablespoons butter
½ teaspoon ground allspice	Cinnamon

Boil sugar, 1 cup of the cranberry juice and the ground spices for 10 minutes. Add cranberry jelly and beat or blend until smooth. Add remaining cranberry juice and pineapple juice and heat to boiling. Serve hot in 6 mugs with 2 cloves in each portion and a small pat of butter floated on each. Sprinkle butter with additional cinnamon if preferred. Makes 6 servings.

❧ Spiced Elderberry Juice

Unfermented

4 quarts ripe elderberries, stems removed

Sugar

Piece of fresh gingerroot (about 2-inches long)

7 whole cloves

3 allspice berries

Spread elderberries in a wide pan and heat in a 250° F. oven until they are soft and juicy. Press and crush them with a wooden potato masher or mallet to extract all juice. Strain off the juice into a kettle, squeezing remaining juice from the pulp. To every cup of juice add 1 cup sugar. Tie spices into a small muslin bag and hang it in the juice by a little kitchen string. Boil the juice and sugar gently for 30 minutes. Taste after 10 minutes and every 5 minutes thereafter. When the juice is spiced to taste, remove the spice bag. Cool the wine; when cold, strain it well and funnel it into bottles. Cork tightly and store in refrigerator. Makes about 2 quarts.

❧ Mystic Salads

Salads were served in Mystic only during the summer months, and then they appeared in a separate course after the meat. A tomato in winter created a furor in Mystic as late as 1922.

The early Mystic settlers remembered the "sallets" of England and used their gourds and root vegetables when green vegetables were not available. Pickled beet salads and onion salads were eaten during the winter. Fresh window-box herbs or dried herbs from the herb garden were used to change their flavors. The whalers' wives' spice cupboards produced cloves, mustard seeds and peppers. The results were sometimes a cross between a salad and a relish, but they went far to enhance the winter meals. Potatoes were not introduced to the United States until 1719, but they were common in Connecticut before the Revolution and potato salads were as popular as warm potato dishes.

New England taverns and inns introduced the custom borrowed from the South of placing a little appetizer or salad, hot breads and a relish tray before the guest awaiting his dinner. This was thought by some to be a ruse to lessen the appetite, while others believed it was used as a sop to prevent impatience. The style was not generally followed in the Mystic homes.

Present-day pre-dinner salads are usually a combination of 3 or 4 crisp greens—Boston lettuce, romaine, endive, cress, sometimes spinach. Radishes and/or cucumbers are sometimes sliced into them and the top is often adorned with a wedge of tomato. The dressings vary the taste and there is usually a choice of French, Italian, Russian and Roquefort.

Mixed Salad

1 head of Boston lettuce
½ head of iceberg lettuce
4 radishes, sliced

½ small cucumber, diced or sliced

The following ingredients may be added according to your taste and according to the season.

¼ bunch of watercress
2 heads of Belgian endive, sliced across
2 celery stalks, diced

2 tomatoes, peeled and quartered
2 hard-cooked eggs, sliced

Prepare all salad ingredients, arrange in a bowl, and chill. Mix dressing, pour over salad, and toss well before serving.
Makes 6 to 12 servings, depending on the added ingredients.

DRESSING

Increase quantity of dressing if more than above quantities are used.

1 teaspoon salt
¼ teaspoon pepper
2 teaspoons mixed herbs—dried or fresh mint, chervil, tarragon, orégano, chives or parsley

2 tablespoons lemon juice
¼ cup oil

Stir salt and pepper with herbs; gradually stir in lemon juice and stir in oil last of all.
Makes about ⅓ cup.

✕ Grandfather's Potato Salad

From Mrs. Reed Whitney

His specialty for a Sunday night supper, it took all afternoon to prepare.

15 fair-sized potatoes, boiled, peeled and sliced
12 hard-cooked eggs, whites diced fine
3 bunches of celery, with outside leaves removed, chopped fine

2 onions
1 bottle of stuffed olives, chopped fine
1 cucumber
1 bottle piccalilli
4 slices of bacon, diced and fried until crisp

Combine all ingredients and mix well before adding dressing.
Makes 12 servings.

DRESSING

1 cup olive oil, or more
12 hard-cooked egg yolks
1 teaspoon dry mustard

1 teaspoon salt
Vinegar

Stir oil little by little into egg yolks until smooth. Add mustard and salt and enough vinegar to make dressing medium thick. Stir well into the salad.

Makes about 2 cups.

Egg-stuffed Tomato

6 medium-sized tomatoes
Salt and pepper
1¼ cups mayonnaise
6 eggs, cooked for 6 minutes, chilled and peeled
2 tablespoons chopped chives or capers

12 lettuce leaves
½ bunch of watercress
12 radishes
⅓ cup Basic French Dressing (p. 19)

Peel tomatoes by submerging them in boiling water for 10 seconds and then drawing off the skin with a sharp knife. Cut off tops and scoop out pulp with a teaspoon. Turn tomatoes upside-down and drain them well. Salt and pepper interiors and put 1 tablespoon mayonnaise into each tomato. Place an egg on top of the mayonnaise and spread 1 tablespoon mayonnaise on top of each egg. Sprinkle with chives or capers and arrange the tomatoes on lettuce leaves. Garnish with cress and radishes. Serve a dressing made of the remaining mayonnaise mixed with the French dressing.

Makes 6 servings.

Filled Tomatoes

6 medium-sized tomatoes
1 bunch of watercress (leaves only)

4 to 6 tablespoons mayonnaise
Salt and pepper

Cut off tops of tomatoes, scoop out pulp and press out the seeds. Chop the pulp with watercress and bind with mayonnaise. Season with salt and pepper and fill the tomato shells.

Makes 6 servings.

⚓ Chicken Salad

From the *Providence Journal-Bulletin*

1 fowl (5 pounds), or 2 broilers (2½ pounds each), simmered and boned	⅔ cup mayonnaise
	Salt and pepper
1 small Bermuda onion	Lettuce leaves
2 stalks celery (diced)	12 olives
4 hard-cooked eggs, sliced	1 cucumber, sliced
⅓ cup Basic French Dressing (p. 19)	12 radishes
	4 tomatoes, peeled and sliced

Cut chicken meat into 1-inch cubes. Place in a large mixing bowl. Slice Bermuda onion paper-thin and add to mixing bowl. Cut celery into ½-inch dice and mix in. Add eggs. Beat French dressing and mayonnaise together and pour over salad. Toss lightly, adding salt and pepper to taste. Chill.

Serve in a lettuce-lined salad bowl garnished with olives, cucumber slices and radishes. Serve with homegrown tomatoes and hot biscuits. Makes 6 servings.

⌘ Mary Greenman Davis's Fruit Gelatin

2 envelopes of unflavored gelatin
¼ cup lemon juice
1¾ cups water
1 whole lemon, sliced
1 cup sugar

2 cups drained fruits (orange and grapefruit sections, fresh berries, sliced peaches and diced apple)
2 or 3 slices of canned pineapple, cut into wedges
1 banana, sliced

Soften gelatin in lemon juice for 15 minutes. Boil water, lemon slices and sugar until sugar is dissolved. Take from heat, strain, and stir in softened gelatin until dissolved. Arrange fruits in a shallow bowl. Pour gelatin mixture over fruit and chill.
Makes 6 to 8 servings.
NOTE: Do not use fresh pineapple.

⌘ Molded Salad and Fruit Dressing

From Mrs. Reed Whitney

1 cup diced avocado pear
1 cup diced celery
1 pear, canned or fresh, diced
1 tablespoon grated onion
2 tablespoons minced green pepper
1 cup hot water

1 package (3 ounces) lime-flavored gelatin
1 tablespoon lemon juice
2 tablespoons mayonnaise
½ cup heavy cream, whipped
1 cup grapefruit sections
1 cup hulled strawberries

Chop first 5 ingredients extremely fine. Pour hot water over gelatin. Let gelatin get chilled until syrupy before adding chopped ingredients, lemon juice, mayonnaise and whipped cream. Chill until set. Garnish with grapefruit and strawberries.
Makes 10 to 12 servings.

DRESSING

2 eggs
½ cup sugar
Juice of 1 large lemon, strained

1 tablespoon butter
1 cup heavy cream, whipped

Beat the eggs very light, add sugar, and beat until smooth. Add lemon juice and butter. Cook in the top part of a double boiler over simmering water until mixture drops from a spoon. When cool, add the cream. Stir until mixed.
Makes 2½ cups.

⊘ Basic French Dressing

1½ teaspoons salt
¼ teaspoon pepper
¼ teaspoon dry mustard

⅓ cup tarragon vinegar
⅔ cup oil

Stir dry ingredients in a shallow bowl or place them in a jar. Add vinegar and stir or shake until salt and mustard are dissolved. Add oil and stir or shake vigorously.
Makes 1 cup.

VARIATIONS

1. Add 1 garlic clove to the dressing and remove it before serving.
2. Add 1 teaspoon minced onion to the dressing before shaking it.
3. Add ½ teaspoon paprika to the dressing with the dry ingredients.

⊘ Richard's Blended French Dressing

1 large or 2 small garlic cloves, crushed
1 cup oil
¼ cup tarragon vinegar
2 teaspoons coarse salt

1 teaspoon dry English mustard
1 heaping teaspoon dried orégano
1 teaspoon coarse black pepper
1 teaspoon Maggi seasoning

Combine all ingredients in a blender container. Blend at high speed for 2 minutes. Pour into cruet and keep cool until needed.
Makes about 1¼ cups.

Italian Dressing

¼ cup vinegar
¾ cup olive oil
½ to 1 teaspoon salt
¼ teaspoon roughly ground pepper
½ teaspoon dry mustard
½ teaspoon prepared mustard

½ garlic clove, crushed
½ teaspoon orégano, dried or minced fresh
½ tablespoon minced pimiento or sweet red pepper
¼ cup grated Parmesan cheese (optional)

Shake all ingredients in a covered jar. Chill and shake well before pouring over greens in a salad bowl.
Makes about 1¼ cups.
VARIATION: Slice 1 hard-cooked egg over the salad.

Roquefort Dressing

1 cup olive oil
¼ cup wine vinegar
¼ cup lemon juice
2 teaspoons salt

¼ teaspoon pepper
¼ teaspoon paprika
3 ounces Roquefort cheese, crumbled

Shake ingredients in a covered jar. Chill and shake well before serving.
Makes about 1⅔ cups.

⬥ Cream Roquefort Dressing

⅔ cup mayonnaise   ⅓ cup crumbled Roquefort
⅓ cup Basic French Dressing   cheese, or more
   (p. 19)

Beat mayonnaise and dressing together. Bring cheese to room temperature, crush to a paste, and blend or beat into mayonnaise dressing. Makes about 1⅓ cups.

⬥ Dressing Made Over Salad

½ garlic clove   ¼ teaspoon dry mustard
3 tablespoons olive oil   ⅛ teaspoon salt
1 tablespoon tarragon vinegar   Freshly ground black pepper

Rub salad bowl with garlic; discard garlic. Add salad ingredients to bowl. Sprinkle oil over salad and lift with salad servers to coat all leaves lightly with oil. Sprinkle vinegar, mustard, salt and pepper over salad and fatigue (lift and turn) the salad until the dressing is well mixed through the salad.

⬥ Bacon Salad Dressing

From Mrs. George F. Ruth

1 slice of thick-sliced bacon, or   1 egg, mixed well with spoon,
   2 slices of thin-sliced bacon,   not beater
   or 1 to 1½ tablespoons diced   3 tablespoons granulated sugar
   ham fat   3 tablespoons cider vinegar
                                      Dash of salt

Cut bacon into small squares and brown well in small saucepan. Do not pour off the fat. Mix egg, sugar, vinegar and salt together in a small bowl. Add egg mixture to browned bacon and cook, stirring constantly, until mixture is thickened. If too thick, it may be thinned with either cream or evaporated milk. This recipe may be varied to suit the taste by increasing or decreasing the sugar and vinegar. A good proportion for a slightly sweeter dressing is 4 tablespoons sugar to 3 tablespoons vinegar.

Bacon Salad Dressing is especially good when used for these salads:

Warm Lettuce: Fill large bowl with well-drained lettuce which has been torn into bite-sized pieces. Pour warm dressing over the lettuce *immediately* before serving.

Dandelion: Cook early spring dandelion leaves until tender. Add sliced hard-cooked egg and warm dressing.

Potato: Mix together diced cooked potatoes, diced hard-cooked eggs, fine-chopped onion and green pepper, fine-diced celery, a pinch of salt, and a dash of freshly ground pepper. Pour warm dressing over vegetables for a very tasty and different potato salad.

Spinach: Pour warm dressing over cooked spinach.

CHAPTER II

〜

Soups, Stews and Chowders

ALL cooking in New England started on the hearth. There was a bake oven for bread, a spit for meat, and various trivets and devices for keeping food warm. The central position over the fire was occupied by the heart of the home, the cookpot. It hung from a pivoting arm and could be lowered or swung away from the fire as needed.

The early settlers of Mystic lived largely on two kinds of foods—breads, beans and pies from the bake oven and stews and chowders from the cookpot. In an era where inventiveness was needed to produce a meal, housewives developed specialties that made New England's cook-

ery famous. Even after every Mystic home had a big black iron stove and such undreamed-of innovations as a sink right in the kitchen, the cookpot still stood on the stove and the stew or chowder was still the mainstay of the meal.

ℰℳ Winter Soup

1 ham bone
2 cups diced ham
Cinnamon stick
4 peppercorns
3 whole cloves
4 potatoes, peeled and quartered
4 onions, chopped

½ head of white cabbage, shredded
6 tomatoes, peeled and quartered*
Salt
2 tablespoons herb vinegar, or more

Boil ham bone and ham in a large kettle with a scrap of cinnamon stick, the peppercorns and cloves in water to cover (at least 12 cups) for 2 hours. Add potatoes, onions and cabbage and boil gently for 30 minutes longer. Add tomatoes and simmer until they fall apart, about 30 more minutes. Remove the bone. Add salt only if needed. Spike with vinegar and serve in large bowls with hot corn sticks, butter and damson preserves.
Makes about 8 servings.

ℰℳ Oxtail Soup

Yacht ranges are balanced by gimbals but the iron cooking stoves in the galleys of the whaleships stood firm. With four legs nailed to the planking, they followed every motion of the ship and so did whatever was cooking on them or in them. Soups were stirred by the motion of the sea.

* The original recipe called for a quart jar of home-preserved tomatoes. A 28-ounce can of tomatoes may be substituted for the fresh ones.

1 oxtail, cut into 1½-inch lengths	2 teaspoons dried thyme
Salt	3 whole cloves
2 tablespoons paprika	8 cups stock, veal or beef
3 tablespoons flour	2 cups red wine
4 tablespoons butter	¼ cup sherry
1 onion, chopped fine	½ cup fresh tomato purée
	3 tablespoons minced parsley

Wash and dry oxtail and sprinkle with salt and paprika. Dredge with flour and brown on all sides in butter. Add the onion and stir for 5 minutes. Add thyme, cloves, stock, wine, sherry and tomato purée and simmer very gently for 4 hours. Correct seasoning and serve sprinkled with minced parsley.

Makes about 6 servings.

ℰ𝒳 Dried Vegetable Soups

The Puritans arrived in the New World with the usual settlers' cargo of seeds, staples and animals. But those Separatists who came via Holland had learned the Dutch practice of gathering pod vegetables and roots in the autumn and storing them for the winter in sacks and sand or dry soil. Accordingly they planted peas, beans, turnips, potatoes, beets and carrots, and for a long time dried and root vegetables were their winter sustenance.

ℰ𝒳 Lentil Soup I

Dried vegetable soups and stews were a blessing to the Mystic men when the wind was whistling around the harbor, and a little shot of sherry went into the soup. This is another soup that needs a ham bone, one in the "second stage" when there is still lots of meat on it.

2 cups dried lentils
1 ham bone, with lots of meat on it
4 large potatoes, peeled and cubed
3 carrots, scraped and diced
2 large onions, sliced thin
1 bay leaf
Salt
Sherry

Soak lentils according to directions on box. If they are old-fashioned lentils sold from a sack, soak them in cold water to cover overnight. Use the water they soaked in for the soup and add enough additional water to make 12 cups in all. Boil ham bone and lentils for 1 hour. Add potatoes, carrots, onions and bay leaf and boil for 2 hours longer. Add salt only if ham was very mild. Serve in heated bowls with a shot of old sherry in each serving.
Makes about 8 servings.

Lentil Soup II

2½ cups dried lentils
3 cups diced celery
2 cups diced carrots
2 cups chopped onions
1 turkey carcass
1 teaspoon salt
Turkey scraps
4 tablespoons chopped parsley
Salt and pepper

Soak lentils in water overnight. Pour them with their water into a large kettle. Add celery, carrots and onions, and enough water to make 14 cups in all. Add the carcass of the Thanksgiving turkey and 1 teaspoon salt. Bring to a slow boil and cook for 3 hours. Take out carcass; add turkey scraps, parsley, and salt and pepper to taste; simmer for 15 minutes longer. Serve in heated bowls with corn bread and a decanter of old sherry.
Makes about 10 servings.

❧ Black (or Turtle) Bean Soup

Miss Hyla Snider is a collector of old recipes and has added this to her other generous contributions.

2 cups small black beans
2½ quarts cold water
2 large onions, quartered
Salt and pepper
Sprig of thyme
Butter, the size of a walnut

Cayenne
½ cup sherry or red wine
1 lemon, sliced
2 hard-cooked eggs, sliced
Egg Balls (below)

Wash the beans well and soak in the cold water for several hours. Put them in a pot with the water, onions, a little salt and pepper and the thyme. Let them simmer gently for 3 to 4 hours, until perfectly tender, then press all through a sieve. Return to heat; there should now be 2 quarts. Add the butter, more salt and pepper if needed and a little cayenne; just before serving add the wine. Have ready in a soup tureen the lemon and egg slices and the egg balls. Fill the tureen with the boiling soup. You may add with advantage a scant teaspoon of cornstarch blended with cold water. Boil for 2 or 3 minutes, stirring constantly, and serve.
Makes 8 servings.

Egg Balls
2 hard-cooked egg yolks
Grated lemon rind and juice
1 raw egg yolk
½ cup dried bread crumbs

1 tablespoon minced parsley
Pinch of grated nutmeg
Cayenne

Mix all ingredients together well. Shape into balls the size of a nutmeg; roll in flour and fry in butter. Put these in the tureen.

ℰ𝒳 Pumpkin Soup

4 cups peeled and seeded   1 tablespoon sugar
   pumpkin wedges   Salt and pepper
⅓ cup butter   Pinch of ground allspice
4 cups chicken or beef stock   Milk or thin cream

Boil pumpkin with half of the butter, the stock, sugar, and salt and pepper to taste until tender, about 35 minutes. Stir frequently. Press through a sieve or purée in a blender with the allspice, adding milk to bring the soup to the proper consistency. Correct seasoning. Serve in wide bowls with fried bread croutons.
Makes about 6 servings.

ℰ𝒳 Potato Soup

6 to 8 potatoes, scrubbed   Salt and pepper
6 cups water   Milk
2 onions, sliced   6 bacon slices, fried crisp,
¼ cup butter   drained and crumbled
3 chicken bouillon cubes

Boil potatoes in their jackets in the water until soft and almost falling apart, 20 to 30 minutes. Drain and reserve the potato water. Discard potato skins. Fry onions in butter over low heat, stirring, until tender but not brown, about 5 minutes. Add sliced potatoes and stir just long enough to make them glossy. Add potato water and bouillon cubes and simmer, stirring occasionally for 15 minutes or until cubes are dissolved. Season to taste and purée in a blender or vegetable mill. Add milk to bring to preferred consistency. Serve with bacon crumbled over the top. If served cold, sprinkle with cut chives.
Makes about 6 servings.

✒ Chicken Curry Soup

6 tablespoons butter
4 tablespoons flour
2 chicken bouillon cubes
2 cups boiling water
1 cup light cream
2 tablespoons curry powder, or more

¾ cup diced or slivered cold chicken meat
¾ cup grated coconut
⅔ cup heavy cream
Pinch of salt

Melt 4 tablespoons of the butter in top part of double boiler over boiling water. Stir in flour until smooth. Gradually stir in bouillon cubes dissolved in boiling water. Stir with a French wire whisk until thickened and smooth. Stir in light cream. When soup is hot, ladle out 3 tablespoons into a cup and stir curry powder into it until smooth. Stir back into soup. Repeat if a stronger curry flavor is preferred. Stir in chicken meat, cover, and keep soup hot over boiling water.

Fry coconut in remaining 2 tablespoons butter, stirring, over very low heat. Watch carefully, as it browns suddenly. Take from heat as soon as it starts to brown. The heat of the pan will continue to brown it. Drain on absorbent paper. Whip heavy cream with the salt. Serve soup in wide cups or plates. Garnish with whipped cream and sprinkle coconut over the cream.

The soup can also be served chilled. Chill it after chicken has been added. Serve with cream and coconut in the same way.
Makes 4 servings.

✒ Portable Soup

We are told that concentrated essence of meat, or "portable soup," proved to be a great acquisition and was used for the comfort of the army, the navy, whalers, travelers and invalids.

Housewives boiled, reduced, pressed and dried the soup for weeks before their husbands embarked in order to supply them with soluble nourishment aboard. A German chemist, Baron Justus von Liebig, 1803–1873, invented commercialized meat concentrates and bouillon cubes, and ended the need for this chore, but here is how the original product was made.

Start with 10 pounds of shin and broken bones of beef. Place them in a digester,* cover with cold water, and bring to a boil. Skim off the scum carefully and add a little cold water; continue to skim until broth is clear. Boil for 8 to 10 hours and cool. Remove meat, add 1 teaspoon peppercorns, and boil uncovered until reduced to 4 cups. Skim off any fat that rises. Transfer the broth to a small stewpan and reduce it again to the thickness of syrup. Test a little of the syrup in a spoon. If it turns to a jelly it is done; if not, boil it until it does. Pour into little pots or into a dish about ¼-inch deep. When it is cold, turn it out and weight it until it is quite flattened.

Cut the pressed cake into pieces of ½ ounce each. Dry them in a warm room, turning frequently, for 10 days. When well hardened and kept in a dry place, they may be preserved for several years in any climate.

These portable soups went to sea on many ships or they were used to make Extempor Broth.** We recommend that a bouillon cube be substituted.

☙ Fish Soup I

1 cup melted butter or oil, or ½ cup of each
6 onions, sliced
3 pounds fish, cut into cubes (halibut, flounder, cod, sole or any available fish)

1 pound mussels in shell, bearded and scrubbed (substitute clams if mussels are not available)
3 bouillon cubes
8 cups water

* A digester was a kind of heavy closed kettle, used to heat substances to soften and cook them thoroughly, sometimes under a bit of pressure.
** Extempor Broth is mentioned in old recipes and often turns up in English naval records. The use of dried, hardened Portable Soup predated—and was similar to—the modern use of bouillon cubes.

6 tomatoes, peeled and quartered

¾ cup fine-diced salt pork or
bacon

3 cups noodles

3 cups diced potatoes

1 pound shelled shrimps

¾ cup peeled and diced cucumber

3 tablespoons chopped parsley

Heat butter in a large kettle, add onion slices, and brown lightly. Add
fish and mussels and cook for 5 minutes. Add bouillon cubes dissolved in
the water and simmer for 15 minutes. Add tomatoes, salt pork, noodles
and potatoes. Simmer for 20 minutes longer. Add shrimps, cucumber
and parsley and simmer for 4 minutes longer. Serve from a large
tureen, with toasted Portuguese bread.
Makes about 8 servings.

Fish Soup II

½ cup butter

1 onion, chopped

½ teaspoon dried thyme

½ teaspoon dried sage

1 bay leaf

Salt and pepper

4 tomatoes, peeled, seeded and
diced

2½ cups fish broth or water

2 tablespoons vinegar

3 pounds fish (1 pound each of
cod, salmon, flounder, sole or
any combination)

3 tablespoons chopped parsley

6 slices of white bread, quartered, fried in butter or
toasted until golden

Heat butter in a large soup kettle, add onion, and fry for 5 minutes.
Add herbs, salt and pepper to taste. Stir gently for 5 more minutes. Add
tomatoes, broth or water and vinegar, and boil rapidly until tomatoes
are tender and soup is reduced. Add fish cut into chunks, and reduce
heat. Cook until fish is tender and flakes easily, about 15 minutes.
Correct seasoning. Serve in bowls, sprinkled with parsley and topped
with fried or toasted bread.
Makes about 6 servings.

⚓ Salt-cod Soup

2 pounds salt cod, soaked in water overnight
½ cup butter
1 onion, sliced
4 tomatoes, peeled, seeded and diced
2 celery stalks and leaves, chopped
½ teaspoon dried thyme
1 bay leaf
2 tablespoons chopped parsley
4 potatoes, peeled and sliced
Pepper
2 cups toasted bread croutons

Drain cod, remove skin and bones, and cut into cubes. Heat butter in a large soup kettle and cook onion in it for 7 minutes. Add tomatoes, celery and herbs and stir and cook for about 7 minutes longer. Add potatoes and boiling water to cover and simmer for 15 minutes. Add cod and simmer for about 10 minutes longer. Add pepper to taste. Serve the soup with heated bread croutons.

Garlic croutons may be substituted for plain, and ½ cup white wine can be added with the water.

Makes about 6 servings.

⚓ Quahog Stew

This excellent stew made with creamed butter comes to us from an old issue of *The Vineyard Gazette*.

1 quart rich milk
½ cup butter
3 tablespoons flour
Grated mace
Salt and pepper
1 quart shelled quahogs with their liquor
2 eggs

Heat milk. Cream 2 tablespoons butter and the flour with mace, salt and pepper to taste, and stir into the heated milk. Cook, stirring, until it thickens. Heat quahogs and liquor for 3 minutes, then stir into thickened milk. Put well-beaten eggs in serving dish with remaining tablespoon of butter. Pour in the quahog stew, stir well, and serve.

Makes 4 servings.

Oyster Stew I

3 tablespoons butter	1 teaspoon minced fresh or
3 shallots, chopped fine	dried thyme
1 onion, chopped fine	½ cup oyster liquor
3 cups milk	2 dozen small oysters, shucked
⅛ teaspoon dry mustard	1 cup heavy cream, whipped
Salt and pepper	

Heat butter in a wide saucepan, add shallots, and cook for 4 minutes. Add onion and cook for 3 minutes longer, stirring. Stir 2 tablespoons of the milk into the mustard until smooth. Stir remaining milk into the saucepan; when it boils add the mustard mixture and stir until dissolved. Add salt and pepper to taste, the thyme and oyster liquor. Do not let milk boil for more than 3 minutes in all. Add oysters, reduce heat, and cook for 2 minutes longer. Add whipped cream and serve. Makes 4 servings.

Oyster Stew II

The simplest version

2 quarts shucked oysters and	Cayenne pepper (optional)
their liquor	¼ pound butter, cut into thin
1 quart milk	pats
Salt and pepper	

Strain oyster liquor from oysters, rinse them, and return them to the strained liquor in a large saucepan. Simmer over low heat for 5 minutes. Add milk and heat to just under the boiling point. Take from heat, season to taste, and add a pat of butter to each serving. Makes about 8 servings.

Ҽ҂ Oyster Stew III

3 cups light cream	2 teaspoons celery salt
3 cups milk	2 teaspoons salt
3 pints shucked oysters and their liquor	¼ teaspoon pepper
3 tablespoons butter	2 teaspoons paprika (optional)

This oyster stew requires 3 saucepans, large, medium and small. Before preparing the stew, heat 8 soup bowls or wide soup plates.

Pour cream and milk into the largest saucepan. Drain oysters and place them in the medium saucepan with ¼ cup of their liquor and the butter. Pour remaining liquor into the small saucepan. Scald cream and milk, but under no conditions let it boil. Heat oysters until they are plump and their edges curl. Place the saucepan with the remaining oyster liquor over higher heat to bring it rapidly to a boil. Pour the puffed oysters and boiling oyster liquor into the scalded cream and milk. Stir in salts and pepper and serve immediately in heated bowls or plates. If desired, a little paprika can be sprinkled over the top. Serve with oyster crackers. Stew takes only a few minutes to prepare and must be eaten immediately.
Makes 8 servings.

Ҽ҂ Oyster Bisque

1 pint shucked oysters	2 peppercorns
1 quart milk	6 tablespoons butter
1 small onion, sliced	6 tablespoons flour
2 celery stalks, quartered	Salt
3 parsley sprigs	¾ cup toasted bread croutons
1 bay leaf	

Drain and chop the oysters; set the liquor aside. Heat oysters to boiling and press through a coarse sieve. Scald milk with onion, celery, parsley, bay leaf and peppercorns; let it steep for 15 minutes. Melt

butter in top part of double boiler over boiling water. Stir in flour until smooth. Gradually stir in strained milk and oyster liquor. Cook, stirring occasionally, for 15 minutes. Add the sieved oysters and salt to taste. Cook for 5 minutes longer, stir well, and add more milk if a thinner bisque is preferred. Serve hot with freshly toasted or heated bread croutons.
Makes 4 servings.

ℰ𝒳 Lobster Bisque

The name "bisque" came later than the soup, which was originally called just plain thick lobster soup.

5 cups fish stock or chicken stock
⅔ cup uncooked rice
½ cup butter
3 celery stalks, scraped and cut into fine strips
2 carrots, scraped and cut into fine strips
1 leek, trimmed and sliced fine
1 onion, sliced thin and divided into rings

2 to 2½ pounds lobster, 1 large or 2 small
1 cup white wine
3 tablespoons brandy (optional)
1½ cups heavy cream
Salt, pepper and cayenne
3 tablespoons minced parsley

Boil stock with rice for 45 minutes. Heat half of the butter in a large kettle, add the vegetables, and stir over medium heat for 3 to 4 minutes. Split lobsters (p. 114), take out sac and intestinal vein, and arrange lobster halves cut side down on the vegetables. Cover and simmer for 4 minutes. Turn lobster halves and stir with the vegetables until shells are bright red. Add wine and brandy, cover, and simmer for 7 minutes. Take out lobster, remove meat from shells, and set it aside.

Pound the shells with a mallet and return them to the kettle with the stock and rice. Simmer uncovered, stirring frequently, until liquid is reduced to 4 cups. Strain off the liquid, set it over medium heat, and whip in the cream and remaining ¼ cup butter. Dice lobster meat and add it to the bisque. Add seasoning to taste and cook until lobster is heated through. Sprinkle with parsley and serve in warmed soup cups. Makes about 8 servings.

NOTE: At the season of the year when lobster shells are very soft, or if chicken lobsters are used, the shells can be crushed to a paste and puréed in a blender to add color and flavor to the bisque.

Ⓒ✗ The Big Black Pot

When we were children, we had a bilingual Alsatian governess who taught us both German and French. Apparently our parents thought they could kill two languages with a single governess, and we were trained to address her as Mademoiselle Chaudière in the mornings and Fräulein Martha in the afternoons. Between ourselves we called her "The Black Pot" because my brother had discovered, with utmost delight, that in French *chaudière* meant a big black pot. This personal recollection leads to an American soup, curiously enough.

French fishermen, when they returned to shore, threw some of their catch into a huge communal black pot, or *chaudière*, which was always kept seething over a roaring beach fire. They ladled off mugs of hot fish

stew and broke their stale bread into it. American whalers apparently touched the French shore, ate from the simmering *chaudière,* and returned to New England with a new kind of stew and a new word. I have never eaten a chowder without thinking of Fräulein Martha, The Black Pot.

ℰℋ Fish Chowders

The various fish chowders were all basically the same. They consisted of ingredients that were available in every tidewater household; often they consisted of almost all the ingredients which the larder contained. Except for maple syrup or molasses, honey, eggs, cornmeal, dried peas, and precious tea, everything else went into the chowder. Every householder in Mystic owned a barrel of salt pork, a cache of potatoes and onions in the cellar, a cow in the barn, and all the fish or shellfish he wanted from the sea. To those simple ingredients he naturally added any change that suggested itself—a blade or leaf of herb or spice—anything that could alter or enchance the flavor.

Settling, shipbuilding, whaling and farming were arduous tasks which stimulated enormous appetites, and so housewives set great bowls of steaming chowder before their families. What didn't go into the chowder was served with it. Stale bread and biscuits were broken into it, corn bread was eaten with it, and when there was fresh corn it was added to or substituted for the fish.

Out of all this grew New England's great clam chowders, corn chowders, fish, lobster and crab chowders. Further south tomatoes were later combined with clams and designated as Manhattan clam chowder, but north of Manhattan this innovation was (and still is) frowned upon.

ℰℋ Basic Fish Chowder I

The word "chowder" did not appear in the English language before the New England settlers had created the dish and were eating it happily for every occasion, including breakfast.

The Mysticians used any available fish or combination of fishes for their basic chowder. Spices and herbs were added according to taste.

5 pounds fish, cut into thin slices or chunks

Salt and freshly ground black pepper

½ pound salt pork, sliced thin

10 potatoes, peeled and cut into thick slices

3 to 4 cups broken "hard tack" pilot biscuits

Sprinkle the fish with salt and pepper. Fry the salt pork in a Dutch oven, *chaudière* or kettle until golden. Place a layer of fish on the pork and cover fish with a layer of potato slices; season. Add a layer of broken biscuits and continue layering the ingredients until they are all used. There should be at least 3 layers of fish. Add water just to cover the ingredients. Cover the kettle and simmer, do not boil rapidly, for 1 hour.

Makes 10 to 12 servings.

Basic Fish Chowder II

¼ pound salt pork, diced
1 onion, chopped
4 cups water
3 cups thin-sliced potatoes
3 pounds cod or combination cod and flounder fillets, cubed

3 cups milk
1 cup light cream
Salt and pepper
Chopped parsley (optional)

In a heavy kettle or Dutch oven, brown salt pork and onion for about 7 minutes. Add water and potatoes, reduce heat, and boil gently for 15 minutes. Add fish and boil for 15 minutes longer. Add milk, cream and seasonings to taste and simmer for 5 minutes more. Take from heat, cover, cool, and allow flavors to develop. Reheat before serving, and serve sprinkled with parsley.

Makes 6 to 8 servings.

⅌ Basic Fish Chowder III

½ cup salt pork, diced
3 onions, sliced
½ teaspoon dried thyme
3 parsley sprigs
1 bay leaf
3 peppercorns

6 potatoes, peeled and sliced
4 pounds assorted fish (halibut, cod, salmon, flounder and sole), sliced into fingers
Salt
2 lemons, sliced thin

Heat salt pork in a large soup kettle and brown the onions in it. Add herbs, peppercorns, potatoes, fish and enough boiling water to cover. Boil gently until potatoes are tender. Add salt to taste and serve covered with lemon slices.
Makes 6 servings.

⅌ Mrs. Keator's Fish Chowder

Mrs. William C. Keator has sent a fish chowder recipe which can and should be multiplied to serve at a party. It is far too good to reach only a small family.

This should preferably be prepared the day before it is served.

¼ pound salt pork, sliced thin
5 or 6 large onions
7 or 8 medium-sized potatoes
Salt

6½ pounds whole fish, or 4 pounds haddock fillets
1 quart milk
½ cup butter

Try out the salt pork. Chop onions into coarse pieces and boil in plenty of water for 10 minutes; drain. Cut potatoes into ½-inch cubes and add to drained onions. Salt well and boil together for 10 minutes. Add fat from the tried-out pork. Add boned and skinned fish and more water if necessary. When fish is cooked, add at least 1 quart of milk. Heat through; do NOT boil. Add butter, and serve in soup plates with hard tack.
Makes 4 servings.

໕ Belle's Fish Chowder

From Mrs. Marion G. Larkin

1 small onion, chopped fine
3 cups milk
1 to 1½ cups cubed cooked lobster or fish
2 potatoes, peeled and cubed (optional)

1 cup cream of mushroom soup
½ cup light cream
2 teaspoons butter
Dash of MSG
Salt and pepper

Cook onion in minimum water for 7 minutes. Add milk, lobster or fish and potatoes and boil gently until potatoes are soft, about 15 minutes. Add soup, cream, butter, MSG and salt and pepper to taste. Cook until heated through.
Makes 4 servings.

໕ Foggy Day Special Fish Chowder

"We have long been FRIENDS of Mystic Seaport, and always enjoy our visits there for the dinghy racing, the many wonderful additions, the personnel, and *The Log*. We were slugging it out in foggy Block Island Sound on Columbus Day when we would have liked to have been at the Seaport; our thoughts were with you. But it gave me time to read *The Log* and I happily write our Fish Chowder recipe for a foggy day."

—*Kay and Emery Katzenbach*

3 onions, sliced
¼ pound salt pork, diced
1½ pounds cod or haddock (frozen fillets are fine)
5 white potatoes, peeled and diced
4 teaspoons salt

¼ teaspoon pepper
3 cups boiling water
1 cup scalded milk
1 can (14½ ounces) undiluted evaporated milk
3 tablespoons butter
Grated nutmeg

Brown onions in fried pork; add fish, potatoes and all the rest. Simmer for about 10 minutes. Serve topped with nutmeg.
Makes 4 servings.

ᑧ Judge Drake's Finnan Haddie Chowder

This is Judge Drake's original recipe and he writes, "We enjoy it at least once a week during the winter months. Of course, you have to enjoy the flavor of smoked fish, but it can be made with plain haddock fillet if you wish. Not as good though."

½-inch-thick slices of salt pork, cut into ½-inch cubes
2 medium-sized onions, sliced
2 large potatoes, peeled and sliced medium thick

1 pound smoked finnan haddie fillet, thick end preferred*
Freshly ground black pepper
MSG
1 quart whole milk
Crackers and butter

Try out salt pork in skillet, take out with a slotted spoon, and drain on brown paper. Cook onions in pork fat until they take on color, 6 to 7 minutes. Parboil potato slices in water to cover for 10 minutes; drain and reserve the potato water. Cut fillet across into 1-inch-thick strips and arrange in a complete layer in the top part of a large double boiler. Arrange a layer of potato slices over the fish. Sprinkle well with pepper and MSG and add about ½ cup potato water. Add onions to make a third layer and season as above. Add milk and cook mixture over simmering water for 30 minutes. Add pork cubes but do not stir; merely press them into the chowder so they are submerged. Simmer for another 30 minutes. Do not let the chowder get too hot or it will separate. Serve in bowls over two halves of crackers that have been split and browned with a dab of butter. Serve the rest of the split and browned crackers as an accompaniment. Do not use any salt.
Makes 4 servings.

ᑧ Clam Chowder I

Clam chowder is made up of various prepared ingredients. If fresh clams are available, they have to be steamed. Potatoes must be boiled,

---

* Finnan haddie is dried, smoked and salted haddock.

and pork and onions have to be fried. If possible do these preparations simultaneously, just before the final simmering and serving of the chowder.

When Littlenecks are not available substitute 1½ cups minced Pacific clams or canned minced clams. Always retain the clam juice, whether fresh, shucked or canned clams are used.

4 slices of salt pork or bacon, diced fine	1 cup heavy cream
1 onion, chopped	1 cup milk, or 2 cups light cream
1 quart (2 pounds) Littleneck clams	Pinch of dried thyme
3 small potatoes, peeled and diced	Paprika for garnish
Salt and pepper	3 teaspoons minced parsley (optional)

Fry salt pork or bacon until browned and crisp. Take it out with a slotted spoon and set it aside. Add onion to the fat in the pan and brown it lightly for 6 to 7 minutes. Drain the onion well and set it aside too.

Place scrubbed clams in a kettle with ½ inch of water. Cover kettle and set over high heat. Boil for 5 to 6 minutes, until clams have opened. Strain off the clam juice; there should be at least 1½ cups. Open shells, take out the clams, and set them aside. (Throw clam shells into cold water to scrub later; use for minced-clam and crabmeat appetizers.)

Boil potatoes in water to cover in a large kettle until they are barely soft, 5 to 7 minutes according to size of dice. Take out potatoes with a slotted spoon and boil potato water until it is reduced to 1½ cups.

Add diced potatoes, salt pork or bacon, onion and clam juice to the reduced potato water. As soon as it returns to a boil, reduce heat and simmer for 5 minutes. Add salt and pepper to taste and gradually stir in the cream, or milk and cream. As it returns to an even simmer, add the clams and cook just long enough to heat them through. Stir in the thyme. Serve in heated soup plates or bowls with a sprinkling of paprika on each serving. A little freshly minced parsley may be added.

Makes 4 servings.

⟨ℰ⟩ Clam Chowder II

Clams, quahogs or sea clams make equally good clam chowder. However, many prefer them in the order listed.

6 strips of bacon or 6 ounces salt pork, diced while cold
2 medium-sized onions, diced fine
8 medium-sized potatoes, diced fine
¼ cup flour
Salt and pepper

3 to 4 cups boiling water
2 quarts shucked clams, ground through coarse blade of meat chopper
1 quart milk
¼ cup butter
Paprika

Try out bacon or pork and remove with a slotted spoon. Add diced onions to fat in pan and cook for 3 minutes. Add potatoes which have been dredged with seasoned flour. Add enough boiling water to almost cover the potatoes. Cook over low heat until potatoes are tender. Add clams and cook for just 2 minutes after water returns to a boil. Add heated, not boiled, milk and butter. Stir, let stand for a few minutes, and serve in heated bowls with a dash of paprika on each bowl.
Makes 8 servings.

⟨ℰ⟩ Mystic Lobster Chowder

2½ pounds lobster
2 teaspoons salt
4 dill sprigs
1 whole onion
2 tablespoons butter

¼ cup finest cracker crumbs
4 cups milk
½ onion, sliced
Salt and pepper

Scrub lobster, or lobsters, and drop into a kettle of boiling water. Do not go wild with the water; use just enough to cover the lobster. Add salt, dill and onion and simmer, covered, until lobster is brilliant red, about 20 minutes. Take out lobster and reduce the water in the kettle by boiling rapidly. Break lobster shells, remove sac and intestinal vein, and take out the meat. Return shells and scraps to the water in the kettle and boil, uncovered, while preparing the rest of the chowder.

Cut lobster meat into large dice. Cream butter with cracker crumbs. Scald milk with onion slices and strain. Stir milk into butter mixture; add lobster meat. Strain the reduced liquid from the kettle and add as much of it as needed to make the desired quantity of chowder. Season to taste. Serve in heated bowls with hot biscuits and lots of butter.
Makes 4 to 6 servings.

Corn Chowder

The settlers of Mystic were better off than the families they left behind. Old Englanders had more bread and less meat than New Englanders, who had fish and seafood besides. The settlers also had cornmeal for their bread and corn to feed their cows and hogs. Corn also went into making ardent spirits, namely corn whiskey, and lovely chowders.

½ cup tightly packed diced salt pork
1 large onion, sliced
2 cups diced potatoes
2 cups fresh corn kernels or canned or thawed frozen corn
3 cups boiling water
1 cup light cream
1 cup milk
Salt and pepper

Try out salt pork in a heavy Dutch oven or kettle; take out the pork with a slotted spoon. Brown the onion in the fat for about 7 minutes. Add potatoes, corn and boiling water and cook for 15 minutes. Add cream and milk and season to taste. Garnish with the brown pork dice.
Makes about 6 servings.

Ꮚᎄ Corn Chowder, Hot or Cold

11 ears of fresh corn	4 tablespoons corn flour
4 cups water	½ cup heavy cream
Salt	¼ cup minced green pepper or
2 cups milk	parsley
4 tablespoons butter	Decanter of whiskey or sherry

Slit the kernels on the ears of corn with a sharp knife. Then scrape into a bowl. Boil the scraped cobs with the water and a little salt in a large kettle for 35 minutes. Remove and discard the cobs. Add milk and scraped corn pulp to the kettle and bring back to a boil. Make a paste of the butter and corn flour and stir it into the soup until dissolved. Simmer soup, stirring occasionally, for 15 minutes. Cool and chill the soup until needed. Half whip the cream, then stir it into the soup with minced pepper or parsley. Grate the remaining ear of raw corn over the top. Pass whiskey or sherry to be added to the soup after it is served. If sherry is used, add 1 tablespoon sugar to the boiling soup.
Makes 6 servings.

Ꮚᎄ Chicken Chowder

This was for many years a favorite church supper dish. We are grateful to Mrs. A. Norton and to the *Vineyard Gazette* for being able to include the recipe here.

1 fowl (6 pounds)	4 cups hot water
Leaves from 1 bunch celery	4 cups diced potatoes
1 onion	1 tablespoon salt
½ bay leaf	1 quart scalded milk (or more)
¼ pound salt pork, cubed	2 tablespoons butter
5 to 6 medium-sized onions, sliced	

The day before this is to be served, boil the fowl with celery leaves, onion and bay leaf. Start it in 8 cups cold water and bring it slowly to a boil. Simmer for 3 hours, or until tender. If kettle is large enough, keep the fowl whole. Let it cool in the broth.

The following day remove the fat from the surface. Try out the salt pork, remove the cracklings, drain on paper, and set aside. Fry onions in pork fat until light brown. Pour onions and pork fat into a large kettle; add hot water, potatoes and salt. Simmer until tender, about 10 minutes.

Discard bones and skin of chicken, leaving meat in large pieces. Return it to the broth and boil for 10 minutes. Add the scalded milk and combine mixtures. Add butter just before serving. Add the cracklings to the individual servings.

Makes 10 servings.

CHAPTER III

∼∼

Breads and Pancakes

E VEN in Mystic we have to go back several generations to come to home bread baking. In our age of packaged breads, delivered at the market by a uniformed truck driver, we can hardly visualize a bakery shop with a benevolent baker. The baker and bakery didn't arrive in Mystic until after generations of Mystic wives had baked their own bread each week. Baking day was the same in every home, and anyone coming down the street could smell the mingled aromas of bread and spices. Mystic, like all the Puritan settlements, was a starch-eating community, and breads were a specialty as they are today.

We were asked to reproduce the recipe for the Portuguese Sweet Bread which is sold at Cameron's Coffee Shop on Water Street in Stonington, Connecticut. Mrs. Rebecca Cameron has kindly helped us to obtain the recipe from Mrs. Wilhelmina Arruda. Mrs. Arruda is an artist at baking, and anyone within motoring distance would be wise to drive to the Coffee Shop for one of her loaves. Bread dough is a little like a ship: it responds best when it feels a familiar hand on the wheel.

In this chapter there are corn breads of every description as well as quick breads and yeast breads for a pleasant change from the uniformed truck driver's packaged loaves; also the quickest of all—skillet breads, pancakes, scones and johnnycake.

ℰ⅄ Corn Breads

On page 151 you will find one of those perfectly proper statements, namely that the original habitat of maize, or Indian corn, is unknown. Actually we know exactly how maize originated. It grew out of the headdress of a buried Indian warrior.

Maize has a large golden tuft or panicle at the top which is reminiscent of a feathery Indian headdress. This confirms the legend that a warrior, whose head was adorned with just such a golden panicle, descended from heaven and struggled with a young brave. They wrestled through the night. The brave conquered the warrior, and out of the head of the warrior's grave sprouted the maize for which the starving Indians had been praying.

Roger Williams of Rhode Island fame wrote of the great southwest god Kautanowwit "from whom came Corne and Beans." He also recorded the tradition that the crow, Kaukont, first brought corn to the Indians. Another traditional version of its origin is that corn came from the garden of Kytan to the southwest.

The Indians safeguarded their corn from each other with the greatest ingenuity. They cultivated it carefully and crossed and recrossed it until they developed their own built-in tribal "trademarks." Certain tribes grew certain colors of corn or a certain specified numbers of rows; others grew distinct patterns and sizes. All of these features acted as recognizable patents and prevented theft between the tribes. The Indians branded their horses and trademarked their corn to establish honorable ownership. Fences, barricades, watchmen or other forms of protection were not necessary.

Corn and codfish became Mystic staples. Cornmeal took the place of flour whenever wheat crops were damaged, which occurred frequently. Dishes made of corn, cornmeal or dried beans often took the place of white bread in the settler's diet. White bread was not particularly popular, although one old book has it that "Children were said to like it on their butter."

Cornmeal was often home ground or pounded in a mortar. The ways in which it was prepared should be revived if they are not in use today.

⌇ Corn Bread

2½ cups cornmeal	1 teaspoon salt
2 cups milk	3 eggs, beaten
2 cups flour	½ cup butter, or ½ cup butter
1 teaspoon baking soda	and ¼ cup lard
2 teaspoons cream of tartar	1 cup sugar

Stir cornmeal into milk and let soak overnight. In the morning, beat in flour sifted with dry ingredients. Add eggs and creamed butter or butter and lard. Beat in sugar. Pour into 2 well-buttered loaf pans (9 × 5 × 3 inches) and bake in a 425° F. oven until golden, about 25 minutes.

⌇ Thin Crisp Corn Bread

1½ cups yellow cornmeal	1 tablespoon baking powder
1½ cups flour	1½ tablespoons melted butter
¾ cup sugar	1¾ to 2 cups milk
1 teaspoon salt	

Stir all dry ingredients together in a bowl. Stir butter into 1¾ cups of the milk and beat it into the cornmeal. Add a little more milk if necessary to make a batter of spreading consistency. Spread batter in 2 buttered 10-inch layer-cake pans and bake in a 400° F. oven until crisp and golden, about 20 minutes. Cut into wedges and butter while still warm.

❦ Light Corn Bread

From Miss Margaret Mallory's *The Old Gem Cookbook*

2 cups cornmeal
2 cups flour
½ teaspoon salt
½ teaspoon baking soda
1 teaspoon cream of tartar
2 tablespoons butter

¼ cup tightly packed brown sugar
1 egg
2 cups milk
1 tablespoon molasses (optional)

Sift dry ingredients together. Beat in butter, sugar and egg. Beat in milk until smooth. Add molasses if desired. Bake in 2 well-buttered loaf pans (9 × 5 × 3 inches) in the center of a 400° F. oven until golden, about 30 minutes. Check after 20 minutes.

❦ Apple Corn Bread

This used to hit lots of spots on a blustery autumn morning. It is another recipe descended from Puritan settlers who came to New England via Leyden. It is a combination of the Dutch apple cake they left behind and the Indian maize meal they found here.

2 cups white cornmeal
2 tablespoons sugar
½ teaspoon salt
1 teaspoon cream of tartar
1 teaspoon baking soda

1½ cups milk
3 to 4 tart apples, peeled, cored and sliced thin
2 tablespoons sugar
1 teaspoon ground cinnamon

Sift dry ingredients together into a bowl, beat in the milk until smooth, and pour the batter into a well-buttered shallow pan (11 × 8 inches). Cover with overlapping circles of apple slices. Sprinkle with combined sugar and cinnamon, and bake in a 375° F. oven for 35 minutes.

ℰ⅄ Galley Corn Bread

1 cup yellow cornmeal	¾ cup sugar
2 cups flour	2 eggs, beaten
1 tablespoon baking powder	1 tablespoon melted butter
½ teaspoon salt	1½ cups milk

Sift together cornmeal, flour, baking powder and salt. Beat sugar into eggs until smooth. Add butter and milk and beat in dry ingredients. Pour into buttered shallow pan (14 × 9 inches), and bake in a 425° F. oven until golden, about 20 minutes. Cut into squares and serve with lots of soft butter; no use making it crumble by trying to spread with cold, unspreadable butter.

ℰ⅄ Fred's Upside-down Corn Bread

From Frederick B. Thurber

¼ cup butter	6 slices of ham
½ cup brown sugar	1 package (12 ounces) corn-
8 slices of canned pineapple	bread mix
8 maraschino cherries	

Melt butter in a 10-inch skillet; sprinkle sugar over butter. Place pineapple slices on sugar in a single layer, arranging a cherry in the center of each slice. Place layer of ham over pineapple. Prepare corn bread according to package directions. Pour over ham. Bake in a 300° F. oven for 35 to 45 minutes. Serve with mushroom sauce if desired. Makes 6 to 8 servings.

ℰ⅄ Corn Crisps

2 cups boiling water	⅓ cup butter
1¾ cups cornmeal	1 teaspoon salt

Pour boiling water over meal, butter and salt in a bowl. Stir well until butter is dissolved. Spread the batter ⅛-inch thick on 2 well-buttered baking sheets (15 × 10 inches). Bake in a 375° F. oven until golden, about 8 minutes. Cut into squares while hot and serve at once.

CORN CRISP ROUNDS

The batter can also be dropped onto buttered baking sheets by the tablespoon and spread into ⅛-inch-thick rounds with a spatula dipped into cold water. Sprinkle a little celery salt on each. Bake as above. Take from baking sheet as soon as they come from the oven and serve at once. Excellent with soups and salads.

Simple Corn Pone

2 teaspoons salt
3 cups boiling water

4 cups cornmeal

Dissolve salt in boiling water and stir it into the cornmeal. Add more water if necessary to make a stiff dough. Allow a little time for the meal to "swell." Shape the dough into flat rounds like fish cakes, and lay them 1 inch apart in a buttered baking pan. Bake in a 350° F. oven for 35 minutes.
Makes about 24.

Corn Pone

½ cup lard or vegetable shortening
4 cups cornmeal
1½ teaspoons salt

½ teaspoon baking soda
1½ cups boiling water
1 cup buttermilk

In a bowl, work lard into meal with fingers. Dissolve salt and baking soda in the boiling water. Gradually stir the boiling water into the meal and lard mixture. Add just enough buttermilk to make a stiff dough.

Shape into flat rounds, like fish cakes, and bake 1 inch apart in a buttered baking pan in a 350° F. oven for 35 minutes.
Makes about 24.

INDIAN ASHCAKES I

Shape the same dough into oval cakes, wrap in grape or cabbage leaves, and bake in hot ashes for 40 minutes.
Makes 24.

INDIAN ASHCAKES II

The dough is very much like Simple Corn Pone, but cakes are baked on hot ashes.

4 cups cornmeal	1 tablespoon melted lard
1 teaspoon salt	Cold water

Scald meal with salt, lard and enough cold water to make a stiff dough. Shape into flat oval cakes and wrap in cabbage or grape leaves. Bake on hot ashes for about 40 minutes, turning once. Pull off the leaves and serve cakes hot with butter.

Cornmeal Mush

Not perhaps the most imaginative name in the world, but speed up the cooking and it turns into hasty pudding. It is also a sort of samp, saump, or nasaump. There were those with whom hasty pudding did not agree, due to the short cooking.

4 cups yellow cornmeal	1 tablespoon salt
2 cups cold water	1 tablespoon butter

Stir meal and cold water until thoroughly soaked. Put 6 cups water on to boil in a Dutch oven with salt and butter. Stir in the cornmeal mixture until smooth, cover, and boil gently for 1½ hours.

Eat hot with thick cream and sugar or with butter and maple syrup.
Makes 6 to 8 servings.

FRIED MUSH

When fried mush is contemplated, pour cooked cornmeal mush into a buttered loaf pan (9 × 5 × 3 inches) so that the slices will be even. Cool, and chill, then slice.

10 to 12 slices of cold cornmeal mush, ¾-inch thick	¾ cup butter
½ cup fat or butter for frying	¼ cup sugar
Heated maple syrup	1 tablespoon lemon juice

Fry sliced mush in fat or butter in a wide pan until golden. Turn and fry the second sides. Serve hot with heated maple syrup or with a pitcher of melted butter, beaten with sugar and lemon juice.
Makes about 6 servings.

CRUMBED FRIED MUSH

Prepare cornmeal mush and pour into a buttered loaf pan. Cool and chill. Cut into ¾-inch slices and dip into a mixture of 2 eggs beaten with ¼ cup milk. Turn the slices in bread crumbs to coat both sides evenly and fry in fat or butter as for fried mush.

૯ Brown Corn Balls

1 teaspoon salt	¼ cup butter
1 quart water	2 tablespoons melted butter
1 cup yellow cornmeal	2 teaspoons celery salt

Add salt to water and bring to a rapid boil. Slowly "rain" or sprinkle the cornmeal into the boiling water, stirring constantly with a wooden spoon. Add cornmeal slowly so that water does not stop boiling. Continue to boil and stir the batter for 5 minutes. Take from heat and beat in the butter until melted.

Shape the mush into small walnut-sized balls and place at least 2 inches apart on 2 well-buttered baking sheets. Brush balls lightly with a pastry brush dipped into melted butter and sprinkle with a little celery salt. Bake in a 475° F. oven until crisp and golden, about 25 minutes. Serve with soups, chowders or stews.

Makes about 2 dozen.

⊄ Cornmeal Fritters

2 cups cornmeal	1 tablespoon soft butter
½ cup flour	3 cups milk
1 tablespoon granulated sugar	Vegetable shortening for deep-
1 teaspoon baking powder	frying
1 teaspoon salt	Confectioners' sugar
4 eggs, separated	

Sift dry ingredients together into a bowl. Beat in the egg yolks, soft butter and milk until smooth. Fold in the stiffly beaten egg whites. Drop by large spoonfuls into shortening heated to 365° F. on a frying thermometer and fry until golden, about 4 minutes. Take out with a slotted spoon and sprinkle with confectioners' sugar. Serve with maple syrup or Spiced Cherry Sauce, page 89.

Makes about 6 servings.

VARIATION

Add to the batter 1 large apple, peeled and grated, or ½ cup fresh blueberries.

⊄ Corn Muffins

2 cups cornmeal	2 cups milk
2 cups flour	1 cup ripe blueberries, cranber-
1 tablespoon sugar	ries, raisins, or chopped dates
1 tablespoon baking powder	(optional) (for cranberries
1 teaspoon salt	increase sugar to 2 table-
2 eggs	spoons)

Sift dry ingredients together into a bowl. Beat in eggs and stir in milk until smooth; add fruit. Pour batter into buttered muffin tins until they are three quarters full. Bake in a 400° F. oven for 15 minutes. Makes about 30.

English Corn Muffins

1 cup cornmeal	1 tablespoon sugar
½ cup flour	2 eggs, separated
1 teaspoon salt	1½ cups milk
2 teaspoons baking powder	2 teaspoons lard

Combine and sift dry ingredients into a bowl. Beat in the egg yolks, milk and lard until smooth. Fold in the stiffly beaten egg whites. Bake until browned in buttered muffin rings set on a hot griddle. Turn with a pancake turner and brown the other side. Serve split, with butter and marmalade.
Makes about 16.

Miniature Blueberry Muffins

1¾ cups flour	5 tablespoons melted butter
6 tablespoons sugar	1 cup fresh blueberries or 1
1 tablespoon baking powder	package (12 ounces) frozen
½ teaspoon salt	blueberries, thawed and very
1 large egg, well beaten	well drained
½ cup milk	

Sift flour into a bowl with 3 tablespoons of the sugar, the baking powder and salt. Beat egg with milk and melted butter until smooth. Make a well in the center of the dry ingredients, pour in the egg mixture all at once, and stir quickly. Combine berries and 2 tablespoons of the sugar. Mix into the batter and pour into 24 lightly buttered, non-stick miniature muffin tins. Sprinkle tops with remaining sugar and bake in a 400° F. oven until brown and loose in the pans, about 20 minutes.

Makes 24.

Church Supper Biscuits

From Pauline Smith

2 cups flour
1 tablespoon baking powder
1 teaspoon salt

6 tablespoons vegetable shortening
¾ cup milk

Sift dry ingredients together into a bowl. Cut in shortening with a pastry blender. Stir milk in gradually with a knife blade. Turn soft dough onto a lightly floured pastry canvas. Roll or pat into a ½-inch-thick sheet and cut into 2½-inch rounds with a floured cookie cutter. Place close together in a buttered baking pan and bake in a 450° F. oven for 15 minutes. Split, butter, and serve hot.

Makes about 18.

Orange Biscuits

2 cups sifted flour
4 teaspoons baking powder
½ teaspoon salt
¼ cup butter
⅔ cup milk

14 to 16 lumps sugar (use sugar "dots")
Juice of ½ orange
Grated rind of 1 orange

Sift dry ingredients together into a bowl. Cut in butter with a pastry cutter and stir in milk with a knife blade. Turn soft dough onto a lightly floured pastry canvas and roll or pat out to ¾-inch thickness. Cut with a 1¾-inch floured cookie cutter, and place the rounds on a buttered baking sheet. Dip sugar "dots" into orange juice and press one down in the center of each biscuit. Brush biscuits with orange juice and sprinkle with the grated rind. Bake in a 425° F. oven until golden and sugar is partly dissolved, about 15 minutes.

Makes about 24.

Minute Biscuits

From *The Old Gem Cookbook*

4 cups flour	¼ cup butter
½ teaspoon baking soda	1 cup milk
1 teaspoon cream of tartar	

Sift dry ingredients together. Cut in butter or work it in with the fingertips; stir in milk and work quickly into a smooth dough. Pat out to ½-inch thickness on a floured pastry canvas and cut into 2-inch rounds with a floured cookie cutter. Place rounds close together in a well-buttered baking pan and bake in a 425° F. oven until lightly browned, 12 to 14 minutes. Split, butter, and serve at once.
Makes about 3 dozen.

Sour Milk

The early farmers of Mystic could not waste spoiled milk or any other food. All milk which was not consumed immediately was used for butter or cottage cheese. Any milk that turned sour found its way into baking. With great resourcefulness the housewives baked sour-milk pancakes, waffles, griddlecakes, muffins, biscuits, cakes and bread. Simple necessities in cooking had a way of turning into improvements, and sour milk lent a special delicacy wherever it was used. In this day of pasteurization it is not possible to obtain raw milk as they did in the early Mystic days and sour it naturally. Now it is necessary to add vinegar or lemon juice:

Remove ¼ cup milk from a quart, replace it with vinegar or lemon juice, stir well, and refrigerate until needed.

❦ Sour-milk Biscuits

From *Island Cooks*

4 cups flour
1 teaspoon salt
2 teaspoons cream of tartar
2 teaspoons baking soda

2 tablespoons lard
1⅓ to 1½ cups sour milk
3 tablespoons melted butter

Sift dry ingredients together in a bowl and rub in the lard with fingertips. Stir in just enough sour milk to make a rollable dough. Do not knead. Roll to ½-inch thickness and cut into 2-inch rounds with a floured cookie cutter. Place biscuits close together in a buttered baking dish and brush tops with melted butter. Bake in a 400° F. oven until golden, about 20 minutes.
Makes about 3 dozen.

❦ Sally Lunn

No one could set out from England to settle anywhere without a good recipe for Sally Lunn.

1½ cups milk
¼ cup sugar
1 teaspoon salt
¼ cup shortening
½ cup warm water

2 packages active dry yeast
5½ cups flour
2 eggs
Grated rind of 1 lemon

Scald milk, take from heat, and stir in sugar, salt and shortening until dissolved. Cool to lukewarm. Pour the warm water into a small bowl, sprinkle dry yeast over water, and stir until dissolved. Add 2 cups of the flour to the milk mixture and beat until smooth. Stir in the dissolved yeast and the eggs and beat for 2 minutes. Add remaining flour and the lemon rind and beat until smooth. Scrape dough together with a rubber scraper, cover, and let rise in a warm place for 1 hour.

Stir down dough and divide into 2 buttered standard bread pans (9 × 5 × 3 inches). Cover and let rise again for 1 hour. Bake in a

350° F. oven for about 45 minutes. Turn onto rack to cool slightly. Serve warm with soft butter. Sally Lunn has to be cut with 2 forks because a knife crumbles the loaf when it is still warm.

⚓ Pumpkin Bread

Mrs. Davis was born Mary Greenman; she is a descendant of the prominent family of shipbuilders who launched ships and sturdy steamers from their yards, now part of Mystic Seaport. Thanks to the famous Greenman generosity, Mrs. Davis shares with us her superb Pumpkin Bread and other recipes in this book.

1⅓ cups granulated sugar	¼ teaspoon baking powder
⅓ cup shortening	¾ teaspoon salt
2 eggs	½ teaspoon ground cinnamon
1 cup mashed or strained pumpkin	½ teaspoon grated nutmeg
	½ teaspoon vanilla extract
1⅓ cups flour	⅓ cup water
1 teaspoon baking soda	½ cup chopped nutmeats

Cream sugar with shortening. Beat in eggs, one at a time, until fluffy. Stir in pumpkin; add flour sifted with dry ingredients. Mix in all remaining ingredients and spoon into a buttered loaf pan (9 × 5 × 3 inches). Bake at 350° F. for 45 to 50 minutes. Cool and store. This bread is easier to slice on the second day.

⚓ Banana Bread

From Mrs. H. S. Dodd

2 soft ripe bananas	2 cups flour
1 cup sugar	1 teaspoon baking soda
Pinch of salt	1 teaspoon baking powder
1 egg, unbeaten	

Beat bananas, sugar and salt thoroughly in mixer or with egg beater. Add egg and beat until fluffy. Sift dry ingredients together and add.

Mix thoroughly and pour into greased loaf pan (9 × 5 × 3 inches). Bake slowly in a 320° F. oven until brown, 45 to 60 minutes. Makes 1 small loaf.

Date Nut Bread

Dried fruits and nuts were recognized as nourishing and healthy even before much was known about proper nutrition. It was believed that dates had properties that could slake thirst and satisfy hunger at the same time. Milton said of them:

> . . . fruits of palm-tree pleasantest to thirst
> And hunger both. . . .

As far as nuts were concerned, we learn from J. S. Forsyth, surgeon, that "They agree best with people advanced in years, and those of a phlegmatic and melancholy constitution." Which we counterbalance with all the energetic, happy children who eat nuts with a passion.

4 cups flour	1½ cups sugar
2 tablespoons baking powder	2 eggs
½ teaspoon salt	2 cups chopped walnuts
2 cups pitted and diced dates	⅓ cup perfect walnut halves
2 cups boiling water	for topping
3 tablespoons butter	

Sift flour, baking powder and salt together into a bowl. Combine dates, boiling water and butter in a large bowl and set aside until cold. Beat sugar with eggs until creamy and smooth. Stir dry ingredients into dates, alternating with the sugar and egg mixture. Add chopped nuts last; stir. Pour batter into 2 well-buttered loaf pans (9 × 5 × 3 inches). Cover and rest batter for 15 minutes. Arrange nut halves down the center of the 2 loaves. Bake in a 325° F. oven for 45 minutes, or until bread tests done when pierced with a cake tester or straw. Cool and wrap bread; store for a day before slicing.

❧ Honey Nut Bread

2½ cups flour, sifted
½ teaspoon salt
1 teaspoon baking soda
2 tablespoons butter
1 cup honey
1 large egg

¾ cup sour milk
¼ cup minced candied orange peel
¾ cup raisins
¾ cup chopped walnuts

Sift dry ingredients together. Cream butter, beat in honey until smooth, then beat in egg until fluffy. Beat in dry ingredients alternately with the sour milk. Add peel, raisins and nuts. Pour into a buttered loaf pan (10 × 5 × 3 inches). Bake in a 300° F. oven for 1¾ hours, or until bread tests done when pierced with a cake tester or straw.

❧ Orange Nut Bread

From Mrs. Reed Whitney

3 cups flour
3 teaspoons baking powder
¼ cup sugar
½ cup orange marmalade
1 cup milk
1 egg

½ cup chopped nutmeats (walnuts or pecans)
Thin rind of 3 oranges, soaked in hot water and diced
Pinch of salt

Mix all ingredients in order listed. Let stand for 10 minutes. Pour into a well-buttered loaf pan (10 × 5 × 3 inches) and bake in a 325° F. oven for about 45 minutes. Test with cake tester before taking from oven.

❧ Tart Lemon Bread

1 cup flour
1 teaspoon baking powder

¼ teaspoon salt
¼ teaspoon baking soda

¼ cup butter

7 tablespoons sugar

Grated rind of 4 lemons

1 egg, beaten

7 tablespoons lemon juice

Sift dry ingredients together. Cream butter with sugar and lemon rind until light and creamy; beat in egg until fluffy. Stir a little of the dry ingredients into the butter mixture, add a little lemon juice, and continue beating in a little of each, ending with the last of the flour mixture. Bake in a well-buttered miniature loaf pan (7½ × 3½ × 2½ inches) in a 350° F. oven until brown and done, about 30 minutes.

Lemon Bread

9 tablespoons vegetable shortening or butter

1½ cups granulated sugar

3 eggs

2½ cups flour

1½ tablespoons baking powder

¾ cup milk

Juice and grated rind of 1 lemon

1 cup broken walnut meats

¾ cup confectioners' sugar

Cream shortening and beat in granulated sugar until light. Beat in eggs, one by one, until fluffy. Sift flour with baking powder and stir into mixture, alternating with milk mixed with 1 teaspoon of the lemon juice. Stir in lemon rind and nuts. Pour batter into 2 buttered loaf pans (9 × 5 × 3 inches) and bake in a 325° F. oven for about 1 hour, or until the bread tests done. Stir remaining lemon juice with confectioners' sugar and pour over tops of loaves. Cool in pans, unmold, and wrap until following day.

ℰ𝒳 Hyla Snider's Oatmeal Bread

2 teaspoons sugar
1 cup lukewarm water
2 packages dry yeast
⅔ cup lard or vegetable short-
    ening
3 cups quick-cooking oatmeal
½ cup honey

1¼ tablespoons salt
3 cups boiling water
5 eggs
Flour, preferably unbleached
Oatmeal to sprinkle over tops of
    loaves

Add sugar to water; sprinkle yeast over top and let stand until foamy. Put lard or shortening, oatmeal, honey and salt in a large mixing bowl. Pour the boiling water over mixture and stir briefly. Let cool to lukewarm. Begin sifting in a little flour to insure mixture is lukewarm only.

Add 4 eggs and yeast to mixture and stir well. Stir in flour gradually until dough leaves sides of bowl. Knead for 10 minutes. Divide into 4 parts; place in greased bowls and cover well to prevent surface harden-ing. Let rise in a warm place until doubled in bulk—this will take several hours. Turn out of the bowls and knead until blisters appear under surface of dough. Put in 4 buttered loaf pans (9 × 5 × 3 inches). Brush tops of loaves with remaining egg beaten with 1 tablespoon cold water. Sprinkle generously with oatmeal. Let rise again until doubled in bulk.

Heat oven to 375° F. and bake bread until brown, approximately 35 to 40 minutes. Test for doneness by tapping with fingertips; the sound on top *and* bottom of loaves should be hollow. Cool on a rack, or eat while hot. This makes excellent toast; use a grill-type toaster or toast lightly in oven. A round "corrugated" bread pan, if available, will produce uniform slices, with a crust all around.

ℰ𝒳 Steamed Brown Bread

Baked beans and brown bread are usually attributed to Boston. This is historically true but also pleasantly alliterative. Actually baked beans and steamed bread were served on Saturday nights in every New England community, and Mystic had as many versions as the rest.

2½ cups cornmeal	2 scant cups dark molasses, or
2½ cups whole-wheat flour	1⅞ cups
2½ cups rye flour	5 cups sour milk or buttermilk
2 tablespoons baking soda	2½ cups raisins
2 teaspoons salt	

Combine dry ingredients and sift into a large bowl. Stir in molasses, milk and raisins until thoroughly mixed. Spoon into 3 well-buttered brown-bread molds or into 3 well-buttered tall coffee cans, filling them three quarters full. Cover the molds tightly, or seal the cans with securely tied foil and tape. This is essential, as bread rises and pushes against the lid or foil. Steam the molds or cans on a rack in a kettle of boiling water for 3½ hours. The water must come halfway up the sides of the molds or cans, and it has to be replaced with boiling water as it steams away; the water level must remain the same. Keep the kettle tightly covered except when water is being added. If necessary put a weight on the lid to hold it down more firmly.

Take molds or cans from kettle, uncover them, and bake them in a 300° F. oven for 15 to 20 minutes to dry. Cool slightly and take carefully from molds. Slice across and serve with baked beans (pp. 158 to 160).

🐟 Steamed Rhode Island Brown Bread

Mary Greenman Davis's rule*

3 cups Indian or yellow corn-meal	1 teaspoon baking soda
	1 cup molasses
3 cups sweet milk	1 cup flour
1 cup sour milk	1 teaspoon salt

Combine ingredients and steam in a 1½-quart double boiler or in a mold in a steam kettle for 4 hours. Allow room in boiler or mold for

---

* A "rule" was the settlers' word for a recipe and still has the same meaning in Mystic.

rising and expansion. Always keep water in bottom of double boiler at the same level. Uncover boiler or mold and dry out bread in a 300° F. oven for 15 minutes.

Mrs. Davis adds, "Sweet milk can be substituted for sour. One-half rule makes plenty." That is what Mrs. Davis thinks, but a full rule makes only just enough.

ℰ𝒜 Steamed Boston Brown Bread

Mrs. Howard Saunier Dodd writes, "These recipes never fail for me!" We have tested them with the same result.

1 scant teaspoon baking soda	1 cup flour
⅔ cup molasses	1 cup sweet milk
1 cup yellow cornmeal	½ teaspoon salt

Stir baking soda into molasses until dissolved. Combine all ingredients in 2 buttered 1-pound baking-powder cans. Steam in a covered kettle, keeping water at the same level, for 3 hours. Fill cans three quarters full of batter to allow for expansion of bread. Open cans and allow bread to cool and dry before taking it out. Cut across.

ℰ𝒜 Steamed Sour-milk Brown Bread

Even Mrs. Lincoln,* who claimed everything for Boston, did not claim her recipes never failed. She suggested that this brown bread be baked in a pail set in a steam kettle. Pails, in her day, apparently came in small sizes.

4 cups white cornmeal	2 cups molasses
4 cups graham or whole-wheat flour	1 quart sour milk or buttermilk
2 teaspoons salt	2 cups dried currants (optional)
1 tablespoon baking soda	

* Mrs. Lincoln was the original author of *The Boston Cookbook*.

Stir the dry ingredients in a large mixing bowl. Stir in molasses and milk. Add or subtract a little milk, if necessary. The batter should be just moist enough to pour. Pour it into 2 well-buttered brown-bread or pudding molds or 3 well-buttered tall 1-pound coffee tins. Fill the molds two thirds full. Butter the lids and tape or tie them on securely. The success of the bread depends on the secure covering, because as it rises it exerts considerable pressure against the lid. Steam the molds in boiling water reaching halfway up the molds in a closely covered steamer or large kettle for 3 hours. Replace the boiling water as it boils away, always keeping it at the same level. Take molds from kettle, remove covers, and bake in a 350° F. oven for 15 minutes to dry the crust. Serve hot with butter and baked beans. Also good with marmalade or vanilla ice cream.

Brown Bread

From the *Providence Journal-Bulletin's Rhode Islander Cookbook*

2 cups Rhode Island cornmeal	1 teaspoon salt
1 cup rye meal	⅔ cup molasses
2 teaspoons baking soda	2 cups buttermilk

Combine dry ingredients; stir in molasses and milk. Pour batter into 2 buttered 1-quart pudding molds or fill buttered cans about three quarters full. Butter lids before closing molds, and tie lids on firmly, so rising bread will not lift lid. Steam in 1 inch of water in a covered kettle for 3 hours. Replace water with boiling water to maintain same level.

Mystic Stickies

This will tie a nice toggle knot around your near and dear ones. They'll always come back for more.

¾ cup milk

3 tablespoons granulated sugar

1½ teaspoons salt

4½ tablespoons shortening

¾ cup warm water

2 packages active dry yeast

4½ cups sifted flour

½ cup dark brown sugar

1 cup honey

¼ cup melted butter

1½ cups chopped pecans

Soft butter

Scald milk, take from heat, and stir in granulated sugar, salt and shortening until dissolved. Cool to lukewarm. Into a second bowl pour the warm water; sprinkle the dry yeast over water and stir until dissolved. Add the milk mixture and stir in half of the flour. Work in remaining flour. Turn the dough out on a lightly floured board and knead until smooth. Place in greased bowl, turn dough until all sides are glossy, cover, and let rise in a warm place until doubled in bulk, about 45 minutes.

While dough is rising, combine brown sugar, honey and butter and divide it evenly over two 8-inch-square pans. Sprinkle each pan with ¾ cup pecans. Punch down dough, turn out on lightly floured board, and divide into halves. Roll out each half to a piece 9 × 12 inches. Brush with soft butter and roll each into a 12-inch-long roll. Cut each roll into 1-inch slices. Place 12 slices, cut sides down, in each of the prepared pans, keeping the slices as far apart as possible. Cover and let rise in a warm place for about 1 hour. Bake in a 400° F. oven for about 25 minutes. Take clustered stickies out of pans at once.

On-board Doughnuts

The expression "don't go overboard" for this or that was, of course, borrowed from the sea. Rash overenthusiasm was considered as foolish as a leap into the ocean. While these doughnuts are well worth enthusiasm, eat them "on board."

3½ to 4 cups flour

1½ tablespoons baking powder

½ teaspoon ground cinnamon

½ teaspoon salt

1 whole egg

2 extra egg yolks

1 cup milk, at room temperature

1 cup granulated sugar
3 tablespoons melted butter
½ teaspoon grated nutmeg
(optional)

3 cups confectioners' sugar
Vegetable shortening for deep-
frying

Sift first 4 dry ingredients into a large bowl. In a small bowl, beat eggs and egg yolks and gradually add milk, granulated sugar and butter. Beat egg mixture into dry ingredients to make a soft dough. If necessary add enough flour so that dough can be rolled out on a lightly floured board. Roll out a little of the dough at a time. Cut with a floured doughnut cutter and set each doughnut on a kitchen towel to dry while cutting the rest. Retain the cutouts, which are called "doughgods," to fry and eat with maple syrup. Return dough scraps to remaining dough, knead lightly, and roll out for a second batch.

When all doughnuts and doughgods are completed, deep-fry a few doughnuts at a time in vegetable shortening heated to 370° F. on a frying thermometer. Turn them *once* and take them out carefully with a slotted spoon when they are brown and puffed. Let doughnuts drain on absorbent paper. Sift nutmeg and confectioners' sugar together into a paper bag. Add a few cooled doughnuts at a time and shake until thoroughly coated.

Makes about 42 doughnuts and 42 doughgods.

Molasses Doughnuts

From Lillian Smith

Another recipe for which we are grateful to *The Food Log*.

3 cups flour
1½ tablespoons baking soda
¼ teaspoon salt
¼ teaspoon ground ginger
¼ teaspoon ground cinnamon
¼ teaspoon grated nutmeg
1 egg, well beaten

¼ cup granulated sugar
1 tablespoon melted butter or
lard
1 cup molasses
Confectioners' sugar for sifting
over doughnuts

Sift first 6 dry ingredients together into a bowl. Beat egg with granulated sugar, butter and molasses, and beat mixture into dry ingredients. Add enough additional flour to make a soft dough which is just stiff enough to roll out on a floured board. Follow directions for shaping and frying On-board Doughnuts (see above), or cut into 7-inch-long fingers and twist. Sift confectioners' sugar over the cooled doughnuts. Makes about 35.

Portuguese Easter Bread

We are grateful to the *Vineyard Gazette* for this recipe.

3 cakes compressed yeast	12 eggs, well beaten
1 cup lukewarm water	2 cups lukewarm milk
12 cups flour	1 cup butter, melted
1 tablespoon salt	Grated rind of 3 large lemons
3 cups sugar	

Dissolve yeast in lukewarm water and set aside. Sift flour and salt together into a large bowl. Beat sugar and eggs with the lukewarm milk and stir into flour. Stir in yeast. Knead until smooth. Add melted butter and lemon rind. Knead a little more, adding more flour if necessary. Cover and let rise in a warm place, until doubled in bulk. Divide into 4 round, slightly flattened loaves and place in 4 buttered pie pans. Let rise again until doubled. Bake in 350° F. oven until golden brown and done, about 45 minutes.

Portuguese Sweet Bread

We have had many requests for Mrs. Wilhelmina Arruda's Portuguese Sweet Bread, which we are happy to include here.

Born in 1891 in St. Miguels, Portugal, Mrs. Arruda came to the United States in 1901 and for sixty-seven years has been a well-known resident of Stonington, Mystic's neighboring village to the east. Commonly known as "Ma" to most of Stonington, Mrs. Arruda is actually a mother of twelve children, has forty grandchildren and thirty-nine great-grandchildren.

"Ma" is an active member of St. Mary's Church and the Portuguese Holy Ghost Society. At the age of 71 she won her first contest for dancing the "twist." She sponsors the annual New Year's Eve party for the Portuguese people of Stonington. At the Annual Labor Day feast, when all the people of Stonington are fed (to symbolize the food bought by Queen Isabella who sold her jewels to feed the famished people of Portugal), Mrs. Arruda has for many years been the chief cook. Today at 78, she is still as spry as ever. She advocates that the secret to a long and productive life is hard work, together with a necessary amount of play.

As for the Sweet Bread, she has been making this practically all her life, and we hope she will keep on baking her lovely loaves for many years. This bread is particularly good toasted, but by the time we have tried it fresh, light toasted, dark toasted, parched, fried, with jam and without jam, the loaf is consumed.

1 dozen whole eggs	½ pound butter
4 cups sugar	½ pound shortening
3 yeast cakes	7 pounds flour
1¼ cups lukewarm water	2 extra egg whites
1 tablespoon salt	

Break eggs into a large bowl and beat. Add sugar to the beaten eggs. Mix yeast with 1 cup of the lukewarm water in a small bowl. Dissolve salt in remaining ¼ cup lukewarm water in another bowl. Melt butter and shortening together in saucepan.

Combine yeast, salt and egg mixtures together with flour in a large pan. Knead mixture until ingredients form a dough. Add melted butter and shortening and keep kneading until all ingredients are thoroughly blended. Cover pan well and let mixture rise for 6 or 7 hours (more or less) making sure to keep mixture away from drafts. Knead bread again and keep it covered and rising for an additional 3 to 4 hours.

Divide into portions of 1 pound or 1½ pounds each, and put into bread pans (9 × 5 × 3 inches). Let rise until nearly doubled in size. Slit tops with a sharp knife. Brush with slightly beaten egg whites. Preheat oven to 350° F. Put in bread, reduce heat to 300°, and bake for 30 minutes. Reduce heat to 250° and bake for an additional 30 minutes until golden.

Makes about six 1½-pound loaves.

NOTE: When mixing ingredients, keep them away from drafts.

Pancakes

The first cookbook written and printed in the United States was published in 1796 in Hartford, Connecticut, and was written by "Amelia Simmons, an American Orphan." While some of the recipes are, inevitably, of English and European origin, there are many that were entirely indigenous to America. There are recipes for slapjacks and flapjacks which remind us that elegant thin pancakes had long ago given way to the more nourishing griddle cakes and had moved from the end of dinner to the beginning of the day at breakfast.

Burnt-sugar Pancake

4 large eggs	Pinch of salt
⅔ cup milk	6 tablespoons butter
7 tablespoons flour	¼ cup toasted slivered al-
6 tablespoons sugar	monds

Beat eggs, milk, flour, 2 tablespoons of the sugar and the salt until smooth. Melt 2 to 3 tablespoons butter in very large frying pan and add batter.* Let it brown slowly for 3 to 4 minutes. Cut into wedges, add 2 tablespoons butter, and turn the wedges over with a spatula. Brown other side for a minute, add almonds and continue to fry, breaking each

---

* Batter should not be over ¼-inch deep in the pan. If pan is not large enough, make 2 batches.

wedge into large bite-sized pieces. Add remaining 4 tablespoons of sugar and fry until pancakes are golden and sugar starts to caramelize. Serve at once on hot plates with cold applesauce.
Makes 4 servings.

Pancakes

An old English recipe

6 tablespoons flour	3 tablespoons sugar
2 cups milk	Grating of nutmeg (optional)
5 eggs, well beaten	Butter for frying
3 tablespoons melted butter	Sugar
¼ teaspoon salt	Lemon slices

Mix batter 2 hours before baking pancakes and put in a cool place until needed. Combine first 7 ingredients and beat until smooth. Heat some butter in a pan, pour in enough batter to make a thin pancake, and tilt pan to spread batter evenly. Cook over medium heat until brown on one side, then turn and brown the other side, about 3 minutes in all.

Place each pancake on a warm plate and sift sugar over it. Place a few thin lemon slices on each pancake and serve immediately.
Makes about 4 servings.

Griddle Cakes

1⅓ cups flour	2 eggs, beaten
1½ teaspoons baking powder	1⅓ cups milk
2 teaspoons sugar	3 tablespoons melted butter
½ teaspoon salt, or more	

Sift dry ingredients together in a bowl, add eggs and milk, and beat until blended. Stir in all but 1 teaspoon of the butter. Use remaining teaspoon butter to brush on a hot griddle or pan. Pour even amounts of batter onto the griddle and bake the cakes until a few bubbles form on the top. With a pancake turner turn and brown the second side.

Makes about 10 pancakes.

VARIATION: For Blueberry or Corn Griddle Cakes add ⅔ cup fresh blueberries or well-drained frozen berries, or ⅔ cup fresh or well-drained canned corn.

⚓ Corn Cakes

From the *Vineyard Gazette*, September 17, 1846

"Corn Cakes.—We know of no more delicious cakes than can be made of the green corn with which our market is so abundantly supplied. Take the hardest ears, grate them on a corn grater, mix the wet meal thus obtained in the same manner and to the same consistence as you mix dry Indian meal, add salt, and bake on a hot griddle. Butter and eat while warm, and you will want to repeat the dose next day."

⚓ Corn Cakes

5 or 6 fresh ears of corn	2 teaspoons baking powder
3 eggs, separated	1½ teaspoons salt
3 tablespoons sugar	¼ teaspoon pepper
2 tablespoons flour	Butter for frying

Slit corn kernels down the center with a sharp knife and scrape off the ears. Measure enough to make 3 cups of kernels. Pour scraped kernels into a sieve and let the superfluous "milk" drain off while beating the eggs. Beat yolks with sugar until light and creamy. Sift flour with baking powder, salt and pepper and beat into yolks. Add a little more flour if necessary to keep batter from being too thin. Beat the egg whites stiff. Add the drained corn to the yolk mixture and fold in the egg whites. Drop by large spoonfuls onto a well-buttered hot griddle or pan and fry until browned to taste. Turn with a pancake turner and brown second side.

Makes about 2 dozen small cakes.

✥ Corn Flapjacks

2 cups cornmeal	2 eggs, separated
1 quart boiling milk	1 cup flour
2 teaspoons sugar	1 teaspoon salt
1 tablespoon butter	1 teaspoon baking powder

Scald cornmeal with boiling milk; mix well. Add sugar and butter and set aside overnight. In the morning, beat in egg yolks and flour sifted with salt and baking powder. Fold in the stiffly beaten egg whites and fry on a well-buttered hot griddle. Make flapjacks larger than griddle cakes. Serve for breakfast with butter, bacon or sausage and maple syrup.

Makes about 12 large cakes.

✥ Potato Pancakes For Two

From Mrs. Franklin Overton Rich

2 large raw potatoes, peeled and grated	Dash of pepper
1 tablespoon minced onion	2 tablespoons flour
½ teaspoon salt	2 eggs, beaten
	¼ cup milk

Mix all ingredients together and fry on buttered griddle. Drain on brown paper in oven.

Makes 2 servings.

ⳤ Potato Scones

1 pound cooked and mashed potatoes	1 cup flour
	½ teaspoon salt, or more
2 tablespoons melted butter	

Mix all ingredients into a soft dough. Roll out to a ½-inch-thick round and cut, pie-fashion, into 8 wedges. Bake on a hot griddle or buttered pan for 3 to 4 minutes on each side. Split and butter. Serve hot. Makes 4 servings.

ⳤ Griddle Scones

J. S. Forsyth, author of *A Dictionary of Diet,* published in 1834, states: "The Potatoe is a perennial plant, best known for the tubers produced by its roots." Furthermore Mr. Forsyth says, "It is supposed to be a native of South America, but Humboldt is very doubtful." There is some doubt as well about the origin of sugar cane and other blessings America gave the world.

Sir Walter Raleigh is presumed to have brought the potato to England in 1586, and the early settlers are presumed to have brought it to the rocky meadows of New England. We do know that the potato was the chief food of the whalemen and went far to sustain their families at home. They made potato bread and potato scones, baked on a hot griddle.

6 cups riced boiled potatoes	1 teaspoon baking powder
½ cup butter	1 teaspoon salt, or more
1 cup flour	Flour

Boil, peel and rice while hot, enough potatoes to obtain 6 cups. Stir in the butter until it is melted. Sift flour, baking powder and salt together and work into the potatoes to form a soft dough. Add flour if it is too soft. Roll dough out on a floured board to ½-inch thickness. Cut out with a floured 3-inch, or larger, cookie cutter. Place rounds on wax paper on a cookie sheet. Cover with wax paper before putting on a second layer. Chill for 15 to 20 minutes. Do not take from wax paper until ready to cook. Butter griddle or pan lightly and brown scones on both sides, turning once with a pancake turner. Serve hot with lots of butter and jam.

Makes about 2 dozen.

ℰ𝒳 Dried Fruit Scones

4 cups flour	¾ cup butter
1 teaspoon baking powder	½ cup raisins
1 teaspoon baking soda	½ cup dried currants
½ teaspoon salt	¾ cup buttermilk
2 tablespoons sugar	¼ cup milk

Sift flour, baking powder, baking soda, salt and sugar into a bowl. Cut in butter until mixture resembles small peas. Add dried fruits. Stir in buttermilk, little by little, with the blade of a knife. Stop adding buttermilk as soon as the dough gathers. Knead gently, only long enough to shape into 2 balls. Roll out on a lightly floured board to ½-inch-thick rounds, and cut each round across into 12 pie-slice wedges. Place on a buttered baking sheet, brush tops with milk, and bake in a 450° F. oven for 20 minutes. Split, butter, and serve with jam.

Makes 2 dozen.

ℰ𝒳 Rhode Island Johnnycakes

From Dorcas Whaley Brogan

"My grandmother Whaley and my mother used these johnnycakes with dried bread and seasonings in making stuffing for turkey and chickens and bluefish. Also pork chops baked with this dressing are a treat."

Into a small saucepan, put 1 cup Kenyon's cornmeal (or other corn-meal), and gradually stir in milk until the right consistency for pancake batter has been reached. Meanwhile heat an iron griddle; when hot put on ½ teaspoon bacon grease or vegetable shortening. Now put 3 soup-spoonfuls of the cornmeal mixture on the griddle, making three johnny-cakes; when they are a lovely shade of brown, turn over and brown the other side. Stack these johnnycakes in a dish which has a cover with holes, so the steam may escape. Keep mixing more cornmeal and milk in the saucepan, depending upon how many johnnycakes you plan to make. Serve with butter or gravy. It is necessary to grease the griddle before making each set of three. These johnnycakes are delicious served with liver and bacon and with fish of all kinds, especially eels which have been dipped into cornmeal before frying. They are good with steak and gravy too.

Splendid Johnnycake

Another recipe from Miss Mallory's *The Old Gem Cookbook*

1 cup flour	1 teaspoon salt
1½ cups cornmeal, approximately	1 tablespoon sugar
2 teaspoons cream of tartar	2 cups sweet milk, sour milk or buttermilk
1 teaspoon baking soda	¼ cup melted butter, cooled

Combine and sift dry ingredients. Beat in milk and cooled butter and beat until well mixed. Pour into a well-buttered 9-inch-square baking pan and bake in a 400° F. oven for about 40 minutes. Check after 35 minutes.
Makes nine 3-inch squares.

Perfect Johnnycakes

Mr. Robert Chapin writes, "This is a popular item in Rhode Island and seems to be hard to find on any menus outside of the state. They go well with steak, chops or any meat. And many people like to serve maple syrup with them. *White* cornmeal is important and can be bought packaged in almost any market in Rhode Island. In the early days the

Narragansett Indians and other tribes raised and used white cornmeal as one of their staple foods. White corn continues to be raised and used here."

For Perfect Johnnycakes these rules should be used:

1 cup Grist Mill Special John-nycake Meal*	1¼ cups boiling water
	¼ cup milk

All utensils should be rinsed in warm water before using. Combine meal and boiling water (water *must* be boiling) and blend well. Stir in milk. When well mixed, drop by tablespoons onto a well-greased hot griddle. Cook until golden brown, turn, and brown the second side. Use less water and milk in warm weather and more water and milk in cold weather.

Makes about 4 servings.

ℰ𝒳 Indian Pudding

5 cups milk	1 egg, beaten
⅓ cup corn meal	1 teaspoon ginger
¾ cup dark molasses	½ teaspoon cinnamon
¼ cup butter	3 tablespoons sugar
1 teaspoon salt	

Boil 4 cups of milk over direct heat; stir in corn meal. Place mixture in top of a double boiler and cook over boiling water for 15 minutes. Stir in molasses and cook 5 minutes more. Remove from heat and add remaining ingredients. Pour batter into well-greased baking dish and pour 1 cup of cold milk over the top. Bake in a 325° Fahrenheit oven for 1 ½ to 2 hours. Serve with thick cream or soft vanilla ice cream.

* Old Grist Mill Pure Rhode Island Johnnycake Meal can be mail ordered from: Clarks Falls Grist Mill, Clarks Falls, North Stonington, Connecticut 06359.

CHAPTER IV

~~~

Sauces

A<small>T</small> a time when everything was cooked in a stewpot and was served in its own liquid, it is no wonder that Mystic did not build up a great repertoire of separate sauces. Some appear with other recipes, however, since that is how they were written.

There is a close relationship between Old England's green sauce and New England's "green sass." The green sauce which the settlers left behind them when they sailed was an overboiled vegetable stew similar to our mushroom or tomato sauce. It was served separately in small saucedishes while meat and starches were served together on a plate. Green sauce was eaten with a spoon. Later on the English saucedish turned into a sauceboat and the spoon turned into a ladle.

Trust the New Englanders to take on the new without abandoning the old. In restaurants and some homes they serve meat and potatoes together on a plate, they serve a sauce in a sauceboat with a ladle, and they surround each diner's plate with "sass" dishes filled with stewed vegetables. The little dishes remind those of us who are old enough of our grandmother's canary-bird's bathtub. A dinner table in Mystic can be so absolutely loaded with such little dishes that the table cannot be seen.

⪫ Tomato Sauce I

Mystic wives served sauces of every kind with noodles and rice. When Italian pasta became available, these same sauces were still good.

¼ cup chopped salt pork
½ small onion, chopped
1 tablespoon flour
8 large tomatoes, peeled, seeded and chopped, or 1 can (28 ounces) Italian tomatoes

½ bay leaf
½ teaspoon crushed thyme
½ teaspoon sugar
1 inch of lemon peel
Salt and pepper

Fry salt pork and onion until golden, about 7 minutes. Stir in flour until smooth and browned. Reduce heat to just over a simmer and add tomatoes and remaining ingredients. Cover and cook, stirring frequently, for about 45 minutes. Serve as it is, press it through a sieve, or purée it in the blender. Season to taste.
Makes about 3 cups.

⪫ Tomato Sauce II

6 tablespoons butter
1 carrot, scraped and diced
2 onions, chopped
1 celery stalk, diced
1 bay leaf
3 sprigs parsley
1 sprig thyme
¼ cup flour

1 teaspoon sugar
4 pounds tomatoes, peeled and seeded, or 6 cups canned tomatoes, drained
3 beef bouillon cubes
2 cups boiling water
Salt and pepper

Melt butter in a heavy kettle; add carrot, onions, celery and herbs; and stir over medium heat until onions begin to brown, about 7 minutes. Sprinkle with flour and sugar and stir until both are absorbed and browned. Add tomatoes, bouillon cubes and water and stir for 5 minutes. Cover and simmer, stirring frequently until sauce is thickened; add salt and pepper to taste. Blend or sieve, or serve as it is.

The sauce can also be made in the oven. Place the covered kettle in a 350° F. oven and let it cook for 2 hours, stirring occasionally.
Makes about 6 cups.

&⚓ Aunt Lizzie Hedges' Green-tomato Sauce

From Mrs. George Washington Pierpont

8 quarts green tomatoes	1 tablespoon ground cloves
1 cup salt	1 tablespoon ground allspice
8 green peppers	1 tablespoon ground cinnamon
6 onions	1 cup sugar
1 cup grated horseradish	Vinegar (about 1 quart)
1 cup dark mustard seeds	

Chop the tomatoes, sprinkle with the salt, and let stand overnight. In the morning pour off the water. Chop the peppers and onions, add them with the spices and sugar, and put all into a kettle. Cover with vinegar. Boil until well cooked, stirring frequently, about 1¾ hours. Add a little boiling water as the vinegar evaporates, if a thinner sauce is preferred. Pour into bottles and seal.
Makes about 12 pints.

&⚓ Mushroom Sauce

6 tablespoons butter	2 cups light cream
1 pound mushrooms, including their stems, sliced	1 teaspoon beef extract
	Salt and pepper
½ onion, chopped	1 tablespoon minced parsley
¼ cup flour	

Melt 2 tablespoons of the butter in a heavy saucepan, add mushrooms and onion, and stir over medium heat until mushrooms are wilted and dark. In a heavy saucepan melt remaining butter; let it brown lightly. Reduce heat, stir in flour, and continue to stir until golden. Gradually add cream and stir until thickened and smooth. Add mushrooms and their juices, beef extract and seasonings to taste; stir to heat through. Add parsley. If sauce is too thick, stir in a little bouillon. Season carefully as beef extract is salty.

Makes about 3 cups.

White Sauce I

For sauce base, casseroles, and cream soups.

¼ cup butter	Salt
¼ cup flour	Pinch of pepper
2 cups milk	

Melt butter in a heavy saucepan over low heat; do not let it brown. Stir in flour until well mixed. Gradually add milk, stirring constantly until sauce thickens. Season to taste. Reduce heat and simmer, stirring occasionally, for 12 to 15 minutes longer.

Makes 2 cups.

THIN WHITE SAUCE

Reduce butter and flour to 2 tablespoons each for thin white sauce.

THICK WHITE SAUCE

Increase butter and flour to 6 or even 8 tablespoons each for thick or very thick white sauce. Use this to bind croquettes and for similar recipes.

White Sauce II

Follow recipe for White Sauce I but melt butter in the top part of a double boiler over boiling water. Stir in flour and milk as directed, reduce heat so that water boils gently under sauce, and cook, stirring, until thickened. Reduce heat and let sauce stand, covered, until needed. Whip with a French wire whisk to make smooth.

✺ Tartar Sauces

Prepare any of the following sauces at least 2 hours before serving, and chill until needed. For mayonnaise, use any good recipe or a good bottled brand.

I

1 cup mayonnaise
½ cup finely-chopped onion,
   Bermuda if possible

1 tablespoon small capers, or chopped large capers
1 tablespoon sweet pickle relish, drained

Whip mayonnaise, stir in remaining ingredients, and chill.
Makes about 1½ cups.

II

1 cup mayonnaise
1 tablespoon lemon juice
Grated rind of 1 lemon

¼ cup finely-chopped onion
2 tablespoons chopped capers

Stir together and chill.
Makes about 1½ cups.

III

1¼ cups mayonnaise
1 small shallot, minced
1 tablespoon chopped capers

1 tablespoon chopped dill pickle
1 tablespoon chopped olives
1 tablespoon minced parsley

Whip mayonnaise, stir in remaining ingredients, and chill.
Makes about 1 ½ cups.

IV

1 cup mayonnaise
½ teaspoon minced tarragon (or ½ teaspoon scalded, dried tarragon)
1 tablespoon minced parsley

1 tablespoon sweet pickle relish
2 teaspoons minced onion
1 teaspoon minced green pepper
1 teaspoon chopped chives

Whip and chill.
Makes 1 ¼ cups.

⒞ Lemon Tartar Sauce

Made in a blender

1 egg
2 tablespoons lemon juice
½ teaspoon salt
Pinch of pepper
½ teaspoon dry mustard
1 cup oil

Rind of 1 lemon, cut paper-thin with a potato peeler and slivered
2 tablespoons drained smallest capers
2 tablespoons minced onion
2 tablespoons well-drained sweet pickle relish

Place egg, lemon juice and seasonings in blender container. Cover and blend for 3 to 4 seconds. Open top without turning off the motor and add oil in a thin stream until sauce is thick and smooth. Turn off, scrape down sides of container, and add slivered lemon rind. Blend only until lemon rind is minced, turn off and on a few times if necessary. Scrape sauce out of container. Stir in capers, onion and pickle relish and serve with deep-fried foods.
Makes about 2 cups.

❧ Mystic Cocktail Sauce

For lobster, crabmeat or seafood cocktails

1½ cups mayonnaise
½ cup chili sauce
2 tablespoons prepared mustard
1 teaspoon minced onion

2 tablespoons sweet pickle relish, all moisture pressed out
½ to 1 teaspoon salt, or more
½ teaspoon pepper
2 teaspoons minced capers (optional)

Stir all ingredients and serve cold. Sauce may be sprinkled with chopped parsley.
Makes about 2 cups.

❧ Mint Sauce

1¾ cups sugar
1½ cups cider vinegar
¼ cup crème de menthe

Chopped leaves from 1 bunch of mint (about ½ cup tightly packed)

Boil sugar and vinegar for 15 minutes, turn down heat, add liqueur, and simmer for 5 minutes longer. Add minced mint and serve at once, or bottle and store.
Makes about 3 cups.

❧ Lemon Herb Sauce

Made in a blender

1 whole egg
2 tablespoons lemon juice
¾ teaspoon salt
Pinch of white pepper
½ teaspoon dry mustard
1 cup salad oil

2 onion slices
Rind of 1 lemon, cut with a potato peeler
2 tablespoons chopped parsley
1 tablespoon chopped chives
1 tablespoon chopped tarragon

Place egg, lemon juice, salt and pepper and mustard in blender container. Whirl for 2 seconds, open top without turning off the motor, and add oil in a thin stream. After oil is added sauce will be thick. Scrape down sides of bowl and whirl again with onion slices and lemon rind, doing only a few pieces at a time. Stir in remaining ingredients. Add more salt and pepper if necessary. Chill.

Makes about 2 cups.

Cold Mustard Sauce

For ham, tongue or fish

2 egg yolks	6 tablespoons mild brown mustard
2 teaspoons dry mustard	tard
2 teaspoons lemon juice	1½ cups heavy sour cream
	Salt and pepper

Place egg yolks in a bowl, turn electric beater to low speed, and add dry mustard and lemon juice gradually. Beat until thick, gradually adding brown mustard and sour cream. Beat in seasonings to taste. Add more cream if sauce is too sharp.

Makes about 3 cups.

Chilled Cucumber Sauce

For hot broiled chicken

¾ cup mayonnaise	3 tablespoons lemon juice
¾ cup sour cream	½ teaspoon celery salt
2 unpeeled cucumbers, seeded and diced fine	¼ cup fine-chopped salted almonds or pecans

Beat mayonnaise with sour cream until light. Pat cucumber dice with a kitchen towel to dry completely. Beat in lemon juice and celery salt. Chill. Serve sprinkled with chopped nuts.

Makes about 4 cups.

ℰ᙭ Cold Bread Sauce

For cold meats, game birds or pheasant

6 slices of white bread | Salt and pepper
1 cup milk | 1 cup heavy cream, whipped
1 onion, chopped fine

Soak bread in milk. Blend in onion until smooth. Season to taste, and chill. Just before serving fold in whipped cream and correct seasoning. Makes about 3 cups.

ℰ᙭ Cumberland Sauce

1 lemon, slivered rind and juice | ½ cup port wine
1 orange, slivered rind and juice | 2 tablespoons tarragon vinegar
1 jar (8 to 10 ounces) red-currant jelly | 1 teaspoon Dijon or brown mustard
 | ½ teaspoon sugar
 | Salt and pepper

Peel lemon and orange with a potato peeler before juicing them. Cut the thin rind into slivers with a sharp kitchen scissors or knife. Scald the slivers in ¼ cup water for 3 to 4 minutes; drain well. Heat jelly, wine, vinegar, mustard and sugar over medium heat until jelly is melted. Add the slivered rinds and season to taste. Serve hot or cold with game, ham or cold meats.
Makes about 2 cups.

ℰ᙭ Spiced Sauce

For ham or tongue

1 jar (8 to 10 ounces) red-currant jelly | ½ teaspoon ground cloves
1 tablespoon tarragon vinegar | ½ teaspoon ground cinnamon
 | ½ teaspoon dry mustard

Combine ingredients in top part of double boiler over boiling water. Heat until jelly is melted. Stir well. Serve hot or cold.
Makes about 1 cup.

VARIATIONS
1. Add juice and slivered rind of 1 orange.
2. Add juice and slivered rind of 1 orange and 1 lemon.
3. Pour variation 2, while still hot, over 1 pint basket of hulled strawberries. Chill and serve as a sauce.

❦ Spiced Cherry Sauce

For ham

1 can (16 ounces) sour red cherries	6 whole cloves
1 jar (8 to 10 ounces) red-currant jelly	Juice and grated rind of 1 lemon
1 cinnamon stick	Sugar

Heat first 5 ingredients in top part of double boiler over boiling water until jelly is melted. Stir well, add sugar to taste, and stir until it is dissolved.
Makes 3 cups.

CHAPTER V

~~~

Fish and Shellfish

THE world divides itself simply into two kinds of people—those who are interested in the sea and those who are not. Those who are feel the fascination even though they may never have sailed on it, seen it, or even smelled sea air. I do not want to generalize as the wise old lady did, when she said towards the end of a full and heavily peopled life, "the only thing I have discovered about people is that the nicest ones like horseradish." But anyone who even opens this book either likes the sea, or Mystic Seaport, or food, and possibly horseradish too, and I can only say in the midst of an equally heavily peopled life, "the nicest ones like the sea and seafood besides."

Unless otherwise specified, all recipes in this chapter will make 6 servings.

NOTE: Substitute frozen lobster or crabmeat where fresh is not available. Always thaw and press out all moisture before using. Shucked clams and oysters can now be purchased in pint and quart containers. Use them exactly as you would use freshly opened clams or oysters, retaining the liquor to use as the recipes require. Minced canned clams are excellent for certain dishes, and frozen fish can be substituted whenever fresh fish is not available.

∂⅄ Baked Striped Bass I

Serve with or without a garnish of stuffed clams, or use the clam mixture to stuff the bass.

1 whole striped bass (5 to 6 pounds)
¾ cup butter, softened
2 cups clam juice, bottled or obtained from stuffed clam recipe
¼ cup shaved almonds
Parsley sprigs for garnish
1 lemon, sliced paper-thin
Salt and pepper
Stuffed Clams (below)

Wash bass under cold running water, pat dry, and spread generously with some of the soft butter. Arrange in a shallow baking pan. If the head or tail project beyond the sides of the pan, cover them loosely with aluminum foil; if covered too tightly, the fish skin will come away with the foil. Add 1 cup of the clam juice to the pan. Melt remaining butter in a saucepan; set aside ¼ cup; the rest is to use for later basting. Bake bass in a 350° F. oven for 1 hour. Baste every 10 minutes with pan juices and melted butter. Add remaining clam juice after 30 minutes. After 1 hour, fry the almonds in the reserved ¼ cup butter until they start to turn golden; pour immediately over the fish. Bake for 10 minutes longer, until almonds are browned.

Transfer bass carefully to a serving platter, using 2 large pancake turners or the narrow side of a baking sheet. The almonds should stay undisturbed. Garnish with parsley and place lemon slices on the eye and down the length of the fish. Surround with stuffed clams. Strain pan juices into a sauceboat and serve.

The salt in clam juice and butter is sufficient for the sauce, but bass can be seasoned to taste before baking. Reduce baking time by 10 minutes per pound for smaller fish. Serve with cucumber salad and parsley potatoes.

✑ Stuffed Clams

1 quart, 2 pounds, Littleneck clams (about 20)	½ garlic clove, crushed (optional)
6 tablespoons butter	Salt and pepper
1 medium-sized onion, chopped	3 tablespoons minced parsley
	½ cup bread crumbs

Place scrubbed clams in a kettle with about ¾ inch of water. Cover tightly and place over high heat. As soon as water boils, hold down cover with a pot holder and let clams steam for 5 to 7 minutes, until all shells have opened wide. Turn off heat. Take out clams with a slotted spoon and strain clam juice. Add water or bottled clam juice, if necessary, to obtain 2¼ cups. Strain the juice and set aside 2 cups to use in preparing Baked Striped Bass I (above). Pull clams from shells and chop or cut roughly; set aside. Break clam shells apart to obtain 40 half shells, wash them, and trim off the muscle which adheres to the shell.

Melt 2 tablespoons of the butter, add onion, and fry gently until just golden, about 7 minutes. Add garlic, parsley, bread crumbs, chopped clams, remaining butter, and seasonings to taste. Stir until crumbs are lightly browned. Add enough clam juice just to moisten. Spoon the mixture into the 40 half shells and place them on a baking sheet. Bake at 400° F. for 5 minutes, until sizzling but not too brown. Arrange around baked striped bass, and serve each guest 5 or 6 stuffed half clams.

✑ Baked Striped Bass II

1 pound fish heads, bones and tails, or fillets for stock	1 striped bass (4 to 5 pounds), drawn
3 celery stalks and leaves, chopped	Soft butter for spreading on fish
1 onion, sliced	¼ cup butter
3 or 4 parsley sprigs	¼ cup flour
1 teaspoon dried thyme	2 egg yolks
½ teaspoon peppercorns	1 cup heavy cream
1 teaspoon salt	Juice of ½ lemon

Simmer fish scraps or fillets with celery, onion, parsley, thyme, peppercorns and salt in just enough water to cover for 20 minutes. Strain and set fish stock aside; there should be 3 cups. If there is more, reduce by boiling rapidly until there are 3 cups. Discard fish scraps; if fillets were used, retain for fish pudding or soufflé.

Spread rinsed and dried bass with soft butter. Arrange fish on a heavily buttered strip of folded aluminum foil, letting the ends extend beyond the fish so that it can be transferred to a serving platter with ease. Place foil package in a well-buttered baking pan and add 1 cup of the fish stock. Bake, basting frequently, in a 350° F. oven for 35 to 40 minutes, or until fish flakes easily when tested on the underside with a fork. If pan becomes too dry, add ½ cup warm water.

While fish is baking, melt ¼ cup butter in top part of a double boiler over boiling water, stir in flour, and gradually stir in remaining 2 cups of fish stock until smooth. Beat egg yolks into cream. Make sure boiling water in lower section of double boiler does not touch bottom of upper section, and then beat yolk and cream mixture into sauce. Stir until thickened, smooth and creamy; add lemon juice and correct seasoning. Serve bass garnished with parsley and lemon wedges, and serve sauce in a bowl. If bass is filleted, pour sauce over the fillets and glaze under the broiler for a minute. Watch during glazing so sauce does not get too browned.

✺ Salt for Salting Cod

The high cost of living sometimes drove a Mystic farmer off on a whaling voyage for the extra money he could earn. In 1787 a farmer was able to raise all he needed to feed his family and farm hands, but he had to buy the salt for his cattle, for cooking and for meat or fish salting. His budget for salt could go as high as the equivalent of ten dollars a year. The need for salt kept farmers near the coast and its sea salt. It was only after salt springs were discovered that the farming frontier moved further inland.

ℰℛ Codfish Pudding

Mariners brought the *chaudière,* or chowder, from France as well as the idea of making a sort of codfish-cake mixture with a few additions. The French served this mixture heaped on a dish surrounded with fried bread and called it a *brandade.* Mysticians omitted the typically French oil and garlic and ate it with toasted bread, or dropped tablespoonfuls of the mixture into hot fat and fried it golden.

1 pound salt codfish	1 cup mashed potatoes, or more
3 tablespoons minced onion	2 tablespoons minced parsley
⅔ cup heavy cream	Salt and freshly ground black
Grated rind of 1 lemon	pepper
Juice of ½ lemon	

Freshen codfish in cold water overnight. Change water every hour for 4 more hours. Cut codfish into strips and arrange in a saucepan. Cover with cold water and bring to a boil. Reduce heat and simmer for 12 minutes. Drain well and flake with a fork. Press out moisture. Whip or blend the codfish with onion, cream, lemon rind and juice until mixture is as smooth as mashed potatoes. Whip in mashed potatoes and parsley and add more cream if mixture is too dry. Season to taste, mound on a dish, and serve surrounded with bread triangles fried in butter and lemon wedges.

ℰℛ Codfish Balls

From *The Providence Journal-Bulletin*

2 cups dried salt codfish	Pepper
2 cups sliced raw potatoes	Flour
2 eggs, separated	Fat for deep-frying
2 tablespoons butter	

Freshen fish in cold water for 6 to 8 hours, changing water two or more times, or follow package directions. Tear freshened fish into small pieces. Cook potatoes and fish together until potatoes are soft. Crush potatoes lightly together with fish. Beat egg yolks into a paste with butter. Add pepper to taste. Stir yolk mixture gently with the fish and potato mixture. Fold in the stiffly beaten egg whites. Flour hands and shape fish into rough balls. Fry in deep fat heated to 425° F. on a frying thermometer until brown. Serve with tartar sauce or coleslaw. For a refreshing change, try applesauce instead.

Makes 4 to 6 servings.

ℰ𝔛 Codfish Cakes

"Fish may be preserved by dry-salting, a method most frequently employed in New England and Newfoundland. The fish are so completely impregnated with salt that they can be packed in barrels with additional large-grained solid salt so as to be fit for the longest voyages to the hottest climates," says an anonymous author in a fragment of an old book. Also they are very good for breakfast on a short voyage in a cold climate.

1 pound salt codfish	1 egg
7 medium-sized potatoes	Fat for deep-frying

Freshen the codfish by soaking it in water to cover for 3 hours or more. Cut it into strips, place them in a saucepan, and cover with cold water. Bring to a boil, pour off the water, repeat. When water reaches a boil, reduce heat and simmer for 15 minutes. Drain, pick to pieces, squeeze out moisture, and set aside. Boil potatoes until very soft, about 25 minutes. Draw off skins and rice potatoes into a large bowl. Whip in codfish and egg. At this point add nothing or any of the following:

2 tablespoons minced onion	Grated rind of 1 lemon
3 shallots, minced	1 to 2 teaspoons ground ginger
4 spring onions, minced	½ cup sautéed minced mush-
¼ cup cut chives	rooms

Shape into small or medium-sized cakes with a tablespoon and drop into deep fat heated to 375° F. on a frying thermometer. Fry until golden and drain before serving. The cakes can be dredged with flour or rolled in crumbs before frying. Serve small cakes as appetizers, large ones for breakfast.

ℰ&✗ Salt-codfish Hash

Hash, whether roast beef, corn beef or salt codfish, is made in much the same way. The important thing is to get a lovely crisp crust on the bottom and to turn it over, like an omelet, with the crust on the top. Do not disturb the hash while it is browning.

1½ pounds salt codfish	Freshly ground black pepper
¼ cup butter or salt-pork fat	Chopped parsley
4 cups cooked diced potatoes	1 recipe homemade Tomato
½ cup chopped onion	Sauce I (p. 81)
½ cup water or fish broth	6 poached eggs (optional)

Soak salt cod in tepid water until soft. Depending on the type used, 3 to 4 hours should do it. Drain well and shred; there should be 3 cups when shredded. Melt half of the butter or salt-pork fat in a wide pan. Combine fish, potatoes, onion, broth, and pepper to taste. Add to pan and stir until heated through. Push aside the hash; add remaining butter or pork fat. Press the hash down evenly and let the bottom brown well. Turn the pan at a right angle to a hot platter and slide the hash out with a final turn. Sprinkle with parsley and serve with tomato sauce. Top with poached eggs, if desired.

ℰ&✗ Stewed Codfish

From the *Vineyard Gazette*, May 8, 1857

"Take a fine fresh cod and cut into slices an inch thick separated from the bones. Lay the pieces of fish in the bottom of a stew pan; season them with a grated nutmeg, half a dozen blades of mace, a saltspoonful of cayenne pepper, and a small saucerful of chopped celery or a bunch of sweet herbs tied together. Pour on half a pint of oyster liquor diluted with two wineglasses or a gill of water, and the juice of a lemon. Cover it close and let it stew gently until the fish is almost done, shaking the pan frequently. Then take a piece of fresh butter the size of an egg, roll it in flour and add to the stew. Also put in a dozen large fine oysters with what liquor is about them. Cover it again, quicken the fire a little and let the whole continue to stew five minutes longer. Before you send it to the table, remove the bunch of sweet herbs."

Rockfish and fresh salmon may also be stewed in this manner.

☙ Baked Fish with Cheese Sauce

From Carolyn Kelley, Food Editor, *National Fisherman*

¼ cup butter
¼ cup flour
2 teaspoons dry mustard
2 cups milk
1 teaspoon salt

¼ teaspoon pepper
1 cup grated cheese (American or other)
2 pounds haddock fillets

Make a sauce of butter, flour, mustard, milk, salt and pepper in the top part of a double boiler. Add the grated cheese and stir until blended. Pour over uncooked haddock fillets in a buttered baking dish. Bake in a 350° F. oven for 25 to 30 minutes.

☙ To Prepare Finnan Haddie

1. Place finnan haddie in a pan, cover with cold water, and place over medium heat. As soon as it comes to a boil, set timer and boil for 10 minutes. Take from heat, drain, remove skin and bones, and flake with a fork.
2. Soak finnan haddie in milk to cover for 1 hour. Set over medium heat. As soon as milk comes to a boil, reduce heat to simmer gently for 25 to 30 minutes. Drain, remove skin and bones, and flake with a fork.

3. Put whole fish in a baking pan, cover with half milk and half water, and allow to soak for 10 minutes. Set over very low heat and let fish absorb warm liquid for 30 minutes. Drain off liquid. Spread fish with soft butter and bake in a 350° F. oven for 30 minutes.

Baked Finnan Haddie

1 pound finnan haddie, prepared by method 1, 2 or 3 (above), flaked
1½ cups White Sauce I (p. 83)
1 cup diced boiled potatoes

Freshly ground black pepper
¼ cup grated Parmesan cheese
1 tablespoon butter
2 tablespoons chopped parsley
4 hard-cooked eggs, sliced

Combine warm, flaked finnan haddie with white sauce, potatoes, and pepper to taste. Spread in a shallow baking dish and sprinkle with cheese and dot with butter. Bake in a 350° F. oven for about 15 minutes, until lightly browned. Garnish with minced parsley and a ring of egg slices. Serve with hot toast.

Fish Turbot

A family recipe donated by Mrs. Howard W. Dickerman

It is interesting to note that the word "turbot" instead of designating the European fish came to mean a baked halibut casserole. American halibut is sometimes called turbot, although it is a different species.

2 pounds halibut fillets
2 cups milk
½ cup flour
2 eggs, beaten

½ cup plus 1 tablespoon butter
Salt and pepper
⅔ cup bread or cracker crumbs

Season fish and steam until you can take the bones out. Pick to pieces. Make a sauce of milk beaten with flour and cooked until smooth. Cool; add eggs and ½ cup butter. Alternate layers of fish and sauce in a baking dish. Add salt and pepper to taste. Cover top with bread or cracker crumbs, dot with 1 tablespoon butter, and bake in a 375° F. oven for 30 minutes.

Salmon Loaf

From Mary Greenman Davis

2 cans (7 ounces each) salmon
2 cups rolled crackers
2 tablespoons melted butter
2 whole eggs, lightly beaten
Salt, pepper and cayenne
4 extra egg whites, beaten stiff

Beat salmon, crackers, butter, whole eggs and seasonings to taste until light. Fold in egg whites and pour into a well-buttered mold. Set mold in boiling water or in top part of a double boiler over boiling water, and steam for 1 hour. Unmold and serve with hollandaise sauce.

Broiled Shad Roes with Bacon

6 fresh shad roes (3 whole roes)
3 tablespoons oil
Salt and pepper
¾ cup Lemon Butter (below)
12 slices of bacon broiled crisp and drained
6 lemon wedges

Wash roes, dry gently, brush with oil, and season well. Place on an oiled broiler rack and broil for 3 to 4 minutes. Turn carefully and brush second side with oil. Broil 2 to 3 minutes longer. Serve on heated plates with lemon butter, bacon, lemon wedges and Filled Tomatoes (p. 16), all previously prepared.

LEMON BUTTER

¾ cup soft butter
1 tablespoon minced parsley
1 teaspoon minced onion

1 lemon, juice and grated rind
Salt and pepper

Cream the butter and beat in parsley, onion, lemon juice and rind. Add salt and pepper to taste. Chill for a short time, but do not chill until hard.
Makes about 1 cup.

Sunday Trout

6 frozen trout, thawed
1 cup flour
⅓ cup butter
½ cup chopped almonds
1 pound frozen raw shrimps, defrosted

Juice of 1 lemon
1¼ cups sour cream
½ teaspoon sugar, or more
½ teaspoon Worcestershire sauce
Salt and pepper

Dredge trout with flour. Heat half of the butter in a wide pan. Brown the trout on both sides, about 5 minutes. Add almonds, shrimps and remaining butter. Fry for 3 to 4 minutes longer, until shrimps are heated through. Place trout and shrimp on a hot platter. Stir pan juices with lemon juice, sour cream, sugar and seasonings to taste until bubbling. Pour over trout. Serve with green or cucumber salad and white wine.

Fish Soufflé I

2 cups tightly packed cooked fish, free of skin and bones
Fish scraps, skin and bones of fish, for stock
1 onion, quartered
¼ cup butter

5 tablespoons flour
5 eggs, separated
Salt and pepper
2 tablespoons minced parsley
Grated rind of 1 lemon

Grind fish, using medium blade of food grinder, and set aside. Boil fish scraps in 4 cups salted water with the onion until reduced to 2 cups. Strain and set aside. Melt butter in top part of double boiler over boiling water. Stir in flour until smooth. Gradually stir in fish stock and stir until thickened and smooth. Stir in the ground fish and take from heat. Cool mixture slightly and beat in egg yolks, seasonings to taste, parsley and lemon rind. Fold in the stiffly beaten egg whites and pour the mixture into an 8-cup soufflé dish. Set dish in a pan of hot water and bake in a 350° F. oven for 45 minutes. Serve at once with a crisp cucumber salad.

For festive occasions, spoon the cucumber salad into peeled and hollowed tomatoes. First pour French dressing into prepared tomatoes and chill them for 1 hour. Empty out the dressing and fill with cucumber salad.

Fish Soufflé II

½ onion	2 pounds flounder, sole or any
½ carrot	other white fish
½ celery stalk	3 tablespoons butter
4 peppercorns	¼ cup flour
1 bay leaf	4 whole eggs, separated
1 tablespoon vinegar	1 tablespoon minced fresh dill
½ teaspoon salt	1 extra egg white
2 cups water	

Combine the onion, carrot, celery, peppercorns, bay leaf, vinegar and salt with the water in a kettle. Boil for a few minutes, reduce heat, and add the fish. Simmer fish until opaque; remove from broth. Continue to boil broth to reduce it to 1 cup; strain it and set aside.

Put fish through food grinder. There should be 1½ cups tightly packed, or 2 cups loosely packed.

Make cream sauce of butter, flour and reserved 1 cup of fish broth. Separate the eggs and beat the yolks into the cooled cream sauce. Add the fish and dill to the cooled cream sauce. Beat the egg whites very stiff; add a pinch of salt while beating. Fold into fish mixture and turn all into an ungreased 2-quart baking dish. Set dish in a pan of water and bake in a 375° F. oven for 1 hour. Serve with dill or lobster sauce.

ℰ𝔛 Dutch Fish

6 tablespoons flour
1 tablespoon salt
1 tablespoon paprika
½ teaspoon white pepper
3 pounds fish fillets or steaks, cut into cubes
1 cup bacon dice
6 onions, sliced
6 tablespoons butter

1 can (6 ounces) button mushrooms, or 1 package (10 ounces) frozen mushrooms, thawed
2 leeks, cut across into thin slices
¼ pound Dutch or hard yellow cheese, diced
3 cups milk
6 eggs, beaten
Salt

Combine flour, salt, paprika and pepper and dredge fish cubes heavily with the mixture. Heat bacon dice in a heavy kettle. Brown the fish chunks in the bacon fat and add the onion slices. Butter a casserole or baking dish generously with 3 tablespoons of the butter. Pour in the fish and onion mixture and add mushrooms, halved, and leek slices. Combine cheese dice with milk and eggs and salt to taste. Pour the mixture over the fish in the casserole. Bake in a 325° F. oven for 40 to 45 minutes. Take from oven, dot with remaining butter, and return to oven for 2 minutes before serving. Serve with rice or potatoes.

ℰ𝔛 Baked Fillet Sandwiches

2 pounds fillets of flounder or sole
1½ teaspoons salt
¼ teaspoon white pepper

1 tablespoon paprika
1 tablespoon minced herbs—parsley, chives, basil, or tarragon

3 tomatoes, peeled and cut into
    thick slices
½ pound (6 slices) cheese

3 eggs
6 tablespoons flour
⅔ cup butter or shortening

Season fish with salt, pepper, paprika and herbs. Cut fish into 12
even-sized pieces about as wide as they are long. Cover 6 fillet pieces
with 6 tomato slices and 6 cheese slices. Cover cheese with a second fish
slice and secure firmly with wooden picks; flatten as much as possible.
Beat eggs with flour and just enough water to make a liquid batter. Dip
fish sandwiches into batter and fry in butter or shortening in a skillet
until pale golden; turn carefully with a pancake turner and continue to
fry on both sides until a rich brown. Butter must be deep enough to
brown the sandwiches up the sides. Serve with potato salad and cucumber relish.

Fish Balls with Horseradish Sauce

9 slices of white bread
¾ cup heavy cream
1½ pounds fish fillets
4 medium-sized onions, sliced
2 tablespoons capers, well
    drained
6 to 8 tablespoons flour

3 eggs
Salt, pepper and cayenne
¼ teaspoon grated nutmeg
3 tablespoons minced parsley
Horseradish Sauce (below)
6 lemon wedges

Soak bread slices in cream and set aside. Put fish, onions and capers
through finest blade of food grinder. Press cream out of the bread and
reserve it. Put bread through food grinder with fish mixture (fish is
ground twice). Beat flour, eggs, seasonings to taste, nutmeg, and reserved cream into the fish mixture until it is smooth. Add more flour if
too moist. Shape into balls with floured hands.

Bring salted water to a rolling boil. Lower fish balls into it; turn off
heat immediately. Cover and let fish balls poach in the gradually
cooling water over the cooling heat unit. After 15 to 17 minutes the
balls should be done. In the meantime make horseradish sauce. Drain

fish balls well, arrange in a heated serving dish, sprinkle with parsley, and serve with horseradish sauce and lemon wedges.

HORSERADISH SAUCE

¼ cup butter
¼ cup flour
2 cups fish stock or milk
1 cup grated fresh horseradish

Juice of 1 lemon
Salt and pepper
Pinch of sugar

Melt butter over low heat; stir in flour until smooth. Gradually stir in stock or milk until thickened and smooth. Reduce heat and simmer, stirring occasionally, for 12 minutes. Stir vigorously with a whisk while adding horseradish, lemon and seasonings to taste. Thin with cream if too thick.

Makes about 3 cups.

Old English Fish Cakes

2 cups milk
2 teaspoons salt
1 package (4 ounces) instant mashed potatoes
9 tablespoons flour
6 eggs
1 tablespoon anchovy paste, or more

3 onions
3 leeks (if obtainable)
1½ pounds fish fillets
7 parsley sprigs, stems removed
¾ cup fat for frying

Bring milk to a boil with salt; stir in mashed potatoes until thick and fluffy. Beat in flour, eggs and anchovy paste; set aside. Boil onions, leeks, fish and parsley in salted water to cover for 20 minutes. Drain well; mince onion, leek, fish and parsley. Mix well with potatoes and shape into balls. Fry in hot fat, turning with a spatula. Serve with a crisp salad and stewed tomatoes.

⚔ Brown Fish Stew

¾ cup butter
8 onions, sliced thin
½ garlic clove, crushed (op-
    tional)
2½ pounds fish, cut into large
    chunks
6 tablespoons flour
2 tablespoons paprika

2 teaspoons bouillon granules,
    or 2 cubes
Salt
½ pound boiled noodles or
    pasta
2 tablespoons chopped parsley
½ cup sour cream, whipped
Extra bouillon, if needed

Heat butter in a large kettle and brown the onions, stirring constantly with a wooden spoon, for about 7 minutes. Stir in the garlic. Dredge fish heavily with flour and paprika and add to kettle. Add bouillon granules or cubes and boil over medium heat for 25 minutes. Add salt if necessary; stir well. Add freshly boiled and well-drained noodles or pasta. Serve in deep plates, sprinkled with parsley and garnished with whipped sour cream.

Depending on the fish and onions used, the cooking should produce enough liquid in the kettle to sauce the stew. If stew seems too dry during 25-minute boiling period, add up to 2 cups bouillon. If the stew is very salty, just add water.

⚔ Clams

The round clam or quahog and the long or soft-shell clam are American mollusks. Clams were eaten by the Indians for centuries before either Indians or clams were discovered by the white man. There are enormous accumulations of clam shells on the eastern coasts of the United States, mounds literally miles long and several feet high.

These shell heaps found by the early settlers were not, as they first suspected, burial mounds. They were, on the contrary, celebration grounds and marked the sites of countless Indian clambakes.

The Indians taught the settlers the important ritual of the pit and the hot stones that are still essentials of the true clambake. Certain shortcuts and simplifications have inevitably set in, and a clambake today is often prepared in a large metal can. While this seems to take away from the old traditions it is one way for inlanders to enjoy a feast that has until recently been limited to shore dwellers.

The secret of the successful metal-can clambake lies in the preparation. Make and gather all necessary materials so they can be used when the fire is just right. A large can (we hate to say garbage can, but that is the size) will hold a generous clambake for 12 people.

Clambake I

Prepare 12 large cheesecloth bags. Put about ½ quart steamer clams in each bag. Tie them loosely. Also have ready:

12 lobsters (1¼ pounds each)
48 ears of corn, husked, silk removed and husks drawn down over ears

12 baking potatoes, scrubbed and in their skins
6 broiling chickens (1½ pounds each) quartered
4 pounds butter
Salt and pepper

Have fire hot. Put a layer of seaweed or cornhusks in the bottom of the can and add 1 quart seawater. Put can on a strong grill over the hot fire. Fill the sacks with layers of clams, lobsters, corn, potatoes and chicken quarters with seaweed or cornhusks in between. Put lid on securely. Weight it with a stone and keep the fire roaring for 1 hour. Have a bucket of water handy, seawater preferred, and pour it on the fire if it becomes too uproarious. You can also add a little more water to the can if food smells scorched.

Give each person his share with lots of butter, salt and pepper shakers, and pickles.

ℰ𝒶 Clambake II

24 scrubbed baking potatoes, in their skins

12 lobsters (1¼ pounds each)

12 whole small fish or fish steaks

12 cheesecloth bags filled with 12 steamer clams each, loosely tied

36 ears of corn, husked, silk removed and husks pulled back over the ears

Salt and pepper shakers

Lots of butter

Pickles and relishes

Dig a pit 3-feet square and 3-feet deep. Line it with even-sized smooth stones, making a 6-inch-thick wall on all sides and across the bottom. Build a driftwood fire in the pit and have enough wood on hand to keep the fire roaring for about 4 hours. Remove wood and charred embers from the pit. Rake it out clean and brush it with a green leaved branch. Lay 3 inches of wet seaweed over the bottom. Place potatoes on top, then a 1-inch layer of seaweed on the potatoes. Arrange the 12 live lobsters on the seaweed and cover with another layer of wet seaweed. Follow with fish, whole or pieces, and cover with 12 cheesecloth bags of steamer clams. Put on more seaweed and cover with corn. Cover with a 3-inch layer of seaweed and cover the pit with heavy canvas. Secure with rocks to prevent steam escaping. Steam for 1 hour, remove canvas, dig up your dinner, and *eat*.

ℰ𝒶 Steamed Clams

Clams must be steamed in a large closed kettle or other metal container; pails are often made to do. Wash clams well and let them drain for a few minutes. Pour ⅛ inch of water into the kettle. Turn stove-top burner on high. Pour clams into the kettle, adjust cover, place over heat, and steam until the shells open, 5 to 7 minutes. Shake and drain clams in a colander over the kettle. Carefully strain the clam juice from the kettle after the clams have drained over it. Serve at once in deep soup plates with melted butter, clam juice and Portuguese bread.

As to the quantity of clams to steam, it isn't worth the effort unless there are at least 10 quarts which can feed 2 or many more, all depending on the day, the weather, the occasion. There are those who are satisfied with a single large soup plateful and others who refill their plates several times.

ⳙ Corn and Clam Fritters

These used to be eaten for breakfast; now they can accompany Bloody Marys at a late Sunday breakfast or brunch.

12 large clams	¼ teaspoon salt
1 cup corn kernels	2 eggs, beaten
1 cup flour	½ cup milk
1 teaspoon baking powder	½ cup clam juice
½ teaspoon sugar	Shortening for deep-frying

Open clams, remove meat, and drain. Pat dry and chop coarsely. Add to corn and set aside. Make the fritter batter. Sift dry ingredients together into a bowl. Beat in eggs, milk and clam juice; add corn and clams. Drop by large spoonfuls into shortening heated to 365° F. on a frying thermometer. Fry until golden, about 4 minutes. Serve with tartar sauce.

ⳙ Clam Fritters I

From *Stonington Cooks and Cookery*

"Aunt Mary Wolfe," as Mrs. Mary Forsythe Wolfe was known throughout the community, was a cripple from childhood, but though a shut-in she was no recluse. Her extensive reading, wonderful memory, and keen sense of humor settled many an argument. A daughter of Captain Peter and Thankful Cheesebro Forsythe, she married Giles Wolfe and lived in the old Wolfe homestead on Gravel Street, Mystic.

1 cup clam liquor
2½ cups flour
2 eggs, beaten
½ teaspoon salt

½ teaspoon baking soda, dissolved in water
25 clams, drained and chopped
Lard for frying

Beat clam liquor, flour, eggs, salt and baking soda into a batter. Add the clams. Fry in smoking hot lard until golden. Drain and serve.

Fried Clams

We are grateful to Carolyn Kelley, Food Editor of *National Fisherman,* for the two excellent clam recipes and their sauces which follow:

1 quart shucked soft clams (steamers)
2 eggs, beaten
2 tablespoons milk

2 teaspoons salt
Dash of pepper
1 cup dry bread crumbs or cracker crumbs

Drain clams and wipe dry. Beat eggs, milk and seasonings. Dip clams into egg mixture and roll in crumbs. Fry in a basket in deep fat heated to 375° F. on a frying thermometer for 2 to 3 minutes, or until golden brown. Drain on absorbent paper. Serve plain, sprinkled with salt, or with Tartar Sauce (see page 110).

Puffy Clam Batter

This second recipe is for those who like clams fried in batter.

2 eggs
1 teaspoon salt
½ teaspoon pepper

1 cup flour
2 teaspoons baking powder
¾ cup milk

Beat eggs with salt and pepper in a bowl. Sift flour and baking powder together and add alternately with milk to egg mixture. Beat until smooth.

Prepare clams as described and dip them into the batter. Fry in same manner as in preceding recipe.

To top off your meal of fried clams, you should prepare a fine tasty sauce to dip them in. Either of the two recipes shown here is excellent.

TARTAR SAUCE

1 egg	6 teaspoons lemon juice
1 teaspoon salt	Pepper
1 teaspoon sugar	Chopped sweet pickles
1 teaspoon dry mustard	1½ cups olive oil
6 teaspoons vinegar	

Combine all ingredients except oil, adding pepper and pickles to taste; beat well. Add oil in a thin stream, beating well until sauce thickens.

LEMON BUTTER SAUCE

Combine and mix well ¼ cup melted butter, 2 tablespoons lemon juice, 1 teaspoon minced onion and a dash of Tabasco.

Stuffed Quahogs

From the *Vineyard Gazette*

Quahogs are pronounced as spelled by the uninitiated, but in Mystic everyone knows they are *co hogs*. Young co hogs are Littlenecks and Cherrystones.

1 cup ground quahogs	3 green onions, minced
1 cup bread crumbs	3 tablespoons chopped parsley
1 egg, beaten	Salt and pepper
1 small onion, chopped	½ teaspoon poultry seasoning,
1 tablespoon butter	or more

Combine ground quahogs, crumbs and egg. Sauté onion in butter for 6 minutes and add it to the mixture. Add green onions and parsley and seasonings to taste. Spoon mixture into quahog shells and bake in a 350° F. oven for at least 30 minutes.

⬧ Steamed Mussels

From Mrs. Harrison W. Boylan

2 pounds mussels
½ cup dry white wine
½ cup water
1 bay leaf

½ carrot, scraped and sliced
3 or 4 parsley sprigs
1 garlic clove (optional)

Clean mussels by removing the "beards" and scrubbing the shells. Put into a large covered kettle with wine, water, bay leaf, carrot, parsley and garlic. Cover and steam for about 20 minutes. Dip mussels into melted butter. Serve with crusty bread and a tossed salad.

⬧ Oysters

American Indians ate oysters, presumably out of the shell, as evidenced by the great hills of oyster shells found along our shores. The native oyster beds have been so depleted that we now eat cultivated oysters; considering that they are not every man's meat, it is notable that we consume over a hundred million pounds a year. Oysters in stew, fritters and stuffing are among the most popular ways of serving them.

⬧ Oyster Fritters

¼ cup flour
2 egg yolks
2 tablespoons melted butter
Salt and pepper
¾ cup liquor from the oysters, strained

4 egg whites
36 to 40 large oysters, shucked
Fat for deep-frying
2 tablespoons minced parsley
2 lemons, cut into wedges

Beat flour, egg yolks, butter, seasoning to taste and oyster liquor until smooth. Set aside for 2½ hours. Fold in the stiffly beaten egg whites. Dip the bearded and well-dried oysters into batter. Fry in deep fat

heated to 365° F. on a frying thermometer. Drain. Sprinkle with parsley, garnish with lemon wedges, and serve plain or with Lemon Tartar
Sauce (p. 85).

Fried Oysters

3 dozen oysters	1½ to 2 cups cornmeal for
2 eggs, beaten	dredging
2 tablespoons heavy cream	½ cup butter
Salt	Fat or vegetable shortening for
Freshly ground black pepper	deep-frying
	Lemon wedges

Shuck oysters and pat them dry with absorbent paper. Beat eggs with
cream and salt and pepper to taste. Dip oysters into the mixture. Roll
them in cornmeal and set them aside to dry for about 7 minutes. Melt
butter and fat or vegetable shortening in a deep-fryer or heavy skillet
and heat to 375° F. on a frying thermometer. Fry oysters, a few at a
time, until golden. Drain well and keep warm until all are completed.
Serve immediately with lemon wedges.

Deep Oyster Pie

2 pints shucked oysters	Pepper
6 tablespoons butter	1 recipe Pastry for 1-crust Pies
6 tablespoons flour	(p. 173)
2 tablespoons minced parsley	1 tablespoon milk
Celery salt	

Drain liquor from oysters and add enough water to make 3 cups
liquid in all. Set oysters aside. Melt butter in top part of double boiler
over boiling water. Stir in flour until smooth and cook for 5 minutes.
Stir in the 3 cups oyster liquid and continue to stir until thickened and
smooth. Add oysters and parsley and season to taste. Pour mixture into a

buttered 2-quart casserole and cover with pastry for 1-crust pie. Cut vents in top, brush with milk, and bake in a 450° F. oven until golden, about 20 minutes.

𝒸𝓍 Scalloped Oysters

A recipe out of Miss Mallory's *The Old Gem Cookbook* of 1875. The cracker crumbs were roughly crushed pilot biscuits or oyster crackers, not today's cracker meal.

⅓ cup butter
3 cups cracker crumbs
1 quart shucked oysters and
   their liquor

Salt and pepper
2 eggs, beaten
1 cup milk
Grated rind of 1 lemon

Butter a 2-quart casserole well. Sprinkle bottom generously with cracker crumbs and cover with a layer of well-drained oysters. Sprinkle with salt and pepper and dot with butter. Cover with another layer of crumbs, oysters, salt, pepper and butter. Continue until all the oysters

are used, and end with a thick layer of crumbs. Beat eggs and milk with a little of the oyster liquor and the lemon rind and pour over the dish. Season to taste and dot with butter. Bake in a 350° F. oven for 30 minutes.

ⅭⅩ Toasted Scallops

When an open fire has burned down to glowing hot coals, spear fresh sea scallops on long two-tined forks and toast them over the coals as you used to toast marshmallows. Dip them into cold tartar sauce and eat immediately. Allow from 6 to 12 per person. Toast scallops to taste; lightly browned for 3 to 4 minutes is best.

ⅭⅩ Crab Cakes

From Mrs. George F. Ruth

1 pound claw crabmeat	1 tablespoon mayonnaise
Salt	1 egg, beaten
Red pepper (just a dash)	1 tablespoon milk
1 scant teaspoon dry mustard, or more	Cracker crumbs for coating

Mix crabmeat, seasonings to taste and mayonnaise, and shape into 8 cakes. Beat egg and milk together. Dip cakes into egg and milk mixture, then coat with crumbs. Fry in deep fat, or brown well on all sides in butter in skillet. Serve with Worcestershire or tartar sauce.
Makes 8 cakes.

ⅭⅩ Lobster

"The lobster is an animal of such extraordinary form that those who first saw it mistook the head for the tail, but it was soon discovered that the animal moves with its tail forward," according to an old book.

Certain lobster dishes, to be at their best, require killing the lobster with a knife instead of submerging it head first (ladies usually close their eyes when they do this) into boiling water, seawater preferably. There is an easy way to kill lobsters with a pointed knife: Spread the lobster right side up on a wooden cutting board. Insert a pointed knife into the cross that marks the meeting of carapace and head. Drive the knife down in one quick motion. Draw it towards yourself to cut the lobster into halves. It is all over in an instant.

ᏧᎳ Lobster Thermidor

2 cups dry white vermouth	3 peppercorns
2 cups water	1 tablespoon dried tarragon
1 onion, sliced thin	3 live lobsters (2 pounds each)
1 carrot, sliced thin	1 tablespoon butter
1 celery stalk, sliced thin	1 teaspoon lemon juice
6 parsley sprigs	½ teaspoon salt
1 bay leaf	½ pound fresh mushrooms,
¼ teaspoon dried thyme	sliced

Simmer vermouth, water, vegetables, parsley, bay leaf, thyme, peppercorns and tarragon in a large kettle for 15 minutes. Bring to a rolling boil and add live lobsters. Cover and steam for about 20 minutes, or until lobsters are cooked and bright red.

While lobsters are cooking, melt butter in a small saucepan. Add lemon juice, salt and mushrooms, and simmer for 10 minutes. Remove mushrooms from sauce with a slotted spoon and set aside.

When lobsters are cooked, remove them from the kettle. Pour butter sauce from mushrooms into kettle and stir well. Boil down mixture rapidly, until liquid in kettle has reduced to about 2 cups. Remove kettle from heat and reserve liquid for use as a base for thermidor mixture.

Prepare lobsters. Split each into halves, separating body from tail section. Remove sand sacs in the head, and intestinal tubes. Remove lobster meat and dice into chunks. Cut away soft underside of body. Keep the shell halves intact.

Wash lobster shells thoroughly and fill with thermidor mixture.

Preheat oven to 425° F. Place lobster shells in roasting pan and heat for 10 to 15 minutes, or until lobster is bubbling and top of sauce is nicely browned.

THERMIDOR MIXTURE

4 teaspoons butter	Paprika
4 teaspoons flour	2 tablespoons dry sherry or Co-
Diced lobster meat	gnac
½ cup heavy cream	Reserved mushrooms
2 cups reserved lobster stock	3 tablespoons butter
Salt	1½ cups shredded white bread
Cayenne	

Melt 4 teaspoons butter in a large saucepan. Stir in flour and blend. Add diced lobster meat. Slowly stir in cream and stock and simmer gently for 10 minutes, stirring frequently. Season to taste with salt, cayenne and paprika. Remove mixture from heat and add sherry or Cognac and reserved mushrooms.

Melt the 3 tablespoons butter and add shredded bread. Cook gently in a saucepan until butter has been absorbed by bread. Fill lobster halves with thermidor mixture. Sprinkle buttered bread on top of each lobster half, and bake as directed.

Whale Meat

An old document tells us that whalers braved "extremes of tempera-ture, Polar bears, starvation, icebergs and whales." Actually they braved every other conceivable peril as well—storms, reefs, broiling sun, pirates, cannibals, hostile natives, the hardships of separation from home and absolutely monotonous food. Naturally whale meat became a part of their diet. To be sure, whale is not fish, but because of its fishy taste it seems to belong in this chapter rather than with meats.

Artemas Ward said of whale meat, "A food which has merit as a novelty and as a wholesome addition when meat supply (from land food-animals) is scarce." He recommends the smaller whales for tenderer meat, ones which would supply only about six tons of edible meat. He goes on to say that the meat resembles beef and if promptly frozen tastes like beef. Mr. Ward continues about whale meat which is not promptly frozen, "It develops a fishy taste which, in its early stages, pleasantly suggests salmon. If unchecked it becomes overstrong." Ask any Englishman who remembers World War II dinners.

Since husbands rarely come home with whale meat these days we will not bother you with more information than that "It is nice boiled with a little sliced onion." Indeed. However, it is available in certain specialty food shops on occasion.

Uses for Whale Oils

"Spermaceti oil," to quote Mr. J. S. Forsyth, "is oil of a particular species of whale, found in a large trunk, four or five feet deep and ten or twelve feet long, filling almost the whole cavity of the head and seeming to supply the office of cerebrum. The oil drawn from the other parts of the same fish is nearly three times the value of the common black whale oil. It is used for chamber lamps; the common whale oil, or train oil, is used for street lamps." (1834.)

Early in the 18th Century, Peleg Folger wrote of the sperm whale, "He has no bone in his head and his brain is all oyl." No wonder there was great rejoicing when a sperm whale was caught—much more money and also light in many chambers.

In spite of having oil for a brain, the sperm whale was a great fighter and dangerous antagonist. His giant jaws, as long as twenty-five feet, were full of enormous teeth, and his flukes or tail could capsize a boat. When he lay alongside he represented the value of three right whales, a new supply of tapers and smoother skins for whalers' wives.

According to J. S. Forsyth's *A Dictionary of Diet,* whalers' wives were cosmeticians as well as everything else. They made ointments and cosmetic pastes from spermaceti oil which were "softening and emollient to abraded surfaces of the skin and made cheeks smooth." We wonder whether or not the smooth cheeks were slightly permeated with the lingering smell of whale oil?

Another recipe for spermaceti, also quoted from *A Dictionary of Diet* is medicinal in nature.

"An unctuous fatty substance found in the head of some species of whales. In a pure state it has no smell and very little taste. Mixed with the yolk of an egg, or Gum Arabic, it forms a useful emulsion against coughs and colds:

Take 2 scruples* of spermaceti	10 drops C. spirits of vitriol-
The yolk of an egg	ated ether
	1½ ounces distilled water

Make a draught to be taken every four hours."

We do not like the sound of vitriol in a cookbook, but vitriolate was an old chemical used in diluted form for brines. This rule only serves to remind us how hardy our forebears were and how well situated the whale man was to get rid of his lingering cold, possibly for good.

* A scruple is an old measure or weight—⅓ of a dram or 20 grains.

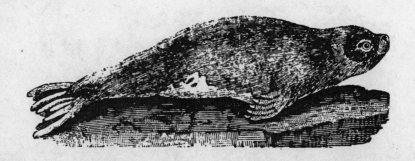

CHAPTER VI

~~

Meats

I N Richard Hakluyt's *The Principall Navigations of The English Nation*, 1598–1600, there is mention of the list of provisions taken on board a "Shippe of 200 tunnes sent to Russia to catch the Whale fish in 1575." The list includes "hogsheds of beefe, bacon, salt fish, herring, pease and beanes, bread, salt, cedar oile, wine and mustard seed."

About two hundred years later, when the New England colonies had been settled and ships had been built, Mystic men went out hunting whale. Their ships were provisioned in much the same way as the "Shippe," with lots of "salt horse" or "salt junk" (an extremely salty dried beef which had to be soaked in water for a day before it could even be boiled), pork, potatoes, codfish, hard bread, rice, tea and coffee, beans, dried fruit, lard and molasses. The captain or master of the ship sweetened his tea or coffee with sugar and early in the voyage he had butter for his bread. Everything was permeated with the powerful smell of whale oil and, as the voyage progressed, the food and water deteriorated.

Rare stops at ports added to the diet fresh meat, fresh fruits and vegetables, water and sometimes even a live pig or some hens; but usually the only diet change in the endless monotony was a lobscouse or a special treat of plum duff. Lobscouse was a sort of hash-stew of salt meat and bread derived from the Norwegian *brun lapskaus* or the Swedish *lapskajs*.

We include three lobscouse recipes because they are ideal for casseroles and for galley cookery. Spice the dish with accompaniments rather than with additions. Lobscouse was, and is, a bland dish that should taste of good black pepper.

⌘ Lobscouse or Lapscouse

3 cups cubed cooked corned brisket of beef, tongue or smoked pork
16 potatoes, peeled and cubed
2½ cups beef stock
2 bay leaves

½ teaspoon black peppercorns, or more
½ teaspoon ground allspice
2 teaspoons dried sage or thyme

Prepare the meat by soaking in water or precooking, depending on the type of meat used. Leftover meat can serve too. Add meat and potatoes to boiling stock in a large kettle. Tie bay leaves and peppercorns in a little cheesecloth bag and hang it into the kettle. Add allspice and sage and cook covered for about 20 minutes, until potatoes are soft and meat is heated through. Serve with pickled cucumbers, pickled beets, or mustard pickles.

VARIATIONS

1. Brown the meat cubes in 4 tablespoons butter before adding them to the boiling stock.
2. Brown the meat cubes in 4 tablespoons butter with 1 cup chopped onion before adding everything to the boiling stock.

⻎ Lapskoda

Finnish

An oven-baked or stove-top stew eaten with traditional accompaniments.

Bacon or salt pork for greasing
1 pound salt pork, sliced thin
1½ pounds beef or veal, sliced thin
6 large onions, cut into thick slices

12 medium-sized or 8 large potatoes, peeled and cut into thick slices
Salt
1 teaspoon black peppercorns
1 teaspoon ground allspice

Rub a heavy cast-iron casserole or Dutch oven well with bacon fat or salt pork. Layer the sliced salt pork heavily across the bottom of the casserole. Cover with a layer of meat slices and continue layering onions, potatoes and meat until the casserole is filled. Salt layers to taste and sprinkle peppercorns between the layers as you go. End with a layer of potato slices and sprinkle allspice over the top. Cover casserole tightly. Bake in a 300° F. oven, or simmer on top of the stove, for 4½ hours. If cooked on top of the stove, the layer of salt pork will keep the *lapskoda* from burning, but only if the heat is very low. The stew can coast for at least another half hour, if necessary. Serve with accompaniments.
Makes 6 servings.

ACCOMPANIMENTS

Hard rye crackers
Thin-sliced cheese. If you cannot find a Finnish cheese, serve Gjetost, caraway cheese or a nice American Sage Cheddar.
Brown mustard, lots of it
Pickled Beets (p. 241)
Sour cream, whipped with salt to taste
Potted cheeses, blended with beer or ale and brandy and ripened in an earthenware pot

✺ Lapskajs

Swedish

3 pounds chuck steak, cut into
　small cubes
½ cup flour
½ teaspoon salt
¼ teaspoon pepper
¼ teaspoon ground allspice
⅓ cup butter

3 large onions, sliced
4 large potatoes, peeled and
　cubed
Salt
6 peppercorns
1 bay leaf
3 cups boiling beef stock

Dredge meat with the flour sifted with salt, pepper and allspice. Melt butter in a heavy casserole or Dutch oven and fry the onions until golden, about 7 minutes. Take out onion slices with a slotted spoon and fry dredged meat, stirring occasionally, until evenly browned on all sides. Take out meat and fry potatoes until lightly browned. Push potatoes to sides of casserole, return meat to the center, and spread onions over the potato border. Add salt to taste, peppercorns and bay leaf and the boiling stock. Cover tightly and simmer for 1½ hours over very low heat without disturbing. Serve with Beet and Red-Cabbage Chutney (p. 243).

Perhaps present-day America is so predominantly carnivorous because its forebears ate very little meat. Cows were needed for milk, butter and cheese, oxen were needed for work, sheep were needed for wool, chickens were needed for eggs. When we consider the long-term value of all these animals it is no wonder that the only ones that reached the table were mature and past their prime. There are no old recipes for lamb, only for mutton; no old recipes for veal, only for salt beef—probably salt old ox or cow.

✺ How to Choose Meat

In America's first cookery book, printed in Hartford in 1796, housewives were told exactly what to look for when buying meat. By this date, of course, animals were being raised for food purposes, since life had become more easy for Americans. In beef they were to select meat of the large stall-fed ox. The test was to dent it with the finger and it would immediately rise again. At this point they were advised that in America the ox was used for labor and cow beef was considered more tender.

Mutton was to be grass-fed and two or three years old, while lamb was to be under six months old. This could be distinguished by its size.

Veal, they were told, would require great care in purchasing since it was so easily "lost." Veal brought to market in a basket or carriage was to be chosen over veal flounced to market "on a sweaty horse." Pork presented no problems: they were to select it by its size and fattened appearance.

Roasting Beef

Here we come upon surprises. The advice was to roast it on a quick fire for 15 minutes for every pound of beef. Rare beef was considered the healthiest and was the most popular way of serving. It was basted with salt and water.

Roasting Veal

Directions for roasting veal were exactly as they are now, even to the buttered paper cover. It was to be served with parsley and sliced lemon.

Roasting Mutton and Lamb

Mystic wives were advised to baste with butter and dust on flour and before taking it up, sprinkle with parsley shreds.

Beef Pot Roast

An adaptation of a 1790 recipe

1 ounce salt pork, minced
¼ teaspoon pepper
½ teaspoon salt
1 teaspoon minced sweet marjoram
½ teaspoon minced thyme
½ teaspoon grated mace
¼ teaspoon ground cloves

5-pound beef round or any preferred pot-roast cut
Beef rib bones
4 cups claret or any dry red wine
4 cups water
2 large onions, sliced
2 cups bread crumbs

On the day before roasting the beef, combine salt pork, pepper, salt, herbs and spices. Mince together until well blended. Cut gashes or holes in the beef; insert the mixture. Cover, store in refrigerator overnight.

Lay beef rib bones across the Dutch oven or roasting pot and place the beef on it. Add wine, water and onion slices. Cover tightly (the old recipe calls for a sealer of dough) and simmer for 2 hours. Open, turn the meat over, seal tightly again, and simmer for 2 more hours. When tender, drain off liquid, cover meat with crumbs, and brown uncovered in a 400° F. oven for a few minutes. Skim the juices, season if necessary, and serve in a separate sauceboat.

Makes 4 servings.

⚓ Barbecued Beef

Mrs. John Putnam Lee's recipe for barbecued beef is excellent for serving aboard ship. It can be made ahead of time and frozen in necessary amounts to be defrosted at mealtime. Mrs. Lee writes that she finds it "much simpler than making sandwiches," and more popular.

¼ cup vinegar
1½ cups water
¼ cup granulated sugar
4 teaspoons prepared mustard
¼ teaspoon black pepper
1 tablespoon salt
¼ teaspoon cayenne pepper
2 thick slices of lemon
2 medium-sized onions, sliced

½ cup butter or margerine
1 cup ketchup or chili sauce
3 tablespoons Worcestershire sauce
4 cups 2-inch strips of cooked pot roast
Celery, sliced on angle
Pitted ripe olives
20 hamburger buns

Early in the day, or on the day before: In Dutch oven, combine first 10 ingredients. Simmer, uncovered, for 20 minutes. Add ketchup or chili sauce, Worcestershire and meat. Refrigerate or freeze.

About 45 minutes before serving: Return to heat and simmer slowly. For a bright touch add celery and olives. Serve on buns.

Makes 10 servings.

NOTE: Mrs. Lee cooks the pot roast until it can be shredded easily.

Beef Casserole

CAROL JAY HARTMAN

1 large onion, sliced
2 pounds ground beef
1 green pepper, shredded
2 cups shredded carrots
1¼ cups uncooked rice

1 can (10½ ounces) condensed mushroom soup
½ pound grated cheese*
3 cups milk

Brown onion and beef in frying pan. Turn off heat and add pepper, carrots, rice, soup and three quarters of the cheese. Mix well. Put into 3-quart casserole. Pour milk over the top; put remaining cheese on top. Bake in 300° F. oven for 1½ hours. Add more milk while baking if it seems necessary to prevent dryness.

Makes 6 to 8 servings as a main dish, and up to 20 servings at buffets and pot-luck suppers.

Roast-beef Hash

2½ cups ground cold roast beef
5 cups diced cold boiled potatoes

½ cup beef bouillon
Salt and pepper
2 tablespoons butter

---

* Velveeta cheese works very well in this recipe; its mild taste appeals to children.

Combine meat, potatoes and bouillon. Season to taste and stir in hot butter in a heavy pan over medium heat until heated through. Cover and cook until underside is brown, about 20 minutes. Fold onto a hot platter like an omelet. Serve with homemade ketchup.
Makes 4 servings.

Beef Stews

During most of the seventeenth century the old stock was slaughtered in autumn to be salted down for the winter. There are constant references to meat (usually beef) preserved by salting, not in salt brine but with dry salt. This type of beef was most frequently used on board ship and by prosperous farmers.

Venison was one of the most obtainable of winter meats, but what good are all those beautiful recipes since it has now become one of the least obtainable?

On shipboard, combinations of broth, salt meat, hardtack and beans were daily fare, the forefathers of many of our stews and casseroles. As shipboard conditions improved there was always bread, cheese and bacon, and very frequently fish. American galley cooks showed no inclination to combine meat and fish in a single stew as many of the Europeans did.

Beef Stew

3 tablespoons butter	3 cups boiling beef stock
4 onions, sliced thin	1 cup cold water
1 tablespoon paprika	¼ cup flour
4 pounds stewing beef, cut into chunks	Grated rind of 1 lemon
½ teaspoon salt	Salt

Melt butter in heavy pan, kettle or Dutch oven over medium heat. As soon as it foams, add onions and fry until puffed and golden. Add

paprika and stir for 1 minute. Add meat and salt and stir occasionally until browned on all sides. Cover pan and simmer until meat juices are extracted. Continue cooking, stirring occasionally, until juices are reduced to half. Add boiling beef stock gradually and boil for 10 minutes. Cover, reduce heat, and boil until meat is tender, about 1½ hours. Stir the cold water into the flour until smooth. Stir it gradually into the stew over reduced heat and continue to stir until stew is thickened. Add lemon rind and salt to taste. Serve at once with noodles, parsley potatoes, rice or pasta. This can be cooled and reheated before serving.
Makes 10 or more servings.

⫶ Marblehead Beef Put-together

Lydia G. Andrews has allowed us to study her copy of *The Food Log,* which she edited for the Baptist Women's Fellowship, Marblehead, Massachusetts. Unfortunately it is out of print. In it we found, among many others, treasures we had long searched for, the truth about Joe Froggers, Snicker Doodles and Bessie MacWilliam's Beef Put-together.

2 pounds stewing beef, cubed	2 cans (10½ ounces each) undiluted condensed tomato soup
3 tablespoons butter	
2 medium-sized onions, chopped	2 cups diced celery
2 green peppers, chopped	2 cups diced carrots
	1 cup small green peas, cooked

Brown beef in butter in a Dutch oven or heavy casserole. Add onions and peppers and cook, stirring, for 5 minutes. Add soup, celery and carrots. Cover and cook slowly, just above a simmer, for 1 hour. Boil rice or potatoes while beef is cooking. Add peas to beef and serve on boiled rice or mashed potatoes.
Makes 6 servings.

ℰ✗ Corned Beef

Corn your own beef, or buy it from a butcher who puts his heart into corning beef. The usual cut of meat is the rump, flank or thick rib. If the flank is preferred, select the piece next to the loin. Place the meat in the kettle in which it will be boiled and cover with fresh water. Take out meat; add 1 whole raw egg in its shell to the water and enough coarse salt to make the egg float. Take out the egg and use it elsewhere. Rub the meat well with more coarse salt. Put the salted meat into the salted water and weight it with anything heavy enough to hold it under the water. Cover and "corn" the beef for any length of time, "not less than 24 hours, not more than 24 days," although it is often corned for a month.

Cook the beef in the salted water in which it was corned, or cook bought corned beef in heavily salted water until tender. Depending on the cut of meat, this can take from 1½ to 3½ hours. Average time is 2 hours.

Serve meat hot, or cool it in the water in which it was boiled. Take it out and serve it cold with hot cooked vegetables and lots of mustard.

ℰ✗ New England Boiled Dinner

From *A Rhode Islander Cookbook*

1½ pounds salt
5 quarts hot water
6-pound brisket, flank or plate of beef
½ pound salt pork
6 small parsnips, peeled and quartered
12 large carrots, scraped and quartered
3 large yellow turnips, peeled and quartered
16 small onions
12 medium-sized potatoes, peeled and quartered
1 head of cabbage, cut into wedges

Dissolve salt in the hot water and rub beef with additional salt. Place beef in an enamelware kettle or stone jar and cover it with the salted hot water. Let water cool, then weight meat to submerge it in the water. Cover the kettle and corn for 48 hours.

Wash corned beef under cold running water to remove surface brine. Drop meat into a kettle of unsalted boiling water and simmer for 4 hours, or until tender. Add salt pork during last 2 hours of cooking. When meat is done, remove it from the kettle. Cook parsnips, carrots and turnips in the stock for 30 minutes. Add onions and potatoes and simmer for 15 minutes longer. Add cabbage and simmer until tender, about 15 minutes. Return meat to kettle to reheat. When meat is warmed, remove it and place on a large platter. Surround with drained vegetables and serve.

Makes 8 to 10 servings.

Boiled Dinner

With cold corned beef

If cold corned beef is to be served with hot boiled vegetables, boil beef the day before, let it cool in the brine, and refrigerate in the brine until about 2 hours before dinner. Take out the meat, bring the brine to a boil, and cook the vegetables in it.

3 carrots, scraped and halved across and lengthwise

2 turnips, sliced

1 small head of white cabbage, cut into 8 wedges

8 potatoes, peeled and cut lengthwise into halves

1 piece (2 to 3 pounds) cold corned beef

3 cups Pickled Beets (p. 241)

Mustard

Homemade Ketchup (p. 244)

Vinegar

Add vegetables to the boiling brine in the order listed above. Start with the carrots about 1½ hours before dinner. Add turnips 30 minutes later and cabbage 30 minutes after that. Add potatoes about 20 minutes before serving. Depending on the season, a thick-sliced summer squash can be added with the potatoes. Drain all vegetables well, serve them around the cold meat, and pass pickled beets, mustard, ketchup and vinegar separately.

Makes 8 servings.

NOTE: If corned beef is to be served hot, boil it as above, starting it about 2½ hours before dinner. Add the vegetables to the boiling brine in the same order as above. Drain meat and vegetables well and serve sliced, surrounded by the vegetables, on a hot platter.

Corned-beef Hash

Beef for hash has to be chopped fine, not ground. Potatoes and onions should be chopped with the meat.

2 pounds sliced corned beef, gristle removed
6 boiled potatoes, peeled and sliced
2 onions, trimmed and sliced
½ cup bouillon or stock
Salt and pepper
4 tablespoons butter
6 hot poached eggs

Chop meat, potatoes and onions together in a large chopping bowl. Add bouillon and season to taste. Heat butter in wide pan, add meat mixture, and stir until heated through. Press down evenly and continue to cook over medium heat until there is a crisp crust on the underside, 20 to 25 minutes. Fold over onto a hot platter like an omelet, and serve with well-drained poached eggs.
Makes 6 servings.

Red Flannel Hash

Serve for breakfast, lunch or dinner.

1 pound cooked corned beef, chopped
1½ cups diced cooked potatoes
1½ cups diced cooked beets, drained
⅓ cup fine-diced onion
Salt and pepper
½ teaspoon Worcestershire sauce, or more
⅓ cup milk
4 tablespoons butter for frying
2 tablespoons chopped parsley

Stir corned beef, potatoes, beets and onion with seasonings to taste and just enough milk to bind. Heat 2 tablespoons butter in a heavy pan, add meat mixture, and cook until heated through. Press hash down evenly in pan, lift with a pancake turner, and let remaining butter run underneath. Let hash brown evenly on underside until there is a crisp crust, about 20 minutes. Fold onto a hot platter like an omelet and sprinkle with parsley.

Makes about 4 servings.

✺ Roast Leg of Lamb

In half an hour

There are knots called sheepshanks used by sailors. Like many other terms, the name was taken straight from the farmyard. A leg of lamb was a mutton or sheepshank until fairly recently.

    1 leg of lamb, 6 to 7 pounds   Salt
    1 garlic clove, split

Have butcher bone leg of lamb and spread it open until it is flattened. Rub cut side with cut side of garlic clove and rub with salt to taste.

Preheat broiler (infrared or oven broiler), as hot as it will go. Spread lamb on oiled rack and place as close to broiler unit as possible. Ideally there should be 1½ inches between highest part of lamb and broiler unit. Broil for 15 minutes on each side and for 17 to 20 minutes for medium or well done. Slice at an angle and serve with Mint Sauce (p. 86).

Makes 10 servings.

⒠ Spiced Roast Fresh Ham

1 fresh ham (10 pounds)	¾ to 1 cup tepid water
1 tablespoon ground cinnamon	2 quarts apple cider
1 tablespoon ground ginger	2 eggs, beaten
1½ teaspoons salt	3 cups bread crumbs
½ teaspoon pepper	½ cup currant jelly
6 cups flour	

Wash and dry fresh ham and rub well with spices and seasonings. Make a dough of the flour by stirring in just enough tepid water so that it can be rolled out to about ⅓-inch thickness. Wrap the ham in the dough and seal the edges with more flour and water, stirred to a paste. Place, fat side up, in a roasting pan. Add 1½ inches of apple cider. Bake in open pan in a 325° F. oven for 20 minutes per pound in all. Add cider when necessary to maintain the same level, and baste frequently for 3 hours.

Take from oven, remove whatever remains of the dough wrapping, and slice off the rind. Pour off the drippings and cider in the pan and brush ham well with beaten eggs. Sprinkle heavily with crumbs, add a little cider, and bake for 20 minutes longer, or long enough to brown the crumbs. While ham is baking, boil down the cider, drippings and flour paste from the pan with additional cider and the currant jelly. Stir with a wire whisk into a smooth gravy. Strain and serve with ham. Garnish ham with parsley and serve with applesauce.

Makes 12 or more servings.

⒠ Honey-glazed Baked Ham

1 pre-cooked ham (10 to 12 pounds)	1 tablespoon cider
	1 tablespoon orange juice
¾ cup brown sugar	½ cup honey
1 tablespoon vinegar	¼ cup whole cloves

Bake the ham according to directions on wrapper, or bake it in an open pan in a 325° F. oven for 20 to 25 minutes per pound. Meat thermometer should register 160° F. Count the longer baking time per pound for a smaller ham. About 45 minutes before baking is completed, heat sugar, vinegar, cider, orange juice and honey until sugar is dissolved. Take ham from oven, cut off rind, and drain off drippings. Cut fat side of ham with a series of diagonal shallow cuts and crosscut in the opposite direction to form diamonds. Spread fat side heavily with the glaze and return to oven. Bake for 45 minutes longer. Whole cloves may be inserted at the points of the diamond cuts in the fat. Make gravy of the ham drippings or serve with any of the sauces made with currant jelly (pp. 88–89).
Makes 15 or more servings.

Ham Gravy

Gravy differs from sauce in that it is made of the drippings and juices left in the pan in which the meat was roasted. In the case of ham the drippings are usually too fat to use in large quantity, but they do impart a rich flavor.

½ cup fat from roasting pan   ½ cup red-currant jelly
½ cup flour   Salt and pepper
6 cups beef stock   1 cup heavy cream
Madeira wine (optional)

Into a small heavy pan, spoon the fat from the roasting pan. Brown gently, unless it is already well browned. Stir in flour until smooth. Gradually stir in stock, add jelly, and stir until jelly is dissolved. Reduce heat to very low and allow to simmer until ham is ready to serve. Depending on saltiness of ham fat and beef stock, season only if necessary. Whip cream into gravy with a wire whisk and pour into a sauceboat as soon as it is warmed through. Add milk or cream if gravy is too thick. Substitute 1 cup Madeira wine for 1 cup of stock if preferred. Makes about 6 cups.

ℰℬ𝒳 Homemade Pork Sausage Meat

2 pounds boneless pork (shoulder preferred)	1 teaspoon dried sage
½ teaspoon pepper	1 teaspoon dried thyme
2 teaspoons salt	1 teaspoon brown sugar

Put pork through medium blade of grinder. Add remaining ingredients and put through grinder a second time. Test flavor by frying small amount until thoroughly cooked. Add more spices to taste, remembering that flavor intensifies after refrigeration.

If sausage meat is to be used within a few days, refrigerate in a bowl. If kept longer, form patties and freeze them on cookie sheets. When frozen hard, store in plastic bags. Use within 3 months.

CHAPTER VII

~~~

Poultry and Game Birds

SOME years after the Pilgrims landed, there were about twenty little tidewater communities between Maine and the Dutch settlements in New York. Among these was Mystic. The small groups of families that broke away from the larger settlements to establish these communities were all of English origin.

The little settlements went through the same growing pains and hardships which the first shipload encountered, but they were more experienced and by then they were not only Pilgrims but pioneers. The first rule was to return to frugal meals. There is not a single recipe for broilers or fat frying chickens. Young poultry had to be kept to produce their quota of eggs. The only poultry recipes that come to us from the early history of Mystic are for fowl, which had led productive lives before they reached the stewpot.

As for game birds, the Pilgrims found some which were nothing less than a godsend. To the whalemen of Mystic, 150 years later, an occasional pheasant was a pleasant change. Everything is relative, and the tough wild pheasant from the fields and forests beyond Mystic was as much of a delicacy for the salt-meat-, pork- and codfish-fed Mystic men as our tender farm-raised pheasant are today.

[135]

Roast Pheasant

3 pheasants (2 pounds each)
1 onion, quartered
1 carrot, quartered
Salt to taste
3 cups dry bread crumbs
1 pound scrapple
½ cup sherry, or to taste

3–6 largest possible slices larding pork*
4 tablespoons butter or fat
4 tablespoons flour
1 tablespoon ground juniper berries
2 teaspoons meat extract
1 cup heavy cream

Put up wing tips, necks and giblets of pheasant in 3 cups water with onion, carrot and salt. Bring to a boil, reduce heat and simmer covered until ready to make sauce. Combine crumbs, scrapple and sherry and stuff body and crop cavities of birds loosely. Secure openings, draw down the neck skin, wrap birds as completely as possible in larding pork and truss. Roast in an open roasting pan in a 350° F. oven for 1 hour. Baste with 2 cups hot water. As pieces of larding pork loosen and drop into pan, drain them well and set them aside for the sauce.

Stir butter or fat in a heavy saucepan over medium heat until brown. Stir in flour until smooth and moisten the roux gradually with the strained broth from the wing tips. Reduce heat and let the sauce simmer, stirring constantly until thickened and smooth. Reduce heat further and let the sauce barely simmer, stirring occasionally for 15 to 20 minutes. Stir in ground juniper, meat extract and cream. Add the sliced giblets and larding pork to the sauce. Remove the trussing threads and serve the pheasant with the sauce.

New England Boiled Chicken Dinner

1 fowl (5 pounds) or 2 broilers (2½ pounds each)
3 quarts cold water

2 tablespoons salt
12 peppercorns
5 large celery ribs

* Order large sheets of larding pork from butcher a day or two before it is needed. One or two slices should suffice to wrap the pheasant completely.

3 parsnips (optional)　　　6 large carrots
4 large onions　　　　　　Homemade noodles, cooked

Wash chicken and place in large kettle. Fill kettle two-thirds full of cold water. Add salt, peppercorns and giblets except liver. Cook liver separately. Bring water to a simmering point and adjust heat carefully so that it simmers but does not come to a full rolling boil. Simmer fowl for 2½ hours before adding vegetables.

Prepare vegetables. Those that take longest to cook should be added first. If broilers are used, add vegetables as soon as simmering begins. Scrub celery carefully, cut into 2-inch lengths, and add to kettle. Scrape and wash parsnips carefully, cut into 1½-inch pieces, and add to kettle. Peel onions, cut into ¼-inch slices, and add to kettle. Scrape and rinse carrots, cut into 1½-inch lengths, and add to kettle. Continue to cook until vegetables and chicken are tender. Allow approximately 1½ hours for total cooking time for broilers. Allow approximately 4 hours for total cooking time for fowl.

Skim fat before serving soup. An easy method is to use a large bulb baster to take up surface fat. To serve soup, place a generous serving of cooked homemade noodles in each soup plate. Add broth and a few pieces of each vegetable. Serve as a first course.

For entrée, arrange chicken on a platter and surround with remaining vegetables; sprinkle freshly milled pepper over all. A green salad and oven-hot baking-powder biscuits should also be served.
Makes 6 servings.

VARIATION

On hot summer days simmer as above in the morning. Remove chicken and refrigerate soup; skim off fat. Remove chicken from bones and use it to prepare Chicken Salad (p. 17). Refrigerate salad. At serving time reheat soup without bringing to a full boil. Serve with noodles as above. Soup flavor will have been improved by refrigeration. Serve chicken salad with sliced homegrown tomatoes and hot biscuits.

⚓ Baked Mystic Chicken

3 broilers (2 pounds each)	1 teaspoon pepper
1 carrot, scraped and quartered	½ cup flour
1 onion, sliced	1 cup salad oil
3 parsley sprigs	3 large onions, sliced paper-
2 teaspoons salt	thin and separated into rings
3 teaspoons paprika	3 tablespoons chopped parsley

Have butcher halve broilers and separate backbones, necks, wing tips and giblets. Put these parts only in 4 cups water with carrot, onion and parsley. Add 1 teaspoon salt, cover, and simmer for at least 2 hours to obtain a strong stock.

Combine 1 teaspoon salt, 1 teaspoon paprika, ½ teaspoon pepper and the flour, and dredge the well-dried remaining broiler parts very thoroughly with the mixture. Dip them into the oil and arrange them in an open ovenware baking pan, meaty sides up. Pour any remaining oil into the pan. Spread the onion rings over the chicken, add salt and pepper to taste, and sprinkle with remaining paprika. Bake in a 450° F. oven for 15 minutes, basting once with stock from giblets. Reduce heat to 375° and bake for about 30 minutes longer, basting frequently with stock until golden brown. Slice giblets, sprinkle them over the top with chopped parsley, and serve out of the baking pan.
Makes 6 servings.

⚓ Fried Chicken

Carol Jay Hartman writes, "This is one of my favorite recipes. I was in the training program aboard the *Gundel* in 1964, and always enjoy my visits to the Seaport."

2 frying chickens (2½ pounds each), disjointed	½ teaspoon pepper
	1 tablespoon salt
1¼ cups flour	Fat for frying
1½ tablespoons paprika	

Rinse chicken pieces and dry thoroughly. Shake in a paper bag with flour, paprika, pepper and salt until well coated. Chill in paper bag for 15 minutes. Heat ½ inch of fat in each of 2 wide skillets. Fry the chicken pieces slowly, turning them occasionally to brown evenly on all sides. After about 25 minutes, when they are uniformly brown, place a cover on each skillet, leaving a ½-inch opening for escaping steam. Reduce heat and continue to cook slowly until tender, about 30 minutes. Drain and serve immediately.
Makes 4 to 6 servings.

Chicken with Mushrooms

2 uncooked double chicken breasts	1 sweet green pepper
1 teaspoon cornstarch	1 can (5 ounces) water chestnuts
¼ teaspoon white pepper	2 tablespoons corn oil
1 teaspoon salt	1 can (4 ounces) mushrooms

Skin and bone chicken breasts. Cut meat into 1-inch pieces. Mix with cornstarch, pepper and salt. Cut green pepper into thin strips, about 1-inch long. Slice water chestnuts. Heat oil in frying pan over high heat. Add chicken; stir constantly until chicken turns white. Add green pepper, drained mushrooms, and water chestnuts. Mix thoroughly and cook for about 2 minutes. If mixture is dry add 1 tablespoon mushroom juice. Serve with rice.
Makes 3 or 4 servings.
NOTE: The raw chicken is easiest to cut if it is slightly frozen. On a boat, putting each piece over an ice cube does the trick.

Chicken Croquettes

From New London, early twentieth century
MRS. B. L. ARMSTRONG
Contributed by Miss Hyla Snider

Dark meat of 1 large chicken,
  cooked and chopped very fine
¼ salt spoon cayenne pepper
10 drops of onion juice
  1 teaspoon lemon juice
  1 teaspoon salt
  1 teaspoon celery salt

2 teaspoons chopped parsley
2 cups hot light cream or milk
½ salt spoon white pepper
2 tablespoons butter
5 tablespoons flour
Pinch of cayenne pepper

Mix chopped chicken, cayenne, onion juice, lemon juice, ½ teaspoon of the salt, ½ teaspoon of the celery salt and the parsley. Melt the butter, stir in the flour until smooth, and add the cream. Cook over low heat, stirring constantly, until smooth and thickened. Season with the white pepper, remaining salt and celery salt and the pinch of cayenne. Mix sauce with chicken mixture until thoroughly blended. Spread out on a platter and set aside to harden a little.

Use 1 tablespoon for each croquette; roll it in bread or cracker crumbs, then in egg, then in crumbs again. This will prevent splitting open when fried. Fry in wire basket in deep fat for 1 minute.
Makes 10 croquettes.

6ℵ Chicken Pie with Cheese Crust

1 large frying chicken, disjointed
2 chicken bouillon cubes
2 celery stalks
1 onion
1 tomato
4 parsley sprigs

5 tablespoons butter
24 small mushroom caps
4 tablespoons flour
6 hard-cooked eggs
¼ cup chopped parsley
1 recipe Cheese Crust for
  Chicken Pie (below)

Put chicken in a kettle with water to cover, bouillon cubes, celery, onion, tomato and parsley sprigs. Poach for about 30 minutes, until tender; (about 1 hour for a stewing chicken). Take out chicken, remove meat, and return skin and bones to broth in kettle. Reduce to 3 cups by boiling rapidly.

Melt butter in a heavy saucepan, add mushrooms, and sauté until dark and glossy, 5 to 7 minutes. Take out mushrooms with a slotted spoon. Stir flour into butter in saucepan. Gradually add 3 cups strained reduced stock and cook over low heat, stirring constantly, until smooth and thickened. Put mushrooms and chicken pieces into sauce and pour into baking dish (8 × 12 inches). Slice eggs with an egg slicer but do not spread apart. Place eggs between the chicken pieces and add parsley. Adjust crust and bake.

Makes about 6 servings.

NOTE: Chicken may be left on bones if preferred. A little Madeira wine may be added to the sauce to taste.

CHEESE CRUST FOR CHICKEN PIE

¾ cup grated Cheddar cheese	1 teaspoon salt
¾ cup butter	½ tablespoon paprika
2¼ cups flour	1 egg, beaten with 1 tablespoon
1 egg yolk	water

If grated Cheddar is not available, put block cheese through coarse blade of a food grinder. Work with butter, flour, egg yolk and seasonings into a smooth dough; chill until filling is ready. Arrange filling in baking dish. Roll out dough on a lightly floured board to approximate size of dish. Transfer on rolling pin to dish and spread over pie. Pinch edge down firmly and cut vents for steam. Trim scraps and cut into leaf shapes or fluted rounds. Brush top and edge of pie with egg; press down leaves or rounds. Bake in a 375° F. oven for 35 to 45 minutes, depending on thickness of crust.

Chicken-in-the-Soup-Pot

During a period when a recipe was called a "rule," a cranberry pie was a "cramberry" tart, and cider was "cyder," the pleasures of overeating were said to produce an "irritable stomach which had to be returned to good temper." One way of doing that was with a nice Chicken-in-the-Soup-Pot.

2 broilers, quartered

1 carrot, scraped

1 onion, stuck with 2 cloves

2 celery stalks

Salt and pepper

¼ cup farina, or more

2 tablespoons minced parsley

Bring enough water to boil in a soup kettle to cover the broilers. Add carrot, onion and celery, and boil for 10 minutes. Add broilers and seasonings to taste, cover, and boil for about 20 minutes. Take from heat; skim off fat. Strain broth through a double cheesecloth wrung out in cold water and return broth to the rinsed kettle. Bring back to a boil, sprinkle in farina, and boil for a few minutes according to package directions. Pull skin from chicken pieces and reheat chicken in the soup. Serve in deep soup plates, sprinkled with parsley.
Makes 4 servings.

ℰℛ Chicken Casseroles

We are embarked on a voyage of rediscovery and in our search we are finding forgotten individual touches. You may not have thought you could ever make another chicken fricassee, but here are three early eighteenth-century recipes for delicious casseroles that fit exactly into our present style of cookery.

ℰℛ Chicken Fricassee I

An eighteenth-century "Golden Fricassee"

3 fryers, disjointed, or 12 half chicken breasts

2 chicken bouillon cubes

1 teaspoon tightly packed saffron or ⅜ teaspoon ground saffron shreds

¼ teaspoon grated mace

1½ teaspoons salt

¾ cup butter

1 pound mushrooms, sliced

½ cup flour

Salt and pepper

½ cup light cream (the original recipe calls for ½ cup dry white Rhenish wine)

¼ bunch of parsley

1 lemon, sliced

Early in the day: In a saucepan put necks, backbones, wing tips and giblets of fryers in 4 cups cold water. Cover and bring to a boil. Add bouillon cubes and reduce heat; simmer covered for 2 hours. Strain and chill broth so that fat can be lifted from the top. Slice giblets and set them aside. Reheat broth to a boil; take from heat and infuse the saffron shreds in it until needed, just before the dish is completed.

Wash and dry chicken pieces; pound them lightly with a mallet until they are slightly flattened. Combine mace and salt and rub it into the pieces; set them aside; in warm weather place them in refrigerator.

About 1 hour before serving: Heat butter in a casserole or Dutch oven and brown the chicken pieces gently on all sides. This will take about 30 minutes. Take out the pieces; strain off the butter remaining in pan. Return chicken to pan, add 4 cups cold water, cover, and bring to a boil. Reduce heat and simmer until tender, about 20 minutes. In the meantime, sauté mushrooms in 3 tablespoons of the drained-off butter until glossy but not wilted, about 5 minutes. Add them to the sliced giblets and set them aside.

Measure ½ cup drained-off butter into top part of double boiler over boiling water. Stir in the flour and cook for a few minutes. Stir in the giblet-saffron broth. As soon as the chicken pieces in the casserole are tender, drain off the broth in which they are simmering and stir it, little by little, into the sauce. There should be enough broth to make a medium-thick sauce. Add mushrooms and giblets and season to taste. Stir in the cream (or wine), and pour the sauce over the chicken in the casserole. Garnish with parsley and lemon slices. If wine is used, it must be very dry; a sweet wine does not combine well with saffron. The casserole can be placed in a very slow oven to keep warm before it is garnished.

Makes 6 servings.

๕๙ Chicken Fricassee II

An early eighteenth-century "Red Fricassey"

This is the sort of thing you can only do when you have a large hen lobster full of red coral, the sort of thing Mystic housewives had and made the very best of. Presumably they had the lobster first and then made the fricassey around it.

Prepare the chicken as in the preceding recipe, but omit the saffron and mushrooms. Boil the lobster for about 20 minutes in a large kettle. Take out the meat and press the coral through a strainer into the thickened fricassey sauce. Return the chicken pieces to the casserole, pour the sauce with the sliced giblets added over the chicken, and garnish with parsley. Serve this fricassey with small dumplings.

Although there is no mention of the lobster meat in the old recipe it can be set aside for use in lobster cocktail or salad, but the very best use is to keep it warm, slice it at the last moment, and add it to the casserole just before it is served. Combinations of meat and seafood were so common that we can presume that this is exactly what they did.

❧ Chicken Fricassee III

An early eighteenth-century "Green Fricassey"

The French made this chicken dish with spinach only, and called it *à la bonne femme*. The English record it as "green fricassey" and the recipe came from there to New England in an old cookery book. With sorrel growing wild in the fields, it is no wonder the settlers made this dish when lobster, coral and saffron were not available.

3 fryers, disjointed, or 12 half chicken breasts	3 cups tightly packed sorrel or spinach, or half and half
3 chicken bouillon cubes	2 pounds asparagus, tender green part only
¼ to ½ teaspoon grated mace	
1½ teaspoons salt	½ cup flour
¼ teaspoon pepper	1 cup heavy cream
½ cup butter	Salt and pepper
	10 parsley sprigs

Early in the day: In a covered saucepan, cook necks, wing tips, backbones and giblets with bouillon cubes in 4 cups water for 1½ hours. Chill stock so that fat can be removed easily.

Wash and dry chicken pieces and rub with combined mace, salt and pepper. Brown them slowly in the butter in a casserole for about 30 minutes.

Boil sorrel and/or spinach in 1 cup salted water for 5 to 7 minutes; blend or purée with the water in which it boiled.

About 35 minutes before serving: Drain all butter and chicken fat from casserole; set aside. Add 4 cups cold water to chicken pieces and simmer covered until tender, about 20 minutes. In the meantime, boil asparagus in as little salted water as possible for about 12 minutes, until just tender. Drain and reserve the water.

Drain stock from casserole. Add sliced giblets to chicken pieces, cover, and keep warm in a 200° F. oven. Measure and strain ½ cup butter drained from casserole into top part of a double boiler over boiling water. Stir in flour until smooth; gradually stir in the strained fat-free giblet stock, the green vegetable purée and the cream. Stir until sauce is smooth and medium thin, adding part of stock drained from casserole and part of asparagus water. Season to taste. Arrange asparagus spears around chicken pieces in casserole, pour the green sauce over both, and serve with rice. Garnish with parsley.

Makes 6 servings.

❧ To Stuff and Roast a Turkey or Fowl

The rule was to stuff with 1 pound of wheat bread, mixed with suet, eggs, sweet marjoram, pepper and salt. Sometimes a gill (½ cup) of wine was added. The bird was roasted and frequently basted with salt water until steam was emitted from the breast; then it was dredged with flour and basted with butter. There were oyster stuffings and parsley garnishes and the proper accompaniments were "cramberry" sauce, boiled onions and parsley done with potatoes. There were also pickles or celery. We have tried the salt-water basting, which we interpret as *salted-water* basting, and the late dredging with flour and cannot understand why these excellent procedures were dropped.

❧ Roast Turkey

Roast turkey in an open pan according to the following rules:

Unstuffed birds weighing under 15 lbs.—20 minutes per pound at 325° F.

Unstuffed birds weighing 15 to 16 lbs.—18 minutes per pound at 325° F.

Unstuffed birds weighing over 16 lbs.—15 minutes a pound at 300° F.

NOTE: For stuffed birds, add ½ hour to 1 hour roasting time; less time for small birds, more time for large ones.

Wash turkey, dry, and salt cavity well. Stuff with any appropriate stuffing or dressing and sew or skewer firmly. (Many cooks prefer not to stuff birds over 16 pounds.) Truss and place in an open roasting pan. Rub well with soft butter or brush with melted butter. Dip a cloth into melted fat and spread it over the bird. Half of an old kitchen towel is the perfect size. Roast turkey, basting every 25 minutes with pan drippings. Remove cloth 30 minutes before turkey is scheduled to be done, and continue basting frequently with ¾ cup water in which 1 tablespoon honey has been dissolved.

ⒸⓍ Roast Christmas Goose

From *The Log* of Mystic Seaport, 1967

1 goose (12 to 14 pounds)	4 tablespoons butter
1 medium-sized onion, quartered	3 tablespoons minced fresh sage, or 1 tablespoon dried sage
8 medium-sized potatoes, peeled, boiled and riced	Salt and freshly ground pepper
1 pound small white onions, peeled and parboiled	1 cup port wine, heated
⅓ to ½ cup heavy cream	1 tablespoon Dijon or brown mustard

Put goose liver aside. Simmer wing tips, neck, other giblets and quartered onion in salted water to cover for 2 hours; add water if necessary. Stir together hot riced potatoes, parboiled white onions, cream, 3 tablespoons butter and the sage; season to taste. Stuff goose with the potato mixture and secure the opening. Truss the goose in such a way that the neck skin is folded under and can be opened during the roasting time. Lay the goose on a rack, spread remaining 1 tablespoon butter over the breast, and roast in a 400° F. oven for 10 minutes on each side. Reduce heat to 325° F., add 1 cup boiling water to pan, and roast for 15 minutes per pound, basting frequently. About 20 minutes before the goose is done, open the neck opening and pour in the port wine stirred with the mustard; tilt the goose so that the wine runs over the stuffing.

Sauté the goose liver in goose fat from the pan until lightly browned. Slice liver and giblets for the gravy. Make a brown gravy of 2 tablespoons goose fat, 2 tablespoons flour, and the strained broth from the giblets. Add the sliced giblets and liver and serve the gravy with the goose.

Serve red cabbage and green peas or any other green vegetable with the goose. Pass cold tart applesauce separately, and serve some of the potato and onion stuffing with each portion. Lingonberry, gooseberry or cranberry sauce can also be served instead of or in addition to the applesauce.

Makes 12 or more servings.

ᏋᏋᏦ Roast Stuffed Duck

12 medium-sized white onions
1 cup bread crumbs
Salt and pepper
1 to 2 teaspoons minced fresh or
    dried sage

2 fat ducks (about 3 pounds
    each)
¼ cup butter

Parboil the onions, chop them with the crumbs, and season to taste. Add salt, also to taste, and stuff mixture into the ducks. Truss them securely. Rub them with butter and roast them, breast-sides down, with ½ inch of water in an open pan in a 325° F. oven for 1 hour. Baste frequently with the water in the pan. Turn duck over to brown the breast. Bake until brown and tender, about 1¼ hours longer. Make gravy from pan liquid and serve with the onion dressing.
Makes 4 to 6 servings.

ᏋᏋᏦ Roast Squab

6 jumbo squabs
6 tablespoons butter
Salt and pepper
½ pound scrapple
½ cup bread crumbs
6 chicken livers

¼ cup chopped onion
½ cup chopped mushrooms
3 tablespoons butter
6 slices of salt pork
½ cup brandy with ½ cup
    water

Wash and dry squabs; rub generously inside and out with butter, and season. Crush scrapple with crumbs and chicken livers. Add onion and mushrooms sautéed in the butter for 7 minutes. Season to taste. Stuff mixture into squabs. Cover breast of each bird with 1 slice of the pork, and truss. Arrange in a roasting pan, add brandy and water, and roast, basting frequently, in a 350° F. oven for 50 minutes. Remove pork and baste for 10 minutes longer. Place on a hot platter and serve with Giblet Sauce (below).
Makes 6 servings.

GIBLET SAUCE

Simmer necks, wing tips and giblets of squabs in salted water to cover with 1 small onion and ½ carrot for 35 minutes. While squabs are roasting, brown 4 tablespoons butter or drippings from the pan in a heavy saucepan. Stir in ¼ cup flour and stir until brown. Reduce heat and gradually stir in 2 cups strained broth from the giblets. Stir until thickened. Correct seasoning and stir in the diced giblets. Keep sauce hot in the top part of a double boiler over simmering water.

Partridges in Casserole

From Mrs. Holton Wood Horton, Providence

6 chukar partridges
¾ loaf of stale white bread, ground in a food grinder or blender
1½ lemons, grated rind and juice
1 egg, beaten
Salt and pepper
⅓ cup brandy

¼ cup soft butter
1⅓ cups sherry
1 cup chopped celery
2 cups button mushrooms, sautéed in butter
2 tablespoons red-currant jelly
½ cup sour cream
Lemon slices

Boil wing tips, necks and giblets of partridges with 2 cups salted water. Rinse and dry birds and stuff them with bread combined with lemons, egg and seasonings to taste. Skewer or truss the birds. Brush with brandy and allow to dry. Rub well with butter and arrange them in a casserole. Add part of the sherry, the stock and giblets and the celery. Bake covered in a 325° F. oven for about 2½ hours, basting frequently and adding sherry when necessary. Just before the birds are done, take them out and drain off the liquid into a saucepan. Return birds to casserole and keep them hot in oven reduced to 250°. Skim fat from pan juices, add mushrooms and jelly, and boil up once. Reduce heat, stir in sour cream, and season to taste. Pour over birds in casserole and serve garnished with paper-thin lemon slices.

CHAPTER VIII
~~
Vegetables

THE various settled regions along the Atlantic Coast showed strong variations in their cookery. At first, the settlers' food was uncharacteristic because it depended entirely on what was available and what the land could be made to produce quickly. Later the food customs of the original homelands influenced the kinds of foods produced.

Corn and beans became the staples of the hardworking Mystic settlers. The fact that wheat did not grow well in New England was reflected in all the good things the Mysticians learned to make out of cornmeal. Surrounded by sugar maples, they were able to pour syrup over their corn cakes. They dredged their clams with cornmeal before frying them. Corn also provided food, flour and fodder for cattle and pigs. However, the settlers came from an England which took other vegetables seriously. The new Americans planted seeds and tended vegetable gardens just as soon as they had established roofs over their heads.

It was then held in England and repeated by Dr. Kitchener many years later that the difference between the "Elegant and the Ordinary table" could be seen more clearly in the "dressing of the vegetables" than in anything else, "especially greens." In other words, the lower classes cooked their vegetables together into a sort of limp and colorless mush while the upper classes cooked them separately and only up to the point at which they were still recognizable.

The Puritans did not pretend to elegance but they did cook their vegetables separately and were even inclined to serve them separately, as New Englanders still do today.

⒠⒳ Maize, or Indian Corn

Maize, like many other grains, has been used by man for so many centuries that its original habitat is unknown, but it is generally assumed to have been indigenous to South America. There is a plausible theory that the Spanish explorers brought it back to Spain. Others claim there was maize in Asia and that it was brought to Spain by the Arabs. Whether it came from the East or the West, it did reach Europe and England via Spain.

The maize which the Pilgrims found in New England had been under cultivation by the North American Indians for centuries, presumably brought from South America by whatever civilization predated them.

In writing a cookbook about Mystic Seaport there is a danger of ending by writing a book about corn. The early settlers could not have

survived without it, and present-day Mystic still prepares it in many of the same ways as the Indians did long before Squantz hailed the Pilgrims. It is a little disconcerting to discover that there is nothing very new under the New England sun. We see our movies today in an atmosphere of popping corn, and on picnics we have the pleasure of roasting our ears of corn in the ashes of the fire. The Indians popped corn, they roasted ears in the ashes of their fires, and they made nasaump, which became "samp," a kind of hominy. Their msakwataš became our "succotash," although we omit their diced bear meat and confine ourselves to mingling corn and beans.

Corn Roasted in Ashes

24 even-sized ears of corn	Salt and pepper shakers
24 slices of bacon (optional)	Lots of butter

Pull husks back from ears of corn and remove all the silk. (If you like, wrap 1 slice of bacon around each ear.) Pull the husks back down over the ears and fasten them at the tips with string. Wait until the fire has burned down to ashes. Bury the ears in the ashes and let them roast for 12 to 15 minutes. Fish the ears out of the ashes and let them cool for a moment. Pull back the husks. If roasted with bacon, sprinkle with pepper and eat from the cob. If roasted plain, brush ears with butter and seasonings and eat. Makes 6 to 8 servings.

Fried Corn

This was served with meat dishes or with grilled bacon.

8 to 10 ears of corn, freshly boiled	1 small onion, minced
1 teaspoon salt	1 egg yolk, beaten
1 teaspoon sugar	¼ cup light cream
¼ teaspoon pepper	2 tablespoons butter

Cut kernels from cobs. Measure into a bowl and for every 2½ cups corn kernels, add the above dry ingredients, onion, egg yolk and cream; stir well. Heat butter in frypan, pour in the corn mixture, and stir over medium heat. Continue to stir until evenly browned. Serve at once. Makes about 6 servings.

ᏋᎧᎩ Corn Pudding

Having found Indians and corn in America, the early settlers often tagged "Indian" onto the names of dishes that contained corn. In a roundabout way this explains why the turkey is still called an Indian, pronounced Indee-ahn, in parts of Europe. Americans are startled to find Roast Stuffed Indian on menus of innocent-appearing inns.

6 large ears of fresh corn or 2 packages (10-ounce pack) frozen corn
3 eggs, separated

1 cup light cream
1 teaspoon minced onion
1 teaspoon sugar
Salt and black pepper

Cut kernels from ears of corn, scraping each ear after cutting to obtain the milky juice and seeds. Put in a 2-quart casserole. Beat egg yolks into cream, add onion, sugar and seasonings to taste, and pour over corn. Beat egg whites stiff with a pinch of salt and fold gently into corn. Bake in a 350° F. oven for 45 minutes.
Makes 4 to 6 servings.

ᏋᎧᎩ Meal-in-one Corn Pudding

All around the happy village
Stood the maize-fields, green and shining,
Waved the green plume of Mondamin,
Waved his soft and sunny tresses,
Filling all the land with plenty.
—Longfellow, *The Song of Hiawatha.*

2½ cups frozen or canned ker-　　½ teaspoon salt
　　nel corn　　　　　　　　　　¼ teaspoon pepper
2 eggs, separated　　　　　　　2 cups sliced cooked chicken or
¾ cup heavy cream　　　　　　　　turkey
½ teaspoon sugar

Stir corn with egg yolks, cream, sugar and seasonings. Fold in stiffly beaten egg whites and pour over the chicken or turkey spread out in a wide, shallow baking pan (7 x 11 inches). Bake in a 350° F. oven for 35 minutes.
Makes about 4 servings.

Plymouth Succotash

Mr. Ellis W. Brewster writes, "There is an old Plymouth recipe of some standing for a dish called Plymouth Succotash. This recipe is taken from *The Plimoth Colony Cook Book*, published by the Plymouth Antiquarian Society. It is my mother's recipe.

"Possibly I should explain that, as you may suspect, it is practically a full meal in itself. It continues to be served by both the Old Colony Club and the Pilgrim Society at their annual meeting on Forefathers' Day."

Forefathers' Day is December 21, the anniversary of the landing of the Pilgrims at Plymouth. It was first celebrated in 1769, when the Old Colony Club met and dined together in "commemoration of the landing of their worthy ancestors in this place."

1 quart dried pea beans　　　　1 medium-sized turnip
6 pounds corned beef　　　　　5 medium-sized potatoes (op-
5 pounds fowl　　　　　　　　　　tional)
5 quarts hulled corn

Soak beans in water to cover overnight, then cook and mash. This makes the thickening. Boil beef and fowl until tender, and save liquid. Cut up turnip and potatoes and cook in the broth. Cut the beef and fowl into 1½-inch cubes. Combine all the ingredients and let boil together for about 1 hour. Stir frequently to keep from sticking. Let cool, always

uncovered. Stir occasionally to keep from souring. Serve in soup plates. This is better the second and third day. The Pilgrims used to freeze it, cutting off chunks at a time and reheating.
Makes 24 servings.

ᏧᎳ Old Long Island Succotash

From Mrs. Franklin O. Rich

1 pound salt pork	1 can (16 ounces) kidney beans
3 quarts cold water	(optional)
3 cups shell beans, or 2 cups dried pea or marrow beans	2 cups cut green snap beans
	Corn kernels cut and scraped
2 cups shelled fresh lima beans	from 2 large ears of corn
2 cups shelled green snap beans	½ cup sugar
	Salt and pepper

Combine salt pork, water and shell beans in a large kettle; cover and boil to a mush for 2 to 3 hours. Add limas, shelled green beans and kidney beans 1 hour before completion. About 15 minutes before serving add cut green beans, corn, sugar and salt and pepper to taste. Stir occasionally. This is a stew of beans, and slight variations won't matter much. Better each time it's warmed up.
Makes 8 or more servings.

ᏧᎳ Samp Porridge

Samp is kernels of hulled dried corn and elsewhere may also be incorrectly called hominy. It was an excellent way to preserve the nourishing kernels over the winter.

Mrs. Franklin O. Rich of Stonington, Connecticut, writes, "Samp seems to be known as hull corn by some old-time Mystic people.

"Soak the samp overnight. In the morning put it in a kettle with enough water to allow the samp to swell to 3 times its size. Add a hunk of fresh pork. The old-fashioned way was to use pig's knuckles—but I like better a piece of loin, about 3 chops I'd guess. Add some salt, bring to a boil, then lower heat and let the porridge simmer until the samp is tender, which will be several hours. Stir occasionally and add more water if needed."

ᏟᎢ Hominy

Hominy is similar to samp, but the germ has been removed. It can be found either in whole kernels or ground to various degrees of fineness.

Most recipes call for boiled hominy. In the top part of a double boiler, boil 1 cup whole hominy in 2 cups lightly salted water for about 2 minutes, stirring constantly. Set over boiling water in lower section of double boiler and boil until water is absorbed. Add 1 cup milk or water and boil for 1 hour. Add a second cup of milk or water and boil for 1 hour longer.

Makes about 4 servings.

ᏟᎢ Coarse Hominy

1 cup coarse hominy	2 tablespoons butter
2 quarts water	Salt

Rinse hominy and soak overnight in water to cover. Set over heat and cook covered until tender, stirring often. Hominy needs slow, steady cooking. Remove cover and stir until water is evaporated, being careful that it does not boil. Stir in butter and salt to taste.

Makes about 4 servings. This makes a good accompaniment for meat or poultry.

ᏟᎢ Fine Hominy

1 cup fine hominy	½ teaspoon salt
2½ cups milk	

Rinse hominy and soak overnight in water to cover. Drain in the morning, put with milk in top part of double boiler over boiling water, and boil covered for 1 hour. Add salt and more milk if needed. Serve with cream and sugar.

Makes about 4 servings. This makes a good breakfast cereal.

ॐ Fried Hominy

Ground hominy, when cooked, can also be molded in a bread pan and chilled. Slice and fry in butter until golden. Serve as a vegetable or with sugar and crushed fruit.

ॐ Dried Peas and Beans

The English and the New Englanders cooked fresh vegetables in season, which left them with nothing for long months of the year. The vegetables which were suitable for drying were, therefore, given preference and rated more space in the garden.

ॐ Baked Lima Beans

Make this when there are ham scraps and/or a ham bone.

1¼ pounds dried baby lima beans	2 teaspoons brown mustard
1 teaspoon baking soda	½ cup molasses
1 ham bone (optional)	12 bacon strips
	1 cup ham scraps, diced

Soak beans in water to cover overnight. Add baking soda and heat in the same water until it comes to a boil, then pour through a strainer. When limas are well drained, return them to the kettle with fresh water to cover. Add the ham bone and boil gently until limas are tender, about

40 minutes. Take from heat, and pour the beans again through the strainer set over a saucepan in order to save the bean liquid. Discard ham bone and set beans aside.

Boil 1 cup of the bean liquid in the kettle with the mustard and molasses for 15 minutes. Arrange bacon and beans mixed with ham scraps in layers in a casserole, starting and ending with bacon. Pour over the mustard-molasses mixture and bake, uncovered, in a 350° F. oven for 1 hour, or until bacon is browned. Replace liquid that boils away with the remaining bean liquid.

Makes about 6 servings.

⽊ Mystic Baked Beans

Mysticians say it is no use baking beans for less than a dozen servings. Just heat them up if any are left over.

3 pounds dried pea beans	¾ cup molasses
1½ teaspoons baking soda	1 tablespoon dry mustard
1½ pounds salt pork	2 tablespoons salt
2 onions	1 teaspoon black pepper
¾ cup sugar	

Soak beans in water to cover overnight, or for 8 hours. Add baking soda and boil them for 3 to 4 minutes; pour them into a sieve and pour enough cold water over to rinse them thoroughly. Score the pork rind in a crisscross pattern and place half of it in a 3-quart bean pot. Add 1 onion and half of the beans. Add the second onion and the rest of the beans. Top with remaining salt pork. Stir sugar, molasses, mustard, salt and pepper with 2½ cups boiling water and pour some of it over the beans. Bake in a 300° F. oven for 6 hours, adding just enough of the remaining molasses water at intervals to keep the beans moist. If there is not enough molasses water, add plain hot water.

Makes 12 servings.

⌘ Baked Beans

1 pound dried pea beans	¼ cup brown sugar
5 cups water	¼ cup molasses
2 teaspoons dry mustard	2 tablespoons sweet pickle juice
Pepper	½ pound salt pork
3 medium-sized onions, peeled and quartered	Salt

Pick over beans carefully and wash. Cover with 3 cups water and soak overnight, or for 8 hours. Add 2 cups water and the mustard, ¼ teaspoon pepper to taste, onions, brown sugar, molasses and pickle juice. Cover and boil until the bean skins are soft enough to wrinkle. Test by removing a few beans with a spoon and blowing over them. Allow about 1 hour.

Slice salt pork almost through at ½-inch intervals. Place pork in a 2-quart bean pot or casserole and cover with hot beans and their liquid. Pepper generously over the top. Cover and bake at 250° F., stirring occasionally, until tender. Allow 6 to 8 hours.

After two thirds of the baking time has elapsed, add ¾ cup water or just enough to cover the beans. Add salt to taste. Remove the cover during the last hour of baking.

Makes 4 to 6 servings.

⌘ Sea Cook's Baked Beans

Mr. John F. Leavitt writes, "This was a very old family recipe which I took to sea with me several times when signed on as cook in coasting schooners."

2 pounds dried beans	½ cup sugar
½ to ¾ pound salt pork	½ cup dark molasses
1 apple	1 teaspoon dry mustard
1 medium-sized onion (optional)	½ teaspoon pepper
	1½ teaspoons salt

Soak beans in cold water overnight. In the morning, parboil until skins crack. Transfer to beanpot and add salt pork cut down to the rind in cubes. Cut the apple into chunks and bury them and the onion in the beans. Mix sugar, molasses, mustard, pepper and salt with about 2 cups boiling water and pour over beans and pork. Bake in a 300° F. oven for 6 hours. Add water when necessary. If you like the pork crisp, take off the cover for the last 30 minutes or so.

Makes 8 to 10 servings.

Brandied Baked Beans

For the Second Day of Christmas

From *The Log* of Mystic Seaport, 1967

4 cans (16 ounces each) baked beans	2 tablespoons minced onion
⅓ cup brandy	½ teaspoon dry mustard
⅓ cup black coffee	¼ teaspoon ground allspice
⅓ cup chili sauce	1 can (16 ounces) pineapple chunks, drained

Combine beans, brandy, coffee and chili sauce with onion, mustard and allspice in a 3-quart casserole. Stir well, cover, and set aside for 3 hours. Bake uncovered in a 375° F. oven for 1 hour. Arrange pineapple over beans and bake for 20 minutes longer.

Makes 8 to 10 servings.

Pease Pudding

2 cups dried split peas	2 eggs, beaten
3 tablespoons butter	¼ cup flour for bag
Salt and pepper	½ cup browned butter

Wash peas and soak them in cold water to cover overnight. Tie them in a densely woven pudding bag (see p. 212), leaving enough room to swell but not enough for them to become mushy. Place bag in a kettle with just enough cold water to cover. Adjust lid, bring water to a boil, and boil for 2 hours.

Transfer pudding bag to a colander and drain well. Open bag, empty peas into a saucepan, and purée in a blender or through a sieve. Beat in butter, salt and pepper to taste and eggs. Rinse and wring out the pudding bag and flour the interior well. Pour back the pudding, tie securely, and boil for 1 hour longer. Turn pudding carefully into a serving bowl so that it does not break. Pour butter over pudding and serve at once.

Makes about 6 servings.

Stewed Red Cabbage

1 large or 2 small heads of red cabbage, trimmed and shredded fine	1 teaspoon salt
	¼ teaspoon pepper
5 tablespoons butter	5 sour cooking apples, peeled, cored and sliced
5 tablespoons red-wine vinegar	¼ teaspoon ground cloves
⅓ cup brown sugar	¼ teaspoon ground cinnamon

Cook cabbage, half of the butter and the remaining ingredients with 1 cup water in a large kettle over low heat. Stir frequently and add more water if cabbage becomes too dry. Cook for 1 hour. Stir in remaining butter, correct seasoning, and serve with pork, venison, game birds or goose.

Makes 6 to 8 servings.

Cauliflower Fritters

1 large head of cauliflower	2 tablespoons minced mint leaves, in season
½ cup warm water	
1 tablespoon melted butter	Shortening or fat for deep-frying
1 cup flour	
Salt and pepper	

Boil cauliflower in salted water for 12 minutes. Drain well and divide into flowerets; cool. Beat warm water and butter (or cold water and salad oil) into the flour until smooth. Season to taste and stir in the mint. Dip cauliflower pieces into the batter and fry in shortening heated to 365° F. on a frying thermometer until golden, about 5 minutes. Drain and serve at once.
Makes 6 servings.

☙ Cauliflower Cheese Casserole

From Mrs. Richard C. Palmer, Stonington

1 large or 2 small cauliflowers	3 cups milk
¼ pound mushrooms, sliced	Salt and pepper
¼ cup butter	7 thin slices of American cheese
¼ cup flour	

Separate cauliflower into flowerets and boil in salted water to cover for 10 minutes. Drain well and arrange in a buttered shallow casserole or baking dish. Fry mushrooms in butter for 5 minutes until glossy but not wilted. Reduce heat and stir in flour until smooth. Gradually add milk and stir until smooth and thickened. Add salt and pepper to taste. Pour over cauliflower, top with cheese slices and bake in a 350° F. oven until cheese is melted and browned, about 15 minutes.
Makes 6 to 8 servings.

Or prepare casserole in a few minutes in the following way:
Partially cook frozen cauliflower. Place in greased casserole and add 1 can (10½ ounces) undiluted cream of mushroom soup and ½ teaspoon Worcestershire sauce for each package of cauliflower. Top with slices of American cheese and bake slowly until cheese is melted.

ⳍ Braised Celery

8 small heads of white celery	3 cups good beef stock
3 teaspoons salt	1 loaf of unsliced 3-day-old
3 tablespoons butter	white bread
2 carrots, scraped and diced	⅓ cup butter
¼ teaspoon pepper	

Trim celery heads, scrape off threads, and cut all heads to an even 6-inch length. Discard coarse stalks. Chop tender tops and leaves and set them aside. Blanch trimmed celery in boiling water with 2 teaspoons salt for 10 minutes; drain well. Melt butter in an oblong pan with a lid. Spread the chopped celery tops and diced carrots in the pan and arrange the blanched celery heads on this bed. Season with remaining salt and the pepper and cover tightly. Simmer over low heat for 15 minutes. Add stock and simmer for 2½ hours. Turn heads carefully after 30 minutes and again after 1 hour. As stock reduces it should go down to a glaze. Increase heat slightly towards the end of the cooking time if stock is not sufficiently reduced. Trim crusts from bread; cut lengthwise into 8 slices at least 7-inches long. Fry slowly in butter until golden. Split celery heads carefully down the center. Place 2 braised halves on each slice of fried bread and serve with chicken or game birds.
Makes 8 servings.

ⳍ Cucumbers in Sour Cream

From Lillian Meyer

3 cucumbers	½ teaspoon onion powder
2 tablespoons plus ½ teaspoon salt	3 tablespoons cider vinegar
1 tablespoon sugar	1 cup sour cream
½ teaspoon dry mustard	Paprika

Peel cucumbers and slice paper-thin. Sprinkle with 2 tablespoons of the salt and cover with ice water. Set aside for 2 hours. Drain and press out all moisture. Combine ½ teaspoon salt and other dry ingredients

and beat into vinegar and sour cream. Stir in cucumbers. Sprinkle with paprika to taste and serve cold with chicken or fish.
Makes 6 servings.

⊄ Honey-glazed Onions with Walnuts

36 small white onions, trimmed and peeled	⅛ teaspoon white pepper
½ cup butter	¾ cup honey
¾ teaspoon salt	¼ cup boiling water
	¾ cup chopped walnuts

Parboil onions in salted water to cover for 10 minutes; drain well. Place in a heavy skillet with butter, salt and pepper. Set over medium heat and cook for 5 minutes, shaking pan frequently. Stir honey with boiling water and pour over the onions. Continue to cook and shake the pan until the onions are glazed and tender. Put them under the broiler with the oven door open. Baste with the honey syrup until lightly browned. Sprinkle with nuts and serve.
Makes 6 servings.

⊄ Spinach Pudding

½ cup butter	½ to ¾ cup sour cream
8 eggs, separated	Salt and pepper
1½ cups puréed spinach	1¾ cups bread crumbs
4 tablespoons chopped parsley	6 large lemons, halved and pulp removed
4 slices of white bread	
Milk enough to soak bread	

Stir the butter until creamy. Add egg yolks, one by one, stirring well. Add spinach purée and parsley. Soak the bread in milk, squeeze it dry, and add it to the sour cream. Stir into the spinach mixture and season to taste. Fold in stiffly beaten egg whites and dust in the bread crumbs while folding in the whites. Steam pudding in a buttered mold in a large kettle of water for 1 to 1¼ hours. Unmold and serve garnished with lemon halves filled with hollandaise sauce, or serve with brown butter. Makes 6 to 8 servings.

ᏻᎯ Green-tomato Casserole

Many of the recipes that come from records of early settlers seem to be made for today's casseroles. The settlers were hampered by owning few utensils and a single source of heat. We are hampered by small kitchens and lack of time. Casseroles are a good answer.

2½ pounds green tomatoes	3 cups bread crumbs
4 tablespoons butter	2 teaspoons minced fresh or
1 cup water	dried sage or basil
Salt and pepper	1 cup grated cheese

Dip tomatoes into boiling water for 2 minutes. Place them in cold water for 3 to 4 minutes and drain them well. Draw off the skins with the help of a pointed knife and slice tomatoes across. Simmer tomato slices with 2 tablespoons of the butter, the water and salt and pepper to taste until very soft, about 25 minutes, stirring frequently.

Butter a 2-quart shallow baking dish with 1 tablespoon butter. Sprinkle with 1 cup of the bread crumbs; be sure they adhere to the bottom and sides of the dish. Transfer the tomatoes and their liquid to the dish and sprinkle with herbs. Cover with a heavy layer of 2 remaining cups of crumbs mixed with grated cheese and dot with remaining butter. Bake in a 450° F. oven until bubbling and browned, about 12 minutes. To brown crumbs faster, turn on broiler for last few minutes baking time.

Makes about 6 servings.

ᏻᎯ Potatoes

England was growing carrots, turnips, melons, gourds, cucumbers, radishes, parsnips, cabbages and salad herbs long before the Puritans set sail. There is evidence that the seeds or roots of all these plants came over on the Mayflower. The potato, on the other hand, was brought from Peru to Spain in 1580 and spread from there to Italy and Austria.

Sir Walter Raleigh supposedly introduced it to England but it took 200 years before it was really accepted there.

The sweet potato of Nova Hispania came to England in 1564 and the Virginia potato was mentioned in Gerard's *Herball* in 1597. The English records speak deprecatingly of Ireland's "lazy root," so it would seem that the natural affinity between the Irish and the potato was established soon after its introduction.

Potatoes became a field crop in New England wherever there were friends to receive them after their introduction in 1719. As the settlement of New England extended northward, potatoes improved until the Maine potato became especially prized.

⊄ Potato Puffs

Leftover roast beef means hash to most of us. In Mystic it meant mince meat for pies or filling for dumplings, puffs and turnovers. It was never described as leftover meat but as "meat that has been dressed before." When you have some cold roast beef that has been dressed before, mince it fine and use it to fill fried potato puffs.

1¼ cups ground cooked roast beef or ham	1¼ pounds potatoes
	1¼ cups flour
Salt and pepper	1 egg, beaten
½ teaspoon grated lemon rind	¾ cup butter
2 tablespoons minced pickle, well drained	¼ cup chopped onion
	½ cup bread crumbs

Stir meat with seasonings to taste, lemon rind and pickle; set aside. Boil potatoes in salted water until tender, about 20 minutes. Draw off the skins and rice potatoes onto a pastry board. Let them cool completely. Sift flour and ½ teaspoon salt over potatoes, make a well in the center, and pour in the egg. Work into a smooth dough with the hands. Roll or pat out on a floured pastry board and cut into 8 to 10 squares. Shape meat into 8 to 10 tightly rolled balls and set one on each square. Roll the potato dough around the meat with floured hands. It will shape into a seamless ball. Bring salted water to a boil in a wide kettle and lower the puffs gently into the boiling water. As soon as water returns to a boil, reduce it to a steady, gentle boil. The puffs will be done when they rise to the surface, about 9 to 10 minutes. Take them out with a slotted spoon and drain them well.

Arrange puffs in a heated bowl. Melt butter and heat until brown. Stir onions and crumbs into it while browning. Pour the butter mixture over the puffs.

Makes about 6 servings.

ℰ𝒳 Boiled Rice

1 quart water	1 cup uncooked rice
1 teaspoon salt	

Bring water to a rapid boil in a large saucepan. Add salt and sprinkle in the rice. Do not stir. Boil for exactly 20 minutes. Pour off any remaining water. Partly cover the saucepan and set it on an asbestos pad over lowest heat for about 7 minutes. When rice appears dry on top, shake it well and shake it into a serving dish. Do not touch it with a spoon. Each grain should be separate.

Makes 4 servings.

ℰ𝒳 Bacon Rice

2 slices of bacon, diced	Salt and pepper
3 shallots, chopped	1½ cups uncooked long-grain
¼ cup butter	rice
1 teaspoon minced parsley	3 cups stock or bouillon

Fry bacon and shallots in butter until golden, 5 to 7 minutes. Add parsley and season to taste. Stir in the rice until glossy. Stir in the stock, cover, and bake in a 350° F. oven for 45 minutes. Shake into a serving bowl and serve hot.

Makes 6 servings.

❧ Pasta

A medical authority, as late as 1834, wrote, "Maccaroni and vermicelli are dried combinations of starch and egg yolk, calculated for patients and convalescents to whom they are frequently administered."

Mystic housewives made noodles and served them boiled or baked with various sauces which lend themselves admirably to any preferred pasta. The noodles also went into soups and puddings. The recipes which follow adapt themselves perfectly to that novelty, "maccaroni," which was sometimes used as a drinking straw.

❧ Spaghetti with White Clam Sauce

From Mrs. Harrison W. Boylan

4 dozen medium-sized hard-shell clams (quahogs)
1 or 2 garlic cloves
⅓ cup oil
½ teaspoon salt
¼ teaspoon freshly ground black pepper, or more
3 tablespoons chopped parsley
1 pound spaghetti, cooked to the *al dente* stage
Grated Romano cheese
1 loaf Italian bread

Scrub clams and place them in a kettle with ½ cup water. Cover and boil for about 5 minutes. Take out and chop clams, but retain the clam juices. Sauté garlic in oil; discard the garlic. Add the clam juice and reduce over high heat to 1 cup. Season with salt and pepper and add chopped clams. Simmer for 6 minutes. Add parsley. Pour over freshly cooked and well-drained spaghetti. Serve with grated Romano cheese, crusty bread and a tossed green salad.

Makes 4 servings.

☙ Pasta with Eggplant Sauce

1 medium-sized onion, chopped
¼ cup fine-chopped parsley
⅔ cup butter
2 large eggplants (about 1½ pounds each) peeled and diced
2 cups Tomato Sauce II (p. 81), or 1 can (19 ounces) Italian tomatoes, drained
1 bay leaf
2 teaspoons minced fresh basil, or 1 teaspoon dried basil
Salt and pepper
⅔ pound lean ground beef
1 pound narrow noodles, or 1½ pounds fettucini
1½ cups grated Parmesan cheese

Sauté onion and parsley in ½ cup of the butter for 10 minutes, stirring frequently. Add eggplant, tomato sauce, herbs and seasonings to taste. Cook over low heat, stirring frequently, for 30 minutes. Brown beef in remaining butter, stirring with a fork to prevent lumping. In the meantime, boil pasta according to package directions until tender. Drain well and arrange on a heated platter. Add beef to sauce, season to taste, and stir well. Pour over the noodles and serve immediately with grated cheese.
Makes 4 servings.

☙ Macaroni Pudding

½ pound macaroni
1 cup milk
1 cup heavy cream
1 cup dry bread crumbs
3 eggs, well beaten
1 pimiento, chopped fine
1 green pepper, seeded and chopped
1 teaspoon onion juice
1 teaspoon minced parsley
½ cup grated Parmesan cheese
4 tablespoons butter, melted
Salt and pepper

Cook macaroni in salted water according to package directions; drain and rinse in cold water. Scald milk and cream and pour over the bread crumbs. Combine two-thirds of this mixture with the macaroni and next 7 ingredients; season to taste. Pour into a 2-quart casserole. Spread

remaining crumb mixture over top. Bake in a 350° F. oven for approximately 1 hour. Serve with Tomato Sauce I (p. 81).
Makes 4 to 6 servings.

ℰℛ Mrs. Keator's Church Supper Spaghetti

1 to 2 pounds onions, sliced
Salt
⅓ cup butter
2 large cans (32 ounces each) tomatoes
1 stewing chicken (5 pounds) boiled, or 3 pounds pork, roasted

4 pounds spaghetti
2 pounds mushrooms, caps and stems, sliced
1½ to 2 cups grated Parmesan cheese

Cook well-salted onions in butter until golden brown, about 7 minutes, and put through food grinder; retain butter in pan. Heat tomatoes and push through strainer. Cook meat, bone it, and put half of it through food grinder. Boil spaghetti until barely tender and drain well. Combine onions, tomatoes and ground meat with just enough of the drained chicken stock or bouillon to moisten to taste. Sauté mushrooms in reserved butter and set aside. Cut remaining meat into thin strips and set aside. Add sauce ingredients to the spaghetti and mix well. Let stand overnight.

Arrange alternate layers of spaghetti mixture, mushrooms and strips of meat in a large flat baking dish. Cover with a heavy layer of grated cheese. Bake covered in a 350° F. oven until bubbling, about 15 minutes. Uncover and bake until cheese is browned, about 15 minutes longer.
Makes 16 to 20 servings.

CHAPTER IX

~~~

Pies and Tarts

MEN on ships have always needed a pastime. They whittled and knitted and knotted and built little ships in bottles, but men on whaleships *scrimshawed*. Scrimshawing was an occupation built on the available elements and influences. Whalemen had time, years of time, sharp knives, whale teeth and whalebone. Scrimshaw was the result. They carved and engraved whale ivory and whalebone and did it with great art and skill. They touched at ports where they saw carved ivory and inlaid wood.

The hardships and dangers of whaling are often described, but the story of the endless hours of waiting and watching is told in scrimshaw. Those heavy-handed whalemen were capable of the roughest manual tasks but they could scrimshaw with unbelievable delicacy. Their unique handwork grew from a pastime into an American folk art which expressed their homesickness, their lonely thoughts and their hunger. They portrayed the whalers' world—ships, whales, seals, seabirds—but their predominant thoughts were apparently on baking. There wasn't a whaler's wife from Mystic to New Bedford who didn't have a wooden rolling pin inlaid with whale ivory, as well as scrimshaw pastry wheels, pie crimpers and jaggers, some of which are shown in the illustration section, taken from The Mystic Seaport collection.

On diets of potatoes, salt meat and fish, weak tea and coffee sweetened with molasses, it is no wonder that whalemen dreamt of pies and tarts. They scrimshawed away at pastry wheels, thousands of miles and several years from home, with an eye to the pie that would one day result. Mystic Seaport has a rare collection of these scrimshaw crimping or jagging wheels used to mark the edges of pies and tarts. Recipes for the pie and tart pastes for which they were used have been given to us by descendants of old whaling families.

When the wives of early settlers left England they knew how to bake a fine tart. They descended from generations of housewives who enjoyed what medieval England called a "tarrte" and Chaucer called a "pye."

The pies and tarts of seventeenth-century England were still imposing affairs baked in deep dishes with edges and lids that imitated piecrust. The pastries were light and flaky, made of puff, or puffed, pastry and baked to a golden brown. Pie fillings were made of game, fish, pork, or beef-and-kidneys; fruit tarts were filled with dried prunes, figs, raisins, ginger and minced meats. English housewives had time and fresh butter to "turn" into their paste. Their daughters in America had nothing more than flour and lard. It took courage to add water and necessity to bake it in a shallow pan.

Whaling wives, whose husbands were on voyages that took up to four years, did not welcome them home with mediocre pies. There was plenty of time for experimenting and for acquiring that desirable "light hand with pastry."

Mystic housewives used to bake pies in winter, pack them firmly in ice and snow and freeze them for later use or place them in the unheated back room. When they needed one for breakfast, they chopped or pried it loose, let it thaw out, and heated it in the oven or by the fire.

When ships sailed in winter there were frozen pies on board at least for the early part of the voyage. Pies are the simplest of galley desserts, and may even start the day in the Mystic manner at breakfast.

❧ Pastry for 1-crust Pies

If a one-crust pie is to have a meringue topping, it is usually baked in a 10-inch pie pan, but any size can be used. This recipe makes enough pastry for a 10-inch shell with a high border.

1½ cups flour	½ cup vegetable shortening
¾ teaspoon salt	4 to 4½ tablespoons ice water

Sift flour and salt together; cut in shortening with a pastry blender until mixture resembles coarse bread crumbs. Stir in 4 tablespoons water with a knife blade little by little, until the paste starts to gather. Gather it with your hands; use the ½ tablespoon water if necessary to gather the crumbs in the bottom of the bowl. Shape paste into a ball, wrap in wax paper, and chill.

Roll out the paste on a lightly floured pastry board with a stockinette-covered rolling pin. Start in the center and roll lightly in all directions. Lay rolling pin across center of paste circle, fold over one side and transfer the paste onto the pie pan. Press paste down into the pan with the back of your first finger. Press it down on the edge of the pan and trim it off, leaving a 1-inch overlap all around. Fold the 1-inch overlap back onto the edge to form a thick, high border; a single crust pie needs a high border. Crimp it attractively.

IF A FILLING IS TO BE BAKED IN THE PREPARED PIE SHELL: pour in the filling and bake according to recipe directions. Usually the oven should be set at 350° F. and the open pie should bake for about 45 minutes. If the border is very high, cover it with pie-tape or aluminum foil after 15 minutes.

IF A FILLING IS TO BE POURED INTO A BAKED PIE SHELL: prick the unbaked pastry with a fork and line it with a piece of wax paper. Fill with cherry pits, dried beans or uncooked rice and chill for 20 minutes. Bake in a 450° F. oven for 12 to 14 minutes. Take out wax paper and cherry pits and replace in oven; bake until lightly browned, 5 to 7 minutes longer. Cool and fill.

⚔ Flaky Pastry for Pie Crust

2 cups sifted flour	1 cup cold shortening
¼ teaspoon salt	5 to 6 tablespoons ice water

Sift flour and salt into a bowl; cut in shortening with a pastry blender or 2 knives until mixture resembles oatmeal. Add water, 1 tablespoon at a time, and stir with a knife blade until mixture gathers and holds together. Shape into 2 balls with hands and chill until needed. If necessary the paste can be used immediately.

Roll out each ball as round and thin as possible on a lightly floured board. Transfer one piece to a 9-inch pie pan. Press down with backs of fingers; do not stretch. Trim edges, fill pie, and cover with second round of dough. Cut vents in top to allow air to escape. Press edges down firmly and crimp attractively. Bake in a 400° F. oven for 15 minutes; reduce heat and bake for 30 minutes longer. Baking times and temperatures may vary with the fillings. Follow individual recipe.
Makes enough for a 2-crust pie.

⚔ American Flaky Pie Pastry

The standard recipe for flaky pastry used in America today is still very much like the first one invented when only flour, lard and icy water were available.

Enough for a 2-crust pie in an 8- or 9-inch pie pan:

2 cups flour	⅔ cup lard
¾ teaspoon salt	4 tablespoons cold water

Enough for a 2-crust pie in a 10-inch pie pan:

3 cups flour	1 cup lard
1 teaspoon salt	6 tablespoons cold water

Sift flour and salt into a mixing bowl. Cut in lard with a pastry blender until the mixture resembles course bread crumbs. Sprinkle water, 1 tablespoon at a time, over the mixture and stir with a knife blade until mixture starts to gather. Push mixture aside so that the last of the water can gather the dry crumbs from the bottom of the bowl. Gather dough with hands and press into a smooth ball, or 2 smooth balls. Wrap in wax paper and chill for 35 minutes, or until needed.

Place one of the dough balls, or half of the single dough ball, on a lightly floured pastry board or canvas, pat into a thick round with hands, and roll out lightly with a rolling pin. Start in the center and roll in all directions until dough is ⅛-inch thick. To transfer dough to pie pan, invert pan on dough, lift the corners of the pastry canvas, and turn the whole thing over. Remove canvas and press dough into pan with backs of fingers. Or roll dough over rolling pin and carefully transfer it to the pan, press out air pockets, and trim edge even with outside of pan.

Roll out second dough ball or second half in the same way as the first. Pour filling into pie. Fold dough in half and move it carefully onto the filled pie pan, placing the fold across the center of the pan. Unfold and press edge down gently on lower crust. Cut dough with kitchen scissors ½ inch wider than the pie pan. Lift bottom crust gently with fingers and fold the top edge under it, making a firm, thick edge. Flute or crimp the edge decoratively. Cut steam vents in the top with a sharp pointed knife and bake according to the recipes.

ℰ᷂᷄ Hot-water Pastry

This pastry is used for some of the palest, lightest, most melting of pies.

2 cups sifted flour	⅓ cup boiling water
½ teaspoon salt	⅔ cup shortening
½ teaspoon baking powder	

Sift flour, salt and baking powder into medium-large bowl. Beat boiling water into the shortening in a small bowl until light and creamy. Pour into the bowl of dry ingredients and mix quickly until dough gathers. Shape into a ball and chill for at least 45 minutes. Roll out and use as any pie crust dough. Makes enough for a 2-crust 9-inch pie.

Ꮼ Short Crust

4 cups flour	1 egg
¼ teaspoon salt	1 to 3 tablespoons cold water
1¼ cups butter	

Sift flour and salt into a bowl; rub in or cut in the butter until the mixture looks like fine bread crumbs. Beat the egg with 1 tablespoon water and stir it into the dry ingredients with the blade of a knife. Add just enough more water to gather the paste into a ball. Roll or pat out gently and use as recipe requires.

Makes enough pastry for four 1-crust pies or two 2-crust 9-inch pies.

Ꮼ Rich Pastry for Deep-dish Pie

1⅓ cups flour	1 egg
⅓ cup sugar	¼ teaspoon vanilla extract
⅔ cup butter	

Sift flour with sugar. Cut in butter with a pastry blender or 2 knives until mixture resembles coarse bread crumbs. Beat egg with vanilla and stir into the dry ingredients. Knead into a ball, wrap, and chill for 20 minutes.

As this pastry is short and soft, add a little flour while handling it, and a little more flour than usual in rolling it out. Roll out pastry a trifle thicker than usual and use to cover a deep-dish pie or to line a pie pan. Bake in a 350° F. oven for 45 minutes, or until golden. If necessary cover fluted edge with pie tape or aluminum foil when baking the filled pastry shell.

Makes enough pastry for a single top crust or a lattice top for an 8-inch pie. Good for dried-apricot, mincemeat, huckleberry, or dried-peach pies.

ℰℋ Family Pie Crust

From Mrs. Elizabeth Palmer Loper

4 cups flour	½ cup ice water
½ cup lard	1 cup butter

Sift flour into deep wooden bowl. With a broad-bladed knife or a small keen "chopper" cut the lard into the flour until it is fine as dust. Wet with ice water into a stiff dough, working with a wooden spoon until it can be formed into a roll or ball with the hands. Flour the ball of dough and knead the paste into shape with as few strokes as possible. Lay the lump on a floured kneading board and roll into a thin sheet, always rolling from you with a quick, light action. When thin enough, stick bits of butter in regular close rows all over the sheet. Roll up the paste and fold the ends closed. Flatten it and roll out again as thin as before. Dot with butter as before, roll up and then out, until all butter is used. Finally, roll the dough into rounds to fit pie plates. Butter pie plates, lay paste lightly upon them, and cut paste off evenly around the edges. If pies have a top crust, fill crust with fruit or whatever you have ready, lay top sheet on this, cut it to fit, and press down the edges to prevent escape of juices. Bake in a moderate oven until a light brown. Be sure that the oven heats evenly or the lower crust will be clammy and raw.

Makes enough for two 2-crust 9-inch pies.

ℰℋ Apple Pies

Almost the first thing the settlers did was to plant orchards. As soon as there were apples there was the ubiquitous apple pie, as well as apple fritters, sauces, juices, jellies and above all, apple cider. After that, inevitably, came hard apple cider, which was very good with hot apple pie and cheese.

⳼ Open English Apple Pie

American Flaky Pie Pastry for
2-crust 9-inch pie (p. 174)
3 pounds apples
1¼ cups sugar
1 blade of mace, or pinch of
grated mace

¼ teaspoon ground cloves
1 lemon, grated rind and 1 tablespoon juice
2 tablespoons flour
½ teaspoon ground cinnamon
Whole cloves

Prepare the pastry. Roll out half of it, line a 9-inch pie pan, and trim edge, leaving a 1-inch edge all around. Chill pan and remaining pastry until needed. Peel and core apples and boil the peels and cores, uncovered, with ½ cup sugar, the mace, ground cloves and water to cover. Slice the apples and combine them with the grated lemon rind and juice and the remaining sugar mixed with flour and cinnamon. Spoon the applies into the lined pie pan and chill.

Roll out the remaining pastry, a little thicker than usual, and cut it with a fluted pastry wheel (as the whalers' wives cut theirs with scrimshaw wheels) into ¾-inch-wide strips. Strain the reduced liquid from the apple peels and lemon juice over the pie. Weave the pastry strips into a lattice top. Trim ends of strips evenly and press them firmly on the rim. Turn the 1-inch edge up over the strips, press it down, and flute it attractively. Stick a clove through the pastry at each point where lattice strips cross one another. Bake the pie in a 400° F. oven for 40 minutes. Serve the pie hot, dredged with sugar and accompanied by a pitcher of heavy cream.
Makes 6 to 8 servings.

⳼ English Apple Pie Garnishes

In England the housewives decorated and garnished their pies as elaborately as a curry in India. The hot pies stood on the table surrounded by garnishes to suit everyone's taste. The American settlers simplified the pies, and of the garnishes only the cheese and ice cream remain. They made and served a good strong yellow cheese. Here are some lovely old customs that should be revived.

A pitcher of chilled pouring cream (cream almost too heavy to pour). This custom became the grandfather of our pie *à la mode*.

Fine sugar in a muffineer to dredge over the pie.

Good Port wine in a decanter to pour over the pie.

Two good cheeses, Cheddar and Cheshire.

Toasted hazelnuts.

Blanched almonds.

Melted quince jelly.

Diced candied orange peel.

Sweetened whipped cream.

Plum conserve (damson-plum jelly in Mystic).

Dried currants.

Raisins.

Cinnamon sugar.

ℰ𝒳 American Apple Pie

A nineteenth-century recipe

1 recipe Flaky Pastry (p. 174)	2 tablespoons water
2½ to 3 pounds sour apples	1 tablespoon lemon juice
¼ cup confectioners' sugar	Grated rind of 1 lemon
6 tablespoons granulated sugar	½ cup heavy cream (optional)

Prepare the pastry. Line a 9-inch pie pan and chill the lined pan and remaining pastry dough until needed. Peel, core, and slice apples. Arrange them in the pastry and sprinkle them with confectioners' sugar. Wet edge of lower crust with water, sprinkle it with flour, and cover with the top crust. Trim edge and flute or crimp edge attractively. Gather all dough scraps and cut out a 2-inch round with a fluted cookie cutter. Cut a small hole, about 1 inch in diameter, in center top of pie; cut vents around the sides with a sharp knife. Lay the fluted round over the hole. Bake the pie in a 400° F. oven for 40 minutes. While the pie is baking, boil granulated sugar, water, lemon juice and rind until sugar is dissolved; then boil for 4 minutes longer. When pie is completed take it out, remove round from center top and pour the sugar syrup into the pie. The heavy cream may be poured into the pie after the sugar syrup. Makes 6 to 8 servings.

Apple Pie with Crumble Topping

1 recipe Pastry for 1-crust pie (p. 173) or ½ package (10 ounces) pie crust mix	⅔ cup granulated sugar
	1 cup plus 1 tablespoon flour
	1 teaspoon ground cinnamon
6 to 8 tart apples (about 2½ pounds), peeled, cored and sliced thin	¼ cup raisins (optional)
	⅔ cup dark brown sugar
	½ cup butter

Line a 9-inch pie pan with pastry; crimp edges. Combine apples, granulated sugar, 1 tablespoon flour, cinnamon and raisins and spread mixture evenly in pastry. Combine brown sugar and 1 cup flour and cut in butter with a pastry blender or 2 knives until mixture resembles small peas. Spread mixture over apples. Bake in a 450° F. oven for 15 minutes. Reduce heat to 350° and bake for 25 minutes longer. If a browner topping is preferred, bake for about 10 minutes longer. Serve warm with half-whipped cream or softened and whipped vanilla ice cream. Makes 4 to 6 servings.

VARIATION: Add ½ cup chopped walnuts to the crumble mixture.

Open Apple Tart

PASTRY

2 egg yolks	1 cup butter
⅓ cup sugar	1 tablespoon cold water
2 cups flour	

FILLING

    1 cup mincemeat   2 tablespoons sugar

    1 cup thick applesauce   1/4 cup apricot jam, melted

    2 pounds apples, peeled, cored
    and sliced

TOPPING

    1 cup heavy cream, whipped   1 tablespoon confectioners'

    2 teaspoons Calvados or apple-   sugar, or more
    jack

Beat egg yolks and sugar until sugar is dissolved. Sift flour into a bowl and cut in butter until mixture resembles rough crumbs. Make a well in the center, put in egg yolks and sugar and work into a firm dough with fingertips. Add water, a few drops at a time, but only as much as needed to gather the dough; it should be dry and smooth. Wrap in wax paper and chill for 2 hours.

Roll out two-thirds of dough to about 1/8-inch thickness on a lightly floured board, and transfer it carefully to a deep 9-inch pie pan. Press it down gently and trim edge, leaving 1 inch overhang all around. Spread pastry with a mixture of mincemeat and applesauce and cover with the sliced apples arranged in overlapping rows. Sprinkle with sugar and pour the melted apricot jam over all. Roll out remaining pastry a little thicker than usual and cut it into 1-inch wide strips with a fluted pastry wheel. Lay strips across the pie diagonally, crossing them to form a lattice. Bake in a 350° F. oven for 35 minutes. Cool. Serve with whipped cream flavored with Calvados and sweetened to taste.

Makes 6 to 8 servings.

🙠 Open Peach Tart

1 recipe Short Crust (p. 176)
3 pounds fresh peaches, or 2 pounds well-drained canned peaches
⅔ cup sugar

3 tablespoons cornstarch
1½ cups heavy cream
½ teaspoon vanilla
½ teaspoon ground cinnamon

Prepare the pastry. Line a 9-inch pie pan, crimp border and chill. (Refrigerate remaining pastry for other pies.) Scald peaches, pull off skins, discard pits, and slice the fruit. Arrange peach slices in overlapping circles in pastry. Stir ½ cup sugar with cornstarch and beat with half of the cream and the vanilla. Pour over the peaches. Sprinkle with cinnamon and bake in a 400° F. oven until peaches are tender, about 35 minutes. Whip remaining cream, whip in remaining sugar, and serve warm peach tart topped with the sweetened whipped cream.
Makes 6 to 8 servings.

🙠 Blueberry Pie

1 recipe Flaky Pastry (p. 174)
3½ cups fresh blueberries, preferably hand-picked wild berries
3 tablespoons flour for dredging

¾ cup sugar
Pinch of salt (optional)
1 teaspoon lemon juice (optional)

Line a 9-inch pie pan with half of the pastry and chill it and the remaining pastry. Wash and pick over fresh berries and drain them well by letting them stand in a colander. Shake them frequently. Dredge

berries with flour, pour them into the pastry-lined pan, and sprinkle the sugar over them. Salt and lemon juice may be added. Roll out remaining pastry, cover the pie, trim pastry, and fold under the top. Pinch edges firmly and prick with a fork. Bake in a 450° F. oven for 10 minutes. Reduce heat to 350° F. and bake for 35 minutes longer. Serve warm or cold, with or without vanilla ice cream.

Makes 6 to 8 servings.

⸎ Open Blueberry Pie

The trick when baking on a sailboat is to level with a spoon. Gravity pulls bread loaves into one-sided shapes and makes blueberry pie filling run out. An inverted kitchen spoon placed under the pan to level it is the seaman's answer. Place it under the pan to make it level.

1 recipe Pastry for 1-crust Pies (p. 173)	Pinch of salt
4 cups fresh blueberries	1 cup water, or half water and half fruit juice*
¾ cup sugar	1 tablespoon butter
2½ tablespoons cornstarch	1 teaspoon lemon juice

Prepare pastry and use it to line a 9-inch pie pan. Pinch edge attractively and bake according to directions on page 173.

Wash and pick over berries and let them drain in a colander. Stir sugar, cornstarch, salt and water in a large saucepan over low heat; add 1 cup of the berries and stir until thickened, about 7 minutes. Add butter and lemon juice and stir until butter is melted. Stir remaining fresh berries into the mixture and cook for 1 minute longer. Take from heat and cool. When cold pour into baked pie shell and serve with soft ice cream. Makes 4 to 6 servings.

---

* If blueberries are fresh picked, use only water (without the fruit juice) to retain berry flavor. If purchased blueberries are use, substitute grape juice, orange juice or any preferred fruit juice for half of the water. The reason for this is that wild berries freshly picked are much more flavorful than the cultivated berries that may have been picked some time before.

⳥ Huckleberry Deep-dish Pie

1 cup granulated sugar
2 tablespoons maple sugar or brown sugar
1 teaspoon ground cinnamon
¼ cup flour
1 quart fresh huckleberries
2 tablespoons lemon juice

Grated rind of 1 lemon
3 tablespoons butter
1 recipe Rich Pastry for Deep-dish Pie (p. 176)
½ tablespoon milk for brushing crust

Butter a deep 8-inch baking dish. Sift sugars, cinnamon and flour together. Stir in the berries gently and add lemon juice and rind. Put in the buttered baking dish. Dot surface with butter and cover the dish with unbaked pie crust. Fold under and flute the edges attractively. Cut vents in top and brush with milk. Bake in a 350° F. oven for 45 minutes, or until crust is golden.
Makes 6 servings.

NOTE: As deep-dish pie fillings cook they usually sink in the baking dish and the crust caves in. To avoid this, either fill dish to the brim or trim the crust with an attractive crimped or fluted edge and lay it over the berries, without pressing it to the edge of the baking dish. The crust is then free to sink with the filling.

⳥ Prune Meringue Pie

From Mrs. W. E. Bates

1 recipe Pastry for 1-crust Pies (p. 173)
1 pound dried prunes
¾ cup sugar

2 cups light cream or milk
4 whole eggs, separated
2 extra egg whites

Roll out the pastry and line a 10-inch pie pan with it. Make a high crimped border on the edge of the pan. Stew prunes with ¼ cup sugar in water barely to cover until tender. Drain, stone, and mash them to make 2 cups of pulp. Add cream and the well-beaten egg yolks. Pour into the pastry-lined pan. Bake in a 400° F. oven for 10 minutes. Reduce heat to 325° and bake until crust is golden, about 35 minutes. Cool and chill.

Beat egg whites until they look creamy and show the mark of the withdrawn beater. Beat in the ½ cup sugar, a little at a time, until the meringue is stiff and smooth. Rub a little of the whites between your fingers; if you can still feel the sugar granules, continue to beat until the meringue is smooth. Heap the meringue on the chilled pie, spreading it to the edges but keeping it higher in the center. Bake in a 425° F. oven until edges of meringue are lightly browned, about 7 minutes. Makes 8 servings.

Lemon Sponge Pie

From Mrs. William Westphal, New London

1 recipe Pastry for 1-crust Pies (p. 173)
2 tablespoons flour
½ tablespoon cornstarch
¼ teaspoon salt
1 cup sugar

Juice and grated rind of 1 lemon
1 cup milk
4 eggs, separated

Make the pastry and use it to line a 9-inch pie pan.

Combine the flour, cornstarch, salt and sugar. Add the lemon juice and rind, milk and beaten egg yolks. Mix the ingredients well, then fold in 3 stiffly beaten egg whites. Beat remaining egg white slightly and spread over the inside of the unbaked pastry crust. Pour the filling into the piecrust. Bake at 425° F. for 15 minutes, then at 325° for 35 minutes. Makes 6 or 8 servings.

ᏭᎧ Lemon Pie

1 recipe Pastry for 1-crust Pies   2 tablespoons cornstarch
  (p. 173)   1 tablespoon butter
1 cup cold water   1 egg yolk, beaten
1 cup plus 3 tablespoons sugar   3 egg whites
Juice and grated rind of 1
  lemon

Make the pastry and use it to line a 9-inch pie pan. Bake the crust and cool it.

Combine water, 1 cup sugar, lemon juice and rind and cornstarch in the top part of a double boiler. Bring to a boil, stirring constantly. Set over boiling water in lower section of double boiler and cook, covered, for 20 minutes. Stir in butter and egg yolk and stir until thick and smooth. Cool and pour into the baked pie shell.

Beat egg whites until they peak. Add remaining 3 tablespoons of sugar and beat a little more. Mount on top of pie, spreading to reach edges. Bake in a 350° F. oven for 15 minutes, until meringue is lightly browned.

Makes 6 servings.

ᏭᎧ Baked Lemon Pie

1 recipe Pastry for 1-crust Pies   Juice and grated rind of 1
  (p. 173)   lemon
4 eggs, separated   Pinch of salt
1 cup sugar
3 tablespoons water

Prepare the pastry and line a 9-inch pie pan with it. Bake the crust and cool it.

Mix egg yolks, ⅔ cup sugar, the water, lemon juice and rind in the top part of a double boiler. Stir over boiling water until smooth and thickened, about 10 minutes. Take from heat and cool slightly. Beat egg whites with salt until frothy, gradually add remaining sugar, and beat until stiff. Fold egg whites into cooled yolk mixture, pour into pie shell, and bake in a 375° F. oven until browned. Watch carefully as this will only take a few minutes.

Makes 6 servings.

⚶ Old-Fashioned Lemon Pie

Sandra De Veau of Mystic gives us this lemon pie recipe:

1 recipe Flaky Pastry (p. 174)	1 cup raisins
1 lemon	2 tablespoons flour
1 cup molasses	1 tablespoon butter
1 cup sugar	1 cup water

Make the pastry and use half of it to line a 9-inch pie pan. Roll out the rest of the pastry into a round big enough to cover the top.

Use all of the lemon; grate the rind, squeeze the juice, and chop remainder of the flesh. Mix with remaining ingredients and pour into the lined pie pan. Cover with top crust. Start in a 450° F. oven and bake for 15 minutes. Reduce heat to 350° and bake for 30 to 35 minutes longer, until pie is nice and brown.

Makes 6 to 8 servings.

⚶ Chocolate Silk Pie

Mrs. Alice Palmer sends us this recipe for an unusual pie:

½ cup butter	1 teaspoon vanilla extract
¾ cup sugar	2 eggs
2 ounces (2 squares) unsweetened chocolate, melted over hot water	1 baked 9-inch pie shell
	1 cup heavy cream, whipped
	½ cup shaved chocolate curls

Cream together butter and sugar. Add chocolate and vanilla. Add eggs, one by one, beating for 5 minutes after each addition. Pour into baked pastry shell and chill. When set, top with mounds of whipped cream and shaved chocolate.

Makes 6 to 8 servings.

ℰ𝒳 Mince Pies

3 egg yolks	3¼ cups mincemeat (28-ounce
½ cup sugar	jar)
3¼ cups flour	3 large cooking apples, peeled,
1½ cups butter	cored and diced fine
2 tablespoons ice water	1 quart rum raisin ice cream

Beat yolks with sugar until sugar is dissolved and no sugar granules can be seen or felt. Sift flour into a large bowl and cut in butter until mixture resembles oatmeal. Make a well in center, pour in the egg-yolk mixture, and stir until well mixed. Sprinkle with water and gather into a smooth dough with lightly floured hands. Chill for at least 20 minutes.

Divide paste into halves. Roll out one half on a lightly floured pastry canvas to about ⅟₇-inch thickness, or a little thicker than usual, and line an 8-inch pie pan. Trim to within ¼ inch of edge and keep trimmings. Roll out the second piece of dough and line a second pie pan; keep trimmings. Crimp both edges attractively. Fill the pastry-lined pans with mincemeat mixed with the apple dice. Spread the filling a little higher around the edge to support the sides of the pastry. Roll out the trimmings and cut them into 14 to 18 rounds with a 2-inch cookie cutter. Arrange slightly overlapping circles of rounds on the open surface of each pie, and lay 1 round in the center of each circle. Bake in a 350° F. oven for 45 minutes. Serve with rum raisin ice cream, softened in refrigerator and whipped until light and creamy.
Makes two 8-inch pies.

ℰ𝒳 Butterscotch Pie

From Mrs. Jessie Fish Monroe

1 recipe Pastry for 1-crust Pies (p. 173)	3 eggs, separated
5 tablespoons flour	2 tablespoons butter, lightly browned
1½ cups scalded milk	2 tablespoons granulated sugar
1 cup firmly packed brown sugar	

Bake pie shell according to recipe. Cool.

Beat flour, hot milk and brown sugar until smooth; stir in the top part of a double boiler over boiling water for 15 minutes. Stir a little of the mixture into the egg yolks, then stir it back into the top of the double boiler. Cook, stirring constantly, for 2 to 3 minutes. Stir in butter and pour into prepared pie shell; cool. Whip egg whites stiff with granulated sugar, spread over top of pie, and bake in a 350° F. oven for about 14 minutes.

Makes 6 to 8 servings.

Green-tomato Pie

This sweet and spicy pie is a special treat in late summer and early fall. Mrs. George F. Ruth has kindly given us the recipe.

PASTRY

2¼ cups flour, sifted	¾ teaspoon salt
1½ tablespoons granulated sugar	¾ cup shortening
	5 tablespoons cold water

Sift dry ingredients together. Cut in shortening until mixture is grainy. Add just enough cold water so that mixture will hold together. Gather the mix together and divide into halves. Roll out one half to fit a 9-inch pie pan. Roll out the second half of the pastry. A special touch can be given to the top crust by sprinkling about 1 teaspoon of sugar over the rolled crust and rubbing it in. When baked, this adds a crunchy sweetness to the pie.

FILLING

5 large green tomatoes, approximately 5 cups sliced (These must be green; once they begin to turn red, the flavor is unsuitable for this pie.)	½ teaspoon salt
	1½ teaspoons ground cinnamon
	Dash of grated nutmeg
1½ cups granulated sugar	2 tablespoons flour
	2 tablespoons butter

Peel tomatoes and cut into thin slices. Arrange slices in lined pie pan. Mix dry ingredients well and sprinkle over tomatoes. Dot with butter, put on top crust, cut vents, crimp edges. Bake in a 425° F. oven until brown, about 15 minutes, then reduce heat to 350° and bake until tomatoes are tender, 20 to 25 minutes longer.
Makes 6 to 8 servings.

Squash Pie

1 baked 9-inch pie shell	1 teaspoon ground cinnamon
1½ cups cooked squash	½ teaspoon ground ginger
1½ cups undiluted evaporated milk or heavy cream	⅛ teaspoon ground cloves
	½ cup light molasses
6 tablespoons brown sugar	3 eggs, slightly beaten
2 tablespoons sugar	¾ cup black walnut meats (optional)
½ teaspoon salt	

Prepare and bake a 9-inch pie shell. Combine all other ingredients except nuts in the top part of a double boiler and cook over hot water until thick. Cool slightly; add nuts if desired. Pour into baked pie shell and serve.
Makes 6 to 8 servings.

Cramberry Tart

The spelling of cranberries differs with the age of the recipe. You will find them listed as cramberry, craneberry, and cranberry.

1 cup butter	4 egg whites, stiffly beaten
4 cups flour	Filling (see below)
¼ cup sugar	¼ cup butter for top of filling
2 egg yolks	

Cut ⅓ cup butter into the flour in a large bowl. Make a well in the center. Beat sugar with the egg yolks until dissolved and pour it into the well. Add the stiffly beaten egg whites and stir with a knife until the paste gathers. Work it quickly with the hands until it is as smooth as possible. Roll it out thin on a lightly floured board. Spread ⅓ cup butter over half of the paste in dabs measuring about ½ tablespoon each. Fold over the unbuttered half of the paste and seal the edges by pressing firmly with rolling pin. Roll out again, spread half the paste with dabs of the remaining butter, and seal the edges again. Cool the paste until needed. Cut into 4 equal parts and roll each out to ⅛-inch thickness. Use to line two 9-inch pie pans. Fill with one of the cramberry fillings, dot with butter, and cover the tarts with the 2 remaining rounds of paste. Trim and crimp the edges and cut vents in the tops of the pies. Bake in a 425° F. oven until golden, 40 to 50 minutes.

COOKED CRAMBERRY FILLING

2 cups sugar
⅓ cup cornstarch
1 cup light corn syrup
½ cup orange juice

Roughly rasped rind of 1 orange*
6 cups picked-over cramberries

Combine sugar and cornstarch, then gradually stir in corn syrup and orange juice and rind. Stir over medium heat until smooth and thickened. Add cramberries and cook without stirring until they burst. Take from heat and cool before pouring into pastry-lined pie pans. Cover with a solid or a lattice top.

UNCOOKED CRAMBERRY FILLING

2 oranges
6 cups cramberries
1 cup chopped pecans

3 cups sugar
¼ cup flour
1 teaspoon ground cinnamon

Peel outside rind from oranges with a potato peeler. Over a bowl, cut oranges into halves and scoop out pulp with a pointed spoon; discard white skins and membranes. Grind cramberries and orange rind into the bowl, using coarse blade of food grinder; add the nuts. Mix sugar, flour and cinnamon and stir it into the fruit. Pour mixture into pastry-lined pie pans. Cover with a solid or a lattice top.

* Grate against coarser mesh to obtain little curls of rind.

Cranberry Crunch

From the *Vineyard Gazette*

1 cup quick-cooking oats
½ cup flour
1 cup brown sugar

½ cup butter, softened
2 cups whole-berry cranberry
sauce

Mix oats, flour, sugar and butter together thoroughly. Spread half of mixture in a greased 8-inch square dish; cover with cranberry sauce. Cover with rest of mixture. Bake at 350° F. for 45 minutes. Serve hot with ice cream.

Makes 16 two-inch squares.

CHAPTER X

~~

Cakes and Cookies

THE first settlers lived in wigwams while they built their one-room, thatched-roof houses. Lean-tos and extra rooms were added as they were needed. After that came story-and-a-half and two-story houses, with shingled roofs, that somewhat resembled the homes the settlers had left behind. They were modest and simple. The design was based primarily on building materials available, the climate and the needs of the settlers, who were mostly farmers, ship builders and whalers. The only available building material was wood. The long cold winters and the early threat of Indian attack dictated small windows, strong doors and steep roofs. Windows were made up of small panes of blown glass; floors were composed of wide hand-pegged planks.

As more Mystic men went to sea a new feature was incorporated into their homes, the captain's walk. This became a familiar sight in the tidewater settlements along the coast and all high points behind it. Life gravitated around sailings and landings, and local architecture gradually adapted itself to the constant vigil of the wives and sweethearts, the ship owners and the children, as they paced this lookout atop the houses.

The earliest houses had to be entirely self-contained. Stores could not be kept in an adjoining buttery or distant outbuilding. Every housewife lived and cooked in what was also her larder. Cannisters of condiments, drying bunches of herbs, a small basil plant in the window and jugs of syrup and molasses were as much a part of the decoration as they were ingredients for cooking.

There were no secrets. Everyone knew who was baking, who was drying salt fish and who had the kettle on. The smell of cinnamon and cloves, of ginger and allspice, brought young visitors, and cookie jars were emptied almost as soon as they were filled.

When a whaleship sailed, the whalers carried away enough ginger cookies in their sea chests to last, if not the whole voyage, at least through the first pangs of homesickness.

⬥ Sea Voyage Gingerbread

From the *Vineyard Gazette*, August 28, 1857

"Sift two pounds of flour (8 cups) into a bowl, and cut into it 1¼ pounds fresh butter; rub the butter well into the flour and then mix in a pint of West Indian molasses and a pound of the best brown sugar. Beat eight eggs until very light. Stir into the eggs a gill, or ½ cup, of brandy. Add also to the egg ½ cup of ground ginger and a tablespoonful of powdered cinnamon, with 1 teaspoon of baking soda melted in a little warm water. Moisten the flour with this mixture until it becomes a soft dough. Sprinkle a little flour on your pastry board, and with a broad knife spread portions of the mixture thickly and smoothly upon it. The thickness must be equal all through; therefore spread it carefully and evenly, as the dough will be too soft to roll out. Then with the edge of a tumbler dipped in flour, cut it out into round cakes. Have ready square pans, lightly buttered; lay the cakes in them sufficiently far apart to prevent their running into each other when baked. Set the pans into a brisk oven and bake the cakes well, seeing that they do not burn.

"These cakes will keep during a long voyage and are frequently carried to sea. Many persons find highly spiced gingerbread a preventive to sea-sickness."

✑ Joe Froggers or Sailors' Cookies

Mrs. Dumont Rush reports that she unfortunately does not know the origin of the unusual name of this family favorite recipe. Mrs. Rush writes, "Because of their excellent keeping qualities when stored in an airtight tin, I make up a large quantity at the beginning of each sailing season and store them aboard our sloop. We find these hearty cookies make an excellent midmorning or midafternoon snack, or a great *hold-me-over* when heavy seas delay a meal.

"When cut with a 3-inch cutter the cookies expand in baking to fit snugly into the new 4-inch coffee cans with plastic covers. For immediate use, where breakage isn't a problem, they are delightful when cut with the Mystic Seaport whale-shaped cutter."

7 cups all-purpose flour	¾ cup water
1 tablespoon salt	¼ cup rum
1 tablespoon ground ginger	2 teaspoons baking soda
1 teaspoon ground cloves	2 cups dark molasses
1 teaspoon grated nutmeg	1 cup butter or margarine
½ teaspoon ground allspice	2 cups sugar

Sift the flour with the spices and set aside. Combine the water with the rum. Stir the baking soda into the molasses. Cream the shortening and sugar in a large bowl, add the sifted dry ingredients, the water-rum mixture, and the molasses mixture alternately to the creamed mixture, blending well after each addition. Chill dough in refrigerator overnight.

Roll to ⅛-inch thickness on a floured board. Cut with 3-inch round cutter and place on greased baking sheet. Bake for 10 to 12 minutes in a 375° F. oven. Let cookies stand on cookie sheet for a minute or two before removing to prevent breaking. Store in airtight containers. Makes about 4 dozen.

After receiving Mrs. Rush's recipe for Joe Froggers together with the frustrating note that the origin of the name was unknown, this interesting information came to us from Mrs. P. E. (Lydia G.) Andrews, Acting Librarian of The Peabody Museum in Salem, Massachusetts. Mrs. Andrews edited *The Food Log: Refreshment for Body and*

Soul and has very kindly allowed us to bring you these excerpts and recipes as well as excellent recipes that appear in other parts of the book. Many Mystic recipes seem to have come from elsewhere, but Mystic cooks made them their own.

Joe Froggers

A long time ago there was an old Negro who lived on Gingerbread Hill in Marblehead. His name was Uncle Joe. He lived on the edge of a frog pond called Black Joe's pond.

Uncle Joe made the best molasses cookies of anyone in town, and people called them Joe Froggers because they were as plump and as dark as the fat little frogs that lived in the pond.

Marblehead fishermen would give the old man a jug of rum and he would make them a batch of froggers. The fishermen liked them because they never got hard, and women packed them in sea chests for the men to take to sea.

Uncle Joe said what kept them soft was rum and sea water. But he wouldn't tell how to make them. And when he died, people said, "That's the end of Joe Froggers." But there was a woman named Aunt Cressy, who said she was Uncle Joe's daughter, and Aunt Cressy gave the secret recipe to a fisherman's wife. Then half the women in Marblehead began making Joe Froggers. The cookies were rolled thin, as big as a dinner plate—8 to 10 inches.

With a pitcher of milk, "froggers" became the town's favorite Sunday night supper. Boardman's Bakery, where the Gulf station is now located across from the Town House, sold them for a penny apiece.

ᏩᎥ Joe Froggers (Old Marblehead Cookies)

From Lillian Lucas (via *The Food Log*)

Kindly contributed by Mrs. P. E. Andrews

½ cup shortening	1 teaspoon baking soda
1 cup sugar	1½ teaspoons ground ginger
1 cup dark molasses	½ teaspoon ground cloves
½ cup water	½ teaspoon grated nutmeg
4 cups flour	¼ teaspoon ground allspice
1½ teaspoons salt	

Mix shortening and sugar well. Stir in molasses and water. Stir dry ingredients together; blend into shortening mixture. Chill dough for several hours or overnight. Heat oven 375° F. Roll dough ¼-inch thick on floured board. Cut into 3-inch circles. Sprinkle with sugar. Place on well-greased baking sheet. Bake for 10 to 12 minutes. Leave on baking sheet for a few minutes before removing to prevent breaking. Store in a covered jar.

Makes about 3 dozen.

ᏩᎥ Short Gingerbread

From Dr. Franklin R. Ireson (via *The Food Log*)

Another recipe contributed by Mrs. P. E. Andrews

1 cup sugar	½ teaspoon ground ginger
¼ cup lard	2 cups flour
¼ cup butter	½ teaspoon salt
1 egg, beaten	¼ teaspoon baking soda
⅛ teaspoon ground cinnamon	⅓ cup milk
½ teaspoon baking powder	

Cream sugar with lard and butter. Add beaten egg and beat until fluffy. Mix dry ingredients and add in small amounts, alternating with milk. Pour into a buttered baking pan (9 × 14 inches). Bake at 350° F. for 30 minutes. Cut into squares while warm. The cakes will be about ¾-inch thick.

Makes about 15 three-inch squares.

Gingerbread Men

From *The Providence Journal-Bulletin*

½ cup molasses	½ teaspoon ground ginger
¼ cup shortening	½ teaspoon grated orange rind
1¼ cups sifted all-purpose flour	1 cup confectioners' sugar
¾ teaspoon baking soda	3 teaspoons warm water

Bring molasses and shortening to a boil in a saucepan. Cool slightly and add flour, baking soda, ginger and grated orange rind. Mix well and chill for several hours, or overnight.

Roll chilled dough on floured board to ⅛-inch thickness. With a piece of cardboard make a pattern of a gingerbread man. Lay it on the rolled dough and cut around it. Arrange the men about ½-inch apart on buttered cookie sheets. Bake at 375° F. oven for 8 to 10 minutes. Allow to cool.

Decorate with icing made by mixing confectioners' sugar and warm water, or decorate with a tube of icing equipped with a nozzle, available at all markets. Before the icing has a chance to set, add colored sugar, tiny varicolored candies and raisins or currants for eyes and buttons. Makes about 12 men.

Sugar or White Gingerbread

From Mrs. Lydia G. Andrews

Miss Helen C. Hagar of Salem, Massachusetts, told us that her mother, who came of a seafaring family in Salem, said that the men took this kind of gingerbread aboard ship at the beginning of a voyage.

½ cup shortening

1 cup sugar

1 egg

1 teaspoon cream of tartar

½ teaspoon baking soda

1 teaspoon ground ginger

½ teaspoon salt

2½ cups flour

½ cup milk

Combine all ingredients; mix well. The batter will be stiff. Spread it on a cookie sheet or in a shallow pan. Sprinkle top with sugar before baking and bake in a 350° F. oven for 25 minutes.

Makes about 24 pieces.

Cranberry Applesauce Cake

From *The Providence Journal-Bulletin*

½ cup butter or shortening

1 cup sugar

2 eggs

1 cup sweetened applesauce

1½ cups sifted all-purpose flour

¾ teaspoon baking soda

½ teaspoon salt

1 teaspoon ground cinnamon

½ teaspoon ground cloves

¼ teaspoon grated nutmeg

1 cup quick-cooking oatmeal

¾ cup whole-berry cranberry sauce

Cream butter or shortening; beat in sugar and eggs. Add applesauce and blend thoroughly. (Batter may look curdled.) Sift flour, baking soda, salt, cinnamon, cloves and nutmeg together. Add to creamed mixture, blending thoroughly. Stir in oatmeal and cranberry sauce. Pour batter into greased and floured 9-inch-square baking pan. Bake in preheated 350° F. oven for 50 to 55 minutes. Cool. Top with Maple Glaze or a simple Lemon Icing.

Makes 9 three-inch squares.

MAPLE GLAZE

1½ cups sifted confectioners' sugar

½ cup maple syrup

¼ teaspoon salt

Combine sugar, syrup and salt. Beat well and spread on cooled cake.

LEMON ICING

¼ cup lemon juice   Sifted confectioners' sugar
Grated rind of 1 lemon

Put lemon juice in a bowl with grated rind. Add enough sifted confectioners' sugar to bring to spreading consistency. Spread on cooled cake.

Maple-syrup Icing

1½ cups maple syrup   1 teaspoon vanilla extract
1½ cups sugar   1 teaspoon maple flavor
½ teaspoon cream of tartar   1 cup chopped walnuts or but-
½ cup water   ternuts
3 egg whites, beaten stiff

Boil maple syrup, sugar, cream of tartar and water together until sugar is dissolved and syrup spins a thread, 225° F. on a candy thermometer. Take from heat and pour slowly, in a thin stream, over the stiffly beaten egg whites, beating constantly while adding the sugar syrup. Beat until thick. Add flavorings and nuts and spread quickly over the 2 layers and sides of spice cake or any favorite layer cake.

Ann Greenman's Leopard Cake

From Mary Greenman Davis

White Batter

1 cup white sugar   ½ teaspoon baking soda
½ cup butter   1 teaspoon cream of tartar
4 egg whites   ½ cup milk
2 scant cups flour

Dark Batter

1 cup firmly packed brown   ½ cup butter
  sugar   4 egg yolks

2 cups flour	⅔ cup milk
1 teaspoon cream of tartar	1 cup raisins or dried currants
½ teaspoon baking soda	or diced citron

Prepare batters separately but in the same way. Cream sugar with butter and beat in eggs. Sift flour with dry ingredients and add it alternately with the milk. Stir raisins into dark batter. Drop spoonfuls of the light and dark batters into the same buttered cake pan (13 × 9 inches). Bake in a 325° F. oven for 45 to 50 minutes, or until the cake tests done when pierced with a straw.

Cℛ Dripping Cake

3 cups flour	2 cups raisins
1 tablespoon baking powder	Grated rind of 1 lemon
¾ cup drippings	3 eggs
1½ cups sugar	½ cup milk

Sift flour and baking powder into a bowl, rub in the drippings with fingertips, and stir in sugar, raisins and lemon rind. Add eggs beaten with milk. Pour batter into a buttered large loaf pan (9 × 5 × 3 inches). Bake in a 400° F. oven for 45 minutes. Reduce heat to 350° and bake for 1 hour longer.

Cℛ Gold Cake

From Marjorie K. Guidera

1 cup butter	¼ teaspoon salt
1⅓ cups sugar	1 teaspoon almond extract
5 large eggs	2 tablespoons fine dry bread
1½ cups sifted all-purpose	crumbs
flour	Confectioners' sugar
1¼ teaspoons baking powder	

Cream the butter and sugar in a bowl, beating for 5 minutes. Add

eggs, one at a time, beating well after each addition. Sift together the flour, baking powder and salt. Add to mixture with the almond extract, blending well. Sprinkle the bottom of a well-buttered and floured 9-inch tube pan with the bread crumbs. Pour the batter into the pan. Bake in a 325° F. oven until golden brown, or when a cake tester inserted in the cake comes away clean, 40 to 45 minutes. Turn out on wire rack and cool thoroughly. Sprinkle with confectioners' sugar.
Makes 10 servings.

Walnut Crown Poundcake

From Marjorie K. Guidera

1 cup chopped walnut meats	1 teaspoon salt
2¾ cups sifted all-purpose flour	¾ cup milk
	1 cup shortening
1¾ cups sugar	1 teaspoon vanilla extract
2¼ teaspoons baking powder	4 eggs

Grease and flour a 9- or 10-inch angel-cake pan. Spread walnut meats over bottom. Sift together dry ingredients into a large mixing bowl. Add milk, shortening and vanilla. Beat for 2 minutes, scraping bowl frequently. Add the unbeaten eggs. Beat for 2 minutes more. Pour over walnut meats in pan. Bake in a 375° F. oven for 50 or 60 minutes. Walnut meats form topping; needs no icing.
Makes 10 servings.

Mrs. Reed Whitney's Torte

7 egg whites	1½ cups sugar
Pinch of salt	5 egg yolks
½ teaspoon cream of tartar	1 teaspoon vanilla extract
	1 cup sifted cake flour

Beat egg whites half stiff. Add salt and cream of tartar and beat until very stiff. Fold sugar gradually into stiff egg whites, then fold in beaten yolks, vanilla and flour. Pour batter into 2 well-buttered and floured 9-inch layer-cake pans and bake in a 375° F. oven for 15 minutes. Reduce heat to 350° and bake until straw tests done, 15 to 20 minutes longer. Cool on a cake rack while making filling.

FILLING

2 envelopes gelatin	6 egg yolks
1 cup light cream	1½ cups heavy cream, whipped
1 teaspoon vanilla extract	1 cup chopped toasted almonds
1 cup sugar	Additional whipped cream (optional)

Soften gelatin in ¼ cup of the light cream and the vanilla. Heat remaining light cream to just under boiling and stir in gelatin until dissolved. Beat sugar into egg yolks until light and thick. Beat in gelatin mixture and fold in heavy cream, whipped with a pinch of salt. Spread filling over both layers of the cake. Assemble the layers and spread filling over sides. Sprinkle with toasted almonds. Pipe with additional whipped cream if preferred.
Makes 8 to 10 servings.

Fruitcakes

Mystic ships touched at ports where all the food and every phase of its preparation was different from anything the stout Connecticut seafarers knew. After months of salt cod, salt pork, rotting potatoes and dank

water, it is no wonder that they fell in without the slightest trouble with alien tastes for spices and strange concoctions. A tropical fruit, no matter how unfamiliar, was a glorious change. There were mangoes, persimmons, coconuts, peppers, gourds, pineapples and bananas, spiced chutneys, chowchows and hot relishes. There were the citrus fruits, which, before careful modern cultivation, were unbelievably bitter and citric. But nothing daunted the seamen; they brought home dried figs and dates, ginger, mango root and cinnamon bark, vanilla beans and dried peppers to their women.

Spice and silk trade had opened mysterious and dangerous land routes between Europe and the East. Our whaleships and traders traveled equally dangerous sea-lanes to bring back whale oil, lovely pottery and porcelain, tea chests and ginger jars. As a result Lowestoft, beautiful china, ivory and teak have graced New England homes for generations.

While cinnamon and cloves came from far afield, nearer ports yielded raisins and currants, olives, port wine and rum. Madeira wine shows up in Mystic's cookery along with the fruits of southern orchards and gardens. Mystic housewives were fortunately situated and their cooking soon reflected the voyages of their husbands' ships.

Ⳡᕁ Grandmother's Fruitcake

Mrs. E. Fletcher Ingals sends us her grandmother's recipe dated 1874.

3 cups dark brown sugar	1 pound dried currants
¾ pound butter	1 pound chopped raisins
6 eggs	¾ pound diced citron
3½ cups flour	1 tablespoon ground cloves
½ teaspoon baking soda	1 tablespoon ground cinnamon
1 cup molasses	1 tablespoon grated nutmeg

Cream sugar with butter until light. Add eggs, one at a time, and beat well after each addition. Sift flour and divide it into 2 bowls. Stir baking soda into molasses. Combine the dried fruits with half of the flour and sift the other half with the spices. Combine the fruit-flour mixture with the egg mixture. Sprinkle in the spice-flour mixture and stir well. Beat in the molasses last of all. Pour the batter into 2 buttered loaf pans (9 × 5 × 3 inches), lined with brown paper and rebuttered. Bake in a 250° F. oven for about 2½ hours, or until the cake tests done when pierced with a straw. Place a small can of water in the oven while cake is baking.

Mrs. Pierpont's Fruitcake

1 cup butter
1 cup sugar
4 eggs
2 pounds raisins
1½ pounds dried currants
½ pound citron, diced

2 cups flour
½ teaspoon each of ground cloves, cinnamon and allspice
½ cup molasses
¼ cup brandy

Cream butter with sugar. Beat in eggs, one after the other, until fluffy. Combine fruits with dry ingredients. Stir fruit mixture into the egg mixture, alternating with molasses and brandy. Pour into 2 large (9 × 5 × 3 inches) or 4 small (7½ × 3½ × 2½) loaf pans, lined with triple layers of wax paper. Bake in a 325° F. oven for 1½ hours. Cool in pans before taking out.

Spiced Applesauce Fruitcake

1½ cups flour
½ tablespoon baking soda
½ teaspoon ground cloves
½ teaspoon ground cinnamon
½ teaspoon ground allspice
6 tablespoons butter
¾ cup sugar
1 large egg
1½ cups raisins

¾ cup diced candied peels
¾ cup diced citron
¾ cup diced candied cherries
¾ cup chopped pitted dates
¾ cup chopped pecans or walnuts
3 tablespoons brandy
1¼ cups applesauce

Sift dry ingredients and set aside. In a large bowl, cream butter, beat in sugar, and beat in egg until fluffy. Dredge raisins, peel, citron, cherries, dates and nuts with ¼ cup of the sifted flour mixture and set aside. Stir brandy and applesauce together and add to butter mixture, alternating with dry ingredients. Stir in fruit and nuts and pour batter into a buttered and floured 2½-quart springform or shallow tube pan. Bake in a 325° F. oven for 1½ hours. Cool, unmold, wrap in foil, and store for a few days before cutting.
Makes 8 to 12 servings.

✺ Vanilla-sugar Horns

Whaleships sailed in search of whales but they did touch land and take on supplies in various parts of the world. As a result, whalemen were eating exotic foods and bringing home tales and samples of delicacies that did not reach the average housewife for many years. Among these was the vanilla bean.

1 ¼ cups flour
½ cup filberts* or blanched almonds, ground
½ teaspoon vanilla extract
6 tablespoons granulated sugar

½ cup cold butter, cut into
   flakes
1 cup Vanilla Confectioners'
   Sugar (below)

Sift flour into a bowl. Sprinkle fine-ground nuts, vanilla and granulated sugar over the flour and cover with butter flakes. Work with the hands, rubbing the butter into the dry ingredients, until a smooth dough is obtained. Wrap it in wax paper and chill for about 20 minutes.

Take out small portions of dough and roll on a very lightly floured board into a pencil-thick roll. Cut into 3-inch lengths and bend into little horseshoes or horns. Bake on a buttered heavy baking sheet in a 350° F. oven for about 14 minutes, until cream colored. They should not turn

---

* Heat shelled filberts or hazelnuts in a 250° F. oven for about 15 minutes, then rub off any loose brown inner skin with a rough towel. Only a part of it will come away.

brown. Lift with a spatula and transfer them to a platter sprinkled with vanilla sugar. Sieve more vanilla sugar over the tops.

VANILLA CONFECTIONERS' SUGAR

2 thick vanilla beans

2 pounds 10X confectioners' sugar

Bury vanilla beans, fresh out of the bottle or wrapper, in a canister of confectioners' sugar. Seal tightly and set aside to draw for a few weeks. After that, replace the sugar as you use it. Replace the vanilla beans after a year.

Always use vanilla sugar for sprinkling on pastries, cookies or desserts, or as the recipes require.

✐ Hand-to-mouth Hermits

Mystic men and their families lived from hand-to-mouth for only a short time. They had timber trees and the sea and within a short time they were living decently under conditions that were still not easy, but they were happy. They did not enact any historically important dramas, but they built and launched ships and they worked hard. From all indications they ate the sort of food for which we cross the continent today.

These cookies are called hand-to-mouth only because their progress from plate to mouth is almost instantaneous.

2½ cups flour
1 tablespoon baking powder
Pinch of ground cloves
Pinch of ground cinnamon
Pinch of salt
⅔ cup butter

1¼ cups sugar
2 eggs
¼ cup heavy cream
¾ cup chopped raisins or dried currants

Sift flour, baking powder, spices and salt together twice. Cream butter with electric beater, add sugar, and beat until light. Add eggs, one at a

time, and beat until fluffy; add cream. Add raisins to dry ingredients and beat into the egg mixture. Butter a baking sheet and drop the batter by the tablespoon onto the sheet. Allow space for spreading. Bake in a 350° F. oven for 14 to 15 minutes.
Makes about 7 dozen.

ᑟᗩᐸ Eliza's Sugar Cookies

From Louise Trumbull

"Eliza was cook for the family of John Franklin Trumbull. Her reputation for making sugar cookies spread far and near. The cookie jar was never empty. It had to satisfy omnivorous eaters from Hartford, Black Point, New York, etc., who visited the Trumbull family opposite the Congregational Church in Stonington."—*Stonington Cooks*

1 cup butter	Flour: enough to roll, about 6 cups
1 cup milk	
1 teaspoon baking soda	½ teaspoon vanilla extract
2½ cups light brown sugar	

Mix all ingredients and roll out on a lightly floured pastry canvas. Cut into rounds. Bake on a buttered pastry sheet in a 350° F. oven for 8 minutes.
Makes about 8 dozen.

ᑟᗩᐸ Christmas Brown-sugar Cookies

From *The Log* of Mystic Seaport, 1967

1 cup butter	2 teaspoons dark heavy rum
1 cup dark brown sugar	2 cups flour
1 cup granulated sugar	1 teaspoon baking powder
2 eggs	1 package (6 ounces) blanched almonds, chopped
1 teaspoon vanilla extract	

Cream butter and sugars and add eggs, one at a time. Stir in vanilla, rum, and flour sifted with baking powder. Shape into a block (1¼ × 2 inches) and refrigerate for at least 3 hours, or until needed. Cut into thin slices with a sharp knife. Arrange slices on a buttered baking sheet, sprinkle a few almonds on each, and press almonds down into the dough. Bake in a 400° F. oven for about 10 minutes. Cool cookies on the baking sheet. Store in a closed jar or in refrigerator until needed.
Makes about 6 dozen.

ꏝ Drop Cookies

From Helen Chamberlain

"An up-to-date Stonington recipe, a good one, for Helen Chamberlain is a graduate of the School of Home Economics, Pratt Institute, and teaches homemaking in New York City schools. Not only is she a rare cook, but a gay raconteur."—*Stonington Cooks*

½ cup butter	1 egg
⅓ cup sugar	¾ cup flour
½ teaspoon vanilla extract	1 cup chopped nuts or raisins

Cream butter; add sugar, vanilla and beaten egg. Stir in the flour and mix well. Drop small portions from the tip of a spoon about 2 inches apart onto a greased and floured baking sheet. Sprinkle with chopped nuts or raisins. Bake in a 350° F. oven for about 10 minutes.
Makes about 6 dozen.

ꏝ Palmer Cookies

Mrs. Richard C. Palmer used mixed shortening instead of butter and suggested that the user try the original ingredients and compare the result with modern shortening.

½ cup mixed shortening—half
    butter and half lard—or ½
    cup butter
1 cup sugar
1 egg
½ cup dairy sour cream

1 teaspoon vanilla extract
2 cups flour
½ teaspoon baking soda
½ teaspoon grated nutmeg
Sugar for sprinkling

Cream mixed shortening with sugar until light; beat in egg until foamy. Stir in sour cream and vanilla, alternating with flour sifted with baking soda and nutmeg. Drop by teaspoons onto a buttered baking sheet; spread thin with a knife and sprinkle with sugar. Bake in a 350° F. oven until brittle and brown, 8 to 10 minutes.
Makes about 8 dozen.

Seven-layer Bars

From Mrs. Richard C. Palmer

¼ cup butter
1 cup graham-cracker crumbs
1 cup shredded coconut
1 package (6 ounces) chocolate
    bits

1 package (6 ounces) butter-
    scotch bits
1 can (15 ounces) sweetened
    condensed milk
1 cup chopped walnuts

Melt butter in a shallow baking pan (13 × 9 × 2 inches). Sprinkle graham-cracker crumbs on bottom and sides of pan. Then add remaining ingredients in layers in order listed. Bake in a 350° F. oven for 30 minutes. Cool and chill. Cut into bars.
Makes about 18 bars, 2 × 3 inches.

Old-fashioned Sugar Cookies

From Phebe E. Wilcox

2 cups flour
1 teaspoon baking soda
2 teaspoons cream of tartar
½ teaspoon grated nutmeg

½ cup shortening
1 cup sugar
1 whole egg, or 3 egg yolks
3 tablespoons milk

Sift together the first 4 ingredients; mix in the shortening (butter and lard, or all butter; the latter is best). Beat up the sugar and egg, or yolks, with a fork and add to the first mixture. Add milk, 1 tablespoon at a time, to make rolling easy. Roll the batter into a thin sheet and cut into 3-inch rounds. Put on greased cookie sheets and dust the cookies with sugar. Bake in a 350° F. oven for about 10 minutes.
Makes about 3 dozen.

Brown-edge Cookies

6 eggs, separated	1 cup plus 2 tablespoons flour,
1 cup confectioners' sugar, sifted	sifted 3 times
	1 teaspoon vanilla extract
Pinch of salt	9 tablespoons freshly melted butter

Butter and flour 2 cookie sheets; tap off excess flour. Beat egg yolks until light, then gradually add ½ cup sugar and continue to beat until thick. In a second bowl, beat egg whites with a pinch of salt until just white, then add remaining sugar and continue to beat until stiff. Resift the flour over the yolks and fold it in gently and quickly. Then fold in the stiff egg whites and the melted butter. Drop batter by the half-tablespoon onto the prepared cookie sheets, keeping the cookies at least 2 inches apart. Bake in a 325° F. oven for about 10 minutes, or until the edges are brown. Take quickly from oven and with a spatula remove from cookie sheets to a strip of wax paper. Do not move cookies until they are cold and crisp.
Makes about 6 dozen.

CHAPTER XI

≈≈

Puddings and Other Desserts

A pudding was boiled in a pudding cloth, which compared rather favorably with the long sleeve of a winter nightgown. The pudding cloth was a firmly seamed dense cloth measuring about seven- to nine-inches wide by fourteen- to eighteen-inches long. Splendid pudding cloths can be run up out of old tablecloths, preferably damask.

The pudding batter is dropped into the cloth, which is then tied, allowing room for the expansion of the pudding. The whole thing is lowered into a kettle of boiling water and boiled for hours.

A particularly imaginative housewife made her pudding cloth the usual width by seventy-inches long. She dropped in the batter for a pudding, tied it off like the link of a sausage, then dropped in batter for a second pudding. With a little skill she could end up with a formidable

chain of four puddings, which could all be boiled at once in an enormous kettle. Not the sort of thing we would recommend to the city dweller with a small kitchenette.

ℰ⅄ Save-all Pudding

Make this the day you have cut bread rounds for canapés and have all those good bread scraps left over.

1 pound scraps of bread	Ground allspice or grated nut-
2 cups milk	meg
2 eggs, beaten	½ cup dried currants
⅓ cup sugar	¼ cup fine-minced suet

Bring bread and milk to a boil and beat the mixture vigorously until it is smooth. Reduce heat until the mixture has stopped boiling. Beat in the eggs, sugar, spice to taste, and currants; beat well. Pour the mixture into a well-buttered baking dish and strew the suet over it. Bake in a 350° F. oven until set and browned, about 45 minutes. Serve warm with stewed fruit or raspberry sauce.
Makes about 6 servings.

ℰ⅄ Cape Cod Pudding

From Clara Hinckley Chace

1 cup Rhode Island johnny-	1 teaspoon salt
cake meal, sifted	2 quarts skimmed milk
1 cup molasses	¼ teaspoon salt

Mix the meal, molasses, salt and 1 quart of the milk thoroughly; pour into buttered 2½-quart baking dish. Bake in 250° F. oven until mixture is about to boil. Stir well; add remaining milk and salt. Continue to bake slowly, about 5 hours in all. Serve with cream.
Makes 10 servings.
NOTE: Johnnycake meal is water-ground white cornmeal, which is quite different from the ordinary yellow sort. (See pp. 28–29.)

ℰ𝔛 Baked Cranberry Pudding

Mrs. John Merrill of Waterford writes, "This recipe was given to me by the Librarian at Connecticut College, Miss Hazel A. Johnson. I understand it was originally from a cookbook of old recipes prepared by a Congregational parish in Groton many years ago. It is a recipe my family enjoys and certainly has a New England flavor."

2 cups flour
1 cup sugar
2½ teaspoons baking powder
3 tablespoons melted shortening

⅔ cup milk
1 egg
2 cups cranberries

Sift dry ingredients into bowl; add shortening, milk and egg. Beat for 2 minutes. Stir in cranberries. Bake in a buttered 9-inch-square pan in a 350° F. oven for about 40 minutes. Serve with Hot Butter Sauce (below).
Makes 9 three-inch squares.

HOT BUTTER SAUCE
½ cup butter or margarine
1 cup sugar

¾ cup light cream or top milk

Melt butter or margarine in the top part of a double boiler; add sugar and liquid; mix well. Cook over hot water for about 5 minutes, stirring occasionally. Serve hot over pudding.
Makes about 2 cups.

ℰ𝔛 English Plum Pudding

From Mrs. Ann Borodell Gates

"This pudding was a favorite of the clever hostess of Pequotsepos Manor and always graced her festive board on Christmas Day. The crowning touch of that bounteous dinner was the holly-decked, glowing pudding."

¾ cup stale bread crumbs
¼ cup flour
¼ cup brown sugar
1 teaspoon grated nutmeg
1 pound suet, diced
1 pound raisins

1 pound dried currants
½ pound citron, diced
Rind of 1 lemon, chopped fine
5 eggs
1 cup brandy

Mix dry ingredients thoroughly with suet and fruits. Beat eggs and brandy. Combine mixtures. Steam in basin or mold for 6 hours. Do not allow water to stop boiling for one moment. Steam again for 6 hours on the day it is to be served. To serve, turn pudding out on a platter and let it stand in a 250° F. oven for 10 to 15 minutes to dry. For Christmas dinner decorate with holly and pour warm brandy around but not over it. Ignite the brandy and bring at once to the table.
Makes 12 or more servings.

Toast and Marmalade Pudding

7 slices of white bread
6 tablespoons soft butter
6 tablespoons orange marmalade or raspberry jam
6 eggs

1 cup sugar
2 teaspoons vanilla extract
4 cups milk
1 cup heavy cream, whipped

Toast bread, butter it, and spread with marmalade or jam. Cut into cubes and arrange them in a buttered 2-quart baking dish. Beat eggs with sugar and vanilla until creamy and gradually beat in milk. Do not overbeat. Pour the mixture over the toast cubes. Set baking dish into a pan of hot water and bake in a 350° F. oven for 1¼ hours, or until a knife blade inserted in the center comes out clean. Serve at once, and top each hot serving with cold whipped cream or Vanilla Ice-cream Sauce. Makes 8 to 10 servings.

VANILLA ICE-CREAM SAUCE
1½ pints vanilla ice cream
1 cup heavy cream, whipped

1 tablespoon heavy rum

Let ice cream soften slightly. Beat with rotary beater until light and smooth, and set aside. Whip cream until stiff, and fold cream and rum into ice cream. Serve with pie, hot puddings, wrapped apples and all fruit fritters.

Makes about 2½ cups.

ᘓᕗ Maple-syrup Mousse

1 unflavored gelatin	5 eggs, separated
¼ cup cold milk	1 cup heavy cream, whipped
1 cup maple syrup	Maple flavoring

Stir gelatin into milk and set aside. Beat maple syrup and egg yolks in the top part of a double boiler until smooth. Set over gently boiling water and beat with an electric hand beater or rotary beater until thickened and foamy; this will take at least 5 to 7 minutes. Take from heat and immediately stir in softened gelatin until dissolved. (If gelatin was not carefully stirred into the milk, it will form lumps at this stage.) Cool the mixture but do not allow it to set. Beat egg whites stiff and fold them into mixture with the whipped cream flavored with maple flavoring to taste. Pour into an oiled 4- to 4½-cup mold and chill for at least 2 hours.

Insert knife blade at edge of mold, dip mold into hot water for a moment, and unmold onto a serving plate. Serve with a sauce of softened and whipped maple-walnut ice cream or whipped cream sprinkled with shaved maple sugar and chopped walnuts.

Makes 6 servings.

ᘓᕗ Apricot Mousse with Hot Brandy Sauce

From *The Log* of Mystic Seaport, 1967

1 can (1 pound 14 ounces) skinless apricots	1 teaspoon vanilla extract
2 envelopes unflavored gelatin	2 cups heavy cream
½ cup sugar	1 teaspoon salad oil for mold

Prepare this mousse and sauce the day before Christmas.

Drain apricots, reserving the juice. Pit the fruit and blend or sieve them into a smooth purée. Stir gelatin into ¼ cup of juice and set aside for at least 15 minutes. Boil ½ cup juice with the sugar for exactly 5 minutes; take from heat and stir in softened gelatin until dissolved. Add apricot purée and vanilla and cool, but do not let it set. Whip cream until stiff and fold into apricot purée. Pour mixture into well-oiled 1½-quart melon or pudding mold, and chill for at least 2 hours.

To serve, run a thin knife blade around edge of mold and invert onto a paper doily on a serving platter. Garnish with holly springs and pass Hot Apricot Brandy Sauce (below) separately.

Makes 8 to 10 servings.

Hot Apricot Brandy Sauce

½ cup apricot jam	3 ounces slivered almonds
½ cup apricot nectar	½ cup apricot brandy, or more

Heat apricot jam and nectar in top part of a double boiler over boiling water until jam is melted. Add almonds, cool, and refrigerate until needed. Reheat in top of double boiler over boiling water, stir well, and add brandy. Serve hot with cold Apricot Mousse.

NOTE: Toasted slivered almonds may be substituted for plain slivered almonds.

Rum Cream

From Alice Palmer

2 envelopes gelatin	1 cup sugar
½ cup light rum	½ teaspoon vanilla extract
½ cup water	1 quart heavy cream, whipped
6 egg yolks	

Soften gelatin in ¼ cup of the rum. Heat water to boiling, take from heat, and stir in gelatin until dissolved. Set aside. With an electric mixer beat the egg yolks until creamy. Add sugar gradually and beat until very light and thick. Stir in remaining rum, the vanilla and dissolved gelatin. Chill until beginning to set; fold in the whipped cream. Pour into an oiled 3-quart mold. Chill until firm.

Makes 16 servings.

Cups of Vanilla Custard

From Miss Hyla Snider, recipe dated 1884

Cut a vanilla bean into short pieces, put in a quart of boiling milk, take from the heat and let the vanilla infuse for 1 hour. Break 2 whole eggs and 8 egg yolks into a sauce. Add ½ pound of sugar, mix well, dilute with the vanilla infusion, and pass through a fine strainer. Fill custard cups with the mixture. Put the custard cups in a *sautoir* or other flat deep pan with boiling water to half the height of the cups. Cover, and let simmer slowly until the custard is well set. Let cool, wipe the cups, and serve.

Makes about 8 standard custards.

English Trifle

Settlers came burdened with recipes which they were not equipped to prepare in New England. Many recipes were discarded, but an Englishman and his trifle were not so easily parted. As soon as there were eggs and cream and sherry available, his wife baked spongecake fingers and macaroons and recreated the holiday trifle. The whole thing took a full day. We can buy our ladyfingers and macaroons and recreate it in a well-spent hour.

12 large or 16 small ladyfingers	⅔ cup flour
½ cup blackberry or raspberry jam	6 egg yolks
	¾ cup granulated sugar
⅔ cup sherry	2 teaspoons vanilla
4½ cups milk	4 tablespoons sherry
	½ cup shaved almonds

1 tablespoon butter

8 dried macaroons, crumbled, or 1 cup macaroon crumbs

1 cup heavy cream, whipped

2 tablespoons confectioners' sugar

8 glacéed cherries

Split ladyfingers and spread half with jam. Sandwich them together again and arrange them across the bottom and around the sides of a deep crystal dessert dish. Sprinkle the sherry over the ladyfingers and set the dish aside.

In the top part of a double boiler, stir 1 cup cold milk into flour until smooth. Scald remaining milk and stir into the mixture in a thin stream. Set over boiling water and cook, stirring until steam rises, for about 5 minutes. Beat egg yolks with granulated sugar until very light and creamy. Beat the hot milk mixture into the yolks in a thin stream. Set over boiling water again and stir slowly until custard sauce is smooth and thick enough to coat the spoon, 5 to 7 minutes. Take from heat, stir in vanilla and sherry, and chill.

Toast shaved almonds with the butter in a shallow pan in a 250° F. oven. Shake frequently; when they are browned to taste, after about 1 hour, drain them on absorbent paper.

Pour the cooked custard sauce over the ladyfingers, sprinkle with macaroon crumbs, and chill. Before serving decorate top with cream whipped with confectioners' sugar. Pipe it through a fluted tube if you have time and a fluted tube. Garnish with the toasted almonds and glacéed cherries.

Makes about 8 servings.

ᕮᕮ Warm Sherry Trifle

12 to 15 ladyfingers

3 tablespoons raspberry jam

1 cup heavy cream

6 egg yolks

2 tablespoons sugar

½ cup sherry

Split ladyfingers and spread with jam. Sandwich them together again and arrange them in 6 dessert cups.

Whip cream until soft but not pebbly and place in refrigerator while beating the egg yolks. In the top part of a double boiler over boiling water beat yolks, sugar and sherry with an electric hand beater until light and creamy. Be sure to run the beater around the edges and bottom to prevent a layer of cooked egg. Beat until about tripled in volume. Take from heat, beat for ½ minute longer, and fold into the cold whipped cream.

Pour the cream over the ladyfingers in the dessert cups and serve at once.

Makes 6 servings.

Custard Cherries

2 cans (17 ounces each) black cherries	1¼ cups milk, boiling
2 tablespoons cornstarch	2 tablespoons sugar
3 tablespoons rum	1 tablespoon flour
1 cup shaved almonds	2 egg yolks
3 tablespoons butter	½ teaspoon vanilla extract

Drain juice from cherries into a saucepan. Stir 1 tablespoon of the cornstarch into cold rum until smooth, then stir into cherry juice over low heat until clear and thickened. Pour cherries into a crystal dessert

bowl, pour the thickened sauce over them, and chill. Brown almonds in 2 tablespoons of the butter in a 300° F. oven for about 20 minutes. Stir or shake every 5 minutes. Bring 1 cup of the milk to a boil. Dissolve sugar in boiling milk. Stir remaining cornstarch and the flour into ¼ cup cold milk until smooth, then stir into simmering milk until thickened. Stir in remaining 1 tablespoon butter until melted. Beat in egg yolks and vanilla; chill. Pour over cherries, sprinkle top with almonds, and serve very cold.

Makes about 8 servings.

⌘ Dutch Cherry Dumplings

Some of the Puritans spent a few years in Holland before they came to America. As a result, there are to be found in the tidewater settlements a few recipes that suggest the cookery of the Netherlands.

1¼ pounds baking potatoes	36 sweet red cherries
1¼ cups flour	6 tablespoons butter
1 medium-sized egg	6 tablespoons bread crumbs
¼ teaspoon salt	6 tablespoons sugar

Boil potatoes in their skins until tender, 20 to 25 minutes; drain. Pull off skins and rice potatoes onto a pastry board while hot. When they are cold, make a well in the center, sprinkle in 1 cup of the flour, and break the egg into the well. Stir with fingers, gathering more and more flour and potato into the egg until the dough holds together. Knead it until smooth, working in the salt and remaining ¼ cup flour. While the dough should not be sticky, it should not be floury either. Sprinkle board with flour if necessary. Roll to about ⅓-inch thickness and cut into 3- or 3½-inch squares, depending on the size of the cherries; there will be about 12 squares. Place 3 stemmed cherries on each dough square and with floured hands shape into a perfect round. Bring salted water to a boil in 2 wide saucepans. The dumplings should not be crowded when they boil. Place them in the water and as soon as it returns to a boil reduce heat to medium. Let dumplings boil gently until they rise to the surface and are well done, 10 to 15 minutes. In the meantime, melt butter in a small heavy pan, stir in crumbs, and brown lightly. Take dumplings out of the water with a slotted spoon, arrange in a serving dish, and pour the buttered crumbs over them. Sprinkle with the sugar. Pass more sugar separately.

Makes 12 servings.

Sandra De Veau's Rhubarb Dumplings

2 cups flour	2 to 4 tablespoons butter
4 teaspoons baking powder	⅔ cup milk
¼ teaspoon salt	1 cup very finely sliced rhubarb
1 teaspoon sugar	Sugar Syrup (below)

Sift dry ingredients together. Cut in butter until the lumps are the size of peas. Add enough milk to make the dough stick together. Knead lightly. Knead the sliced rhubarb into the dough. Shape into dumplings with floured hands. Bake in a buttered baking dish in a 450° F. oven for 15 minutes.

SUGAR SYRUP

Boil 1 cup granulated sugar with ½ cup water until syrupy, about 15 minutes; pour over dumplings and serve.

Wine Sauce

From the *Vineyard Gazette*

½ cup butter	1 egg yolk
1 cup sugar	3 tablespoons sherry
1 cup hot water	

Cream butter with sugar. Gradually add hot water and cook to consistency of honey. Beat egg yolk slightly. Take cooked mixture from heat and add egg yolk and sherry; beat well.

Makes about 2 cups.

Serve with puddings, especially bland-tasting ones, and other desserts.

ℰℋ Fudge

It is a known fact that men make the best fudge, so we are doubly grateful to Mr. Robert S. Trullinger for his recipe.

4½ cups sugar
⅓ cup butter
1 can (14½ ounces) evaporated milk
1 teaspoon white corn syrup
Pinch of salt
¾ cup marshmallow cream

1 bar of milk chocolate (13 ounces) grated
2 cups semi-sweet chocolate bits (chips)
3 tablespoons peanut butter
2 teaspoons vanilla extract
2 cups English walnuts, coarsely chopped

Combine sugar, butter, evaporated milk, corn syrup and salt. Boil for 5½ minutes. Remove from heat and add remaining ingredients except nuts. Beat until well mixed, either with spoon or electric mixer. Stir in nuts. Spoon into buttered pans. Cool until firm. Makes 5 pounds. This fudge will keep fresh and soft for weeks if wrapped securely in foil.

Chapter XII

~~~

Beverages

THE *Charles W. Morgan* was built at New Bedford and launched on July 21, 1841. The event was briefly noted in the New Bedford paper of that day, "A fine ship of 350 tons burthen, intended for the whalefishery, will be launched from the yard of Messrs. J. & Z. Hillman this morning at half past nine o'clock."

The Hillman brothers, J. and Z., quite aside from the fact that they could build a ship that could survive her long and arduous career, were named Jethro and Zachariah. They did not know that her long career would be unmatched and that she would live to immortalize the industry and its era at Mystic Seaport, only a few miles away.

Charles W. Morgan, a handsome young Quaker who was the proud owner, wrote in his diary on the same day, "A fine warm day, but very dry. This morning at 10 o'clock my elegant new ship was launched beautifully from Messrs. Hillmans' yard—and in the presence of about half the town and a great show of ladies. She looks beautifully on the water, she was copper-bottomed on the stocks. She is to be commanded by Captain Thomas A. Norton."

We tell you all this here because this is the beverage chapter and the launching of a ship has always implied a celebration and has for a long time included a bottle of champagne. However, the *Charles W. Mor-*

gan came down the ways without a christening ceremony and, for that matter, without a name. She was named for her owner at a later and uncelebrated day. Let us lift a glass of any of these fine beverages, and toast her now for the great ship she is, and for the American whaling industry she represents.

ℰℴ Eggnog

A 1790 recipe

2 cups rye whiskey	8 cups chilled thick cream* (or
2 cups sugar	2 quarts vanilla ice cream)
10 eggs, separated	½ cup confectioners' sugar
1 cup rum	Grated nutmeg
1 cup brandy	

Pour whiskey into a small bowl, add 1 cup sugar, and chill for 3 to 4 hours. Beat egg yolks with remaining cup of sugar until thick and creamy, gradually add whiskey, rum and brandy. Whip thick cream with confectioners' sugar until it starts to thicken, then stir it into the eggnog. Fold in the stiffly beaten egg whites. Serve from a chilled punch bowl with a sprinkling of nutmeg on the top.
Makes about 25 cups.

ℰℴ New Year's Day Eggnog

Enough for all the neighbors

3 dozen eggs, separated	2 cups rum
4 cups sugar	1 quart heavy cream, whipped
3 quarts medium cream	Grated nutmeg
3 quarts rye whiskey	

* Use either 3- or 4-day-old cream which has thickened but not soured in closed containers in refrigerator, or substitute vanilla ice cream for the cream and confectioners' sugar. To bring vanilla ice cream to proper consistency, let it stand in refrigerator for 1 hour before beating it smooth.

Beat egg yolks with sugar until light and creamy; gradually beat in cream, whiskey and rum. Fold in stiffly beaten egg whites and top with whipped cream. Whip cream until it is stiff and smooth, not until it looks like an angry thunderhead. Sprinkle nutmeg over whipped cream. Makes about 50 cups.

ҀЖ Cape Cod Eggnog

A very nice version comes from Cape Cod, where eggnog is made with brandy or bourbon instead of rye whiskey.

12 eggs, separated	2 quarts milk
1 pound sugar	1 quart heavy cream
1 quart brandy or bourbon	Grated nutmeg
2 cups rum	

Beat egg yolks with sugar until creamy; gradually beat in brandy and rum. Beat in milk and cream. Pour into punch bowl and float the stiffly beaten egg whites on top. Sprinkle with nutmeg and serve to your neighbors; then go downstreet and drink of your neighbor's eggnog. Makes 20 to 25 cups.

ҀЖ Rich Eggnog

1 pint vanilla ice cream	1 quart bourbon
18 egg yolks	1½ pints heavy cream
1 cup sugar	Grated nutmeg
1 cup heavy rum	

One hour before serving eggnog take vanilla ice cream from freezer and set in warmest part of refrigerator. Immediately beat egg yolks with sugar until thick, light and creamy. Gradually beat in rum and set in refrigerator also. Just before serving, stir bourbon into the egg-and-rum mixture; beat the softened ice cream until smooth and set it aside. Whip the cream and fold ice cream and whipped cream into the bourbon mixture. Pour into a chilled bowl and sprinkle with nutmeg.

Makes 24 servings, about ⅔ cup each. For a larger party, make several batches. Do not attempt to make one enormous batch.

NOTE: *Sound Advice for Storing and Using All Those Egg Whites*

Prepare yourself to own dozens of egg whites when making eggnog. Funnel them into bottles with the narrowest possible necks so that the air surface on the egg whites will be minimal. Cork the bottles and place in bottom of refrigerator; they will keep for several days. Use for meringue shells, cake layers and small baked items which can be stored. You don't want the entire holiday to be one long angel cake. Use the last of the egg whites on a lovely Mystic specialty, Prune Meringue Pie (p. 184).

६४% Milk Punch

Knowledge of these good combinations of milk and rum and/or brandy came with the settlers from England. The West India trade was well under way by the first half of the eighteenth century and Mystic ships touched at Barbados. These healthful and cheerful drinks were served frequently. Nothing helped a cold in the head or a slight running down of vitality like a nice milk punch.

6 eggs, separated	1 cup rum
1 cup sugar	A nutmeg and a nutmeg grater
4 cups milk	

In a bowl, beat egg yolks with sugar until thick and smooth; beat in milk gradually. Stir in the rum and fold in the stiffly beaten egg whites. Grate a very little nutmeg over the top and serve in the bowl. This was eaten with a spoon and was held to be very nourishing.

Makes about 8 cups.

ℰ𝒳 Ardent Spirits

The word ardent means burning and fierce, and it was applied most frequently to suitors and spirits. What every young Mystic maid longed for was an ardent suitor (even though he be tongue-tied and blushing), and what every Mystic man enjoyed, in moderation, were ardent spirits. The word in this case meant all strong alcoholic liquors that produced a hot, fiery, burning and fierce sensation as they went down the throat. And while we are about the language of the sea as used ashore, we should change that last to read, "as they went down the hatch."

ℰ𝒳 Cherry Brandy

Our forefathers brewed and bottled brandies which they stored in cool cellars or even went so far as to bury in the back garden. The essential thing, of course, was the marker, since no one wanted to dig up the whole garden to locate a bottle of cherry brandy.

12 pounds black cherries   4 pounds sugar
8 quarts brandy

Pit black cherries over a large bowl, or bowls, in order to catch all the juices. Pour brandy over the juice and cherries in the bowls. Place cherry pits in a canvas bag and beat them with a mallet until they are bruised or crushed. Add them to the brandy. Cover securely and store in a cool dark place for 14 days. Line a sieve with a double layer of muslin wrung out in cold water, and pour the mixture through it. Press all moisture out of the fruit and pits before discarding them. Boil sugar in a large kettle, stirring until melted and clear. Add the strained cherry brandy and funnel into 6 sterilized, dry bottles of clear glass. Seal and store in a cool dark place for at least 2 months before tasting.

ℰ𝒳 Raspberry Brandy

  1 quart raspberry juice   1 quart brandy
  1 pound sugar

Steam about 3 quarts raspberries by placing them in a kettle and
setting the kettle into a larger kettle of boiling water. As soon as they are
very soft and the juice is drawn out of them, press them through a fine-
mesh sieve to obtain all juice. To each quart of raspberry juice, add 1
pound sugar and bring to a fast boil. Take from heat, cool, and chill.
Measure cold juice and stir it into an equal quantity of brandy. Stir or
shake again and bottle.

There were those who considered this more healthful in proportions
of 1 part cold raspberry juice to 2 parts brandy.

ℰ𝒳 Potables and Drinkables

"We are sooner recovered by liquid than by solid aliment." Hippocrates said that, and for centuries liquids have been used to help the weak
and the weary to recover and the young to grow. They have also served
to warm the cold, to cool the hot, to soothe, to strengthen and to cheer.

The early Mystic settlers needed all the strength and warmth and
cheer they could possibly get. They drank teas and tisanes for their
health; grogs, mulled wines and hot spiced punches for warmth; and
they brewed dandelion and elderberry wines for a spot of comfort. They
drank "cyder" and perry in summer and nourishing nogs and broths in
winter, and at all times there were milk concoctions, ades and ales.

Hippocrates went a step further and urged that all meals should
begin with a liquid substance, and probably fathered the old custom of
starting off every dinner with soup. The Mysticians went a second step
further (after all, Hippocrates didn't have fresh clams): they added
clam juice, spiced cranberry juice, clam broth and various infusions and
decoctions with which to start or end a meal.

Our central heating and air conditioning should not prevent our re-creating the pleasures of a good hot grog in winter and a cold cider cup in summer. These lovely old recipes are, in their way, just as precious as the antique mugs or porringers in which they were served. It is all very well to collect old tankards and mugs, but it is even better in winter to drink a hot grog out of them.

Hot Grog

3 large lemons	¾ cup heavy rum
¼ cup sugar	6 cups strong hot tea*

With a swivel-bladed vegetable peeler cut 6 long curls of thinnest peel from the lemons. Cut lemons into halves and juice them, to make about ½ cup. Combine sugar, lemon juice and rum and divide mixture among 6 warmed mugs. Fill mugs with boiling hot tea and serve at once, garnished with a curl of lemon rind.
Makes 6 servings.

To Make "Bishop"

Miss Hyla Snider sends us a recipe dated December, 1864, for a sort of lemon pomander-ball punch.

"Procure a large, ripe, sound lemon, pierce the same in various parts, and rub into the peel as much pounded white loaf sugar as will abstract a sufficiency of the essential spirit of the rind into it. Introduce into each puncture a spice-clove, and lay the lemon in a bowl. Have ready at hand, on the side of the fire, a quart of the best port wine, scalding hot, pour the same into the bowl, over the lemon, adding sugar** to taste, and crown the bowl with the whites of half a dozen eggs, whipped up into a consistent froth. This constituted a favorite beverage of the late Professor Person of 'Graeco-literature' celebrity."

* Use a good Lapsang Souchong, or other well-flavored tea.
** We assume that the sugar used is that in which the lemon rind was rubbed.

ᏋᎧᏁ King George I Christmas Punch

A rum punch to be served with Christmas pudding

24 large lumps of sugar
3 cups boiling water
Juice and grated rind of 4 lemons
2 cups Jamaica rum

½ cup brandy
½ cup stout or heavy ale
2 dashes of arrack or apple brandy or hard apple cider

Lay sugar in a punch bowl, pour boiling water over it, and stir until dissolved. Add lemon juice and rind and stir in rum. Follow with brandy. Last of all beat in stout and arrack. (Arrack rated as an ardent spirit.)
Makes about 8 cups.

ᏋᎧᏁ Rum Punch

From Mrs. Richard C. Palmer

1 cup grenadine
2 cups lemon juice
1 bottle (26 ounces) falernum
1 bottle (26 ounces) Barbados rum

1 bottle (26 ounces) Demerara rum
5¾ cups unsweetened pineapple juice
10 dashes of Angostura bitters

Combine all ingredients and chill. Just before serving, pour over lots of ice in a punch bowl and garnish with thin slices of orange. For a bubbly punch, use less ice and just before serving add well-chilled ginger ale to taste.
Makes about 18 cups before adding ice.
WARNING: Demerara rum is very potent!

ᚼ Celebration Punch

From Mrs. Richard C. Palmer

2 bottles chilled champagne
2 bottles chilled Sauterne
1½ quarts lemon or orange
   sherbet

2 limes or oranges, sliced paper-thin

Pour champagne and wine over a block of ice in a punch bowl. Add lemon or orange sherbet by the spoonfuls. Decorate with lime or orange slices.
Makes about 50 half-cup servings.

ᚼ Julep in a Tankard

The julep (from *gulāb*, Persian for rosewater) was known and served in England as far back as 1608. Before there were straws to suck juleps through, a stick of macaroni was used.

1 tablespoon sugar
3 sprigs of fresh mint
Crushed ice to fill the tankard
1 jigger (3 tablespoons) brandy

½ jigger (1½ tablespoons)
rum
1 twist of lemon peel

Macerate sugar with the leaves from one of the mint sprigs in the bottom of the tankard. Fill with ice. Shake brandy, rum and lemon peel well, pour over the ice, and garnish with the 2 remaining sprigs of mint.
Makes 1 julep.

ᚼ An Old Ale Posset

1 cup good sherry
1 cup strong ale
4 cups milk, heated to boiling

1 tablespoon sugar
Grated nutmeg

Combine measured ingredients and stir until sugar is dissolved. Pour into heated mugs and serve at once, sprinkled with nutmeg.
Makes 6 cups.

ℰ⅏ Mulled Ale

These ale drinks are not included purely for amusement—they are meant to be tried. They warmed Mystic seamen and whalemen on land, and many brought home spices from their voyages for purposes like these.

2 quarts ale	½ teaspoon ground cloves
2 tablespoons sugar	½ teaspoon grated nutmeg
1 teaspoon ground ginger	1 cup rum or brandy

Heat ale, sugar and spices to just under a boil; add rum or brandy and serve hot.
Makes 9 cups.

ℰ⅏ Syllabubs

There are solid and liquid syllabubs. The liquid form is a mild soft nog which was served to children and ladies, while gentlemen drank eggnogs laced with heavy spirits. The solid form is a cream dessert. Both should be revived. Serve the solid form, which is similar to a sabayon, in stemmed glasses.

There is mention of innkeepers who charged double for syllabubs served out of doors, due to the breakage of glasses. This leaves us with a picture of a sort of syllabub-curb-service to coaches, wagons and horsemen in days gone by.

The original recipes for solid syllabubs all direct to mix and leave to stand until next day. This would imply that they "stood" for about 24 hours, or that they were eaten early in the day. Since our creams are not as heavy, we suggest using 2- to 3-day-old fresh cream and leaving the syllabub to stand for 7 to 8 hours at most.

Furthermore, a very nice thing to do is arrange cubes of spongecake or dried cake in dessert glasses. Sprinkle them with sherry or wine to taste and pour the syllabub over them. This is a sort of trifle.

A Solid Syllabub

½ cup orange juice
½ cup lemon juice
1 cup sherry or dry wine

⅓ cup sugar, or more to taste
2 cups very heavy cream

Combine all ingredients in a bowl and whisk until the mixture stands in soft peaks. Spoon into syllabub glasses and chill for 8 hours. The syllabub will rise and leave a clear liquid at the bottom.
Makes about 6 cups.

Syllabub I

Solid or liquid eggnog for ladies and children

Amelia Simmons, "the American Orphan," in 1796 wrote "To Make A Fine Syllabub from The Cow." She suggests, very practically, that cider be sweetened with sugar and nutmeg and after that, "Milk your cow into your liquor." You do this to the desired amount and then, "You pour the sweetest cream all over it." She does not go on to say whether you drink it right then and there by the cow, but we do know it has to be drunk before the froth settles.

Whipped Syllabub

2 cups heavy cream
1 cup white wine
Grated rind of 1 lemon

3 egg whites
3 tablespoons sugar, or more to taste

Whip all ingredients in a bowl until the froth rises. Skim it off. Pour into syllabub glasses and serve immediately, topped with the froth. Makes about 4 cups.

Syllabub II

While Amelia Simmons suggests her syllabubs *from* the cow in 1796, Briggs suggests his syllabubs *under* the cow in 1792, but then he wasn't a New Englander.

The whole thing presupposes the drinker's ownership of a cow and his ability to milk. It is also interesting to find that even the earliest eggnog recipes called for something to be cold, either the punch bowl or the ingredients, or both. (As a Christmas and New Year's drink this presented no problem in Mystic. The bowl was chilled in snow.) The temperature of the milder version of syllabub for ladies and children is never mentioned. The ingredients would probably come cold from the larder, but when we come to *from* and *under* the cow, we conjecture that the syllabub was apparently served at the temperature known as *cow warm*.

Very Superior Whipped Syllabub

Eliza Akton in 1855 observed "these proportions are sufficient for two dozen or more of syllabubs: They are often made with almost equal quantities of wine and cream, but are considered less wholesome without a portion of brandy." Trust Eliza.

½ pound lump sugar	1 cup brandy
2 lemons	2 cups heavy cream
1 cup sherry	

A day before the syllabub is to be served, rasp the sugar against the lemon rinds, over a bowl. Drop each saturated lump into the bowl until the surfaces of the lemons are grated off. Halve the lemons and add their juice to the sugar in the bowl. Add sherry and brandy and stir until the sugar is dissolved. Just before serving, add the cream and beat until foamy. Skim the foam into cups and continue until all has turned to foam.

Makes about 6 cups.

NOTE: Lemon rind can be grated into the juice with ½ pound of granulated sugar added if there is not enough time for rasping the lump sugar on the lemons.

🐾 Fruit Syllabub

This was served as a dessert or sauce to children and ladies who did not care for the taste of wine or spirits. There was an "everlasting syllabub" served in England which found its way to Connecticut, where it underwent a very pleasant change: berry juice was substituted for lemon juice.

¾ cup strained berry juice— raspberry, cranberry, boysenberry, blackberry, or currant	Sugar 1½ cups very heavy cream

In a large bowl, stir fruit juice with enough sugar to sweeten to taste. Stir until sugar is completely dissolved. Add cream and whip until the mixture stands in soft peaks. Makes about 4 cups.

To Serve

1. Serve at once in chilled dessert cups.
2. Pour into dessert cups and chill for 8 to 12 hours. The cream will rise and make a "head" on the berry juice.
3. Serve at once as a sauce for hot or cold puddings.
4. Go back to the "everlasting" syllabub and substitute lemon juice, or half lemon and half orange juice, for the berry juice and serve in any of the above 3 suggested ways.
5. Make a berry-juice or citrus-juice syllabub and pour it over poundcake or spongecake fingers in dessert glasses; top with a suitable berry or a little berry jam, or with grated lemon or orange rind.

6. If the purple of some of the berry juice is not liked, apricot juice or nectar, peach juice, or strawberry juice may be substituted.
7. Prepare one of the syllabubs, pour it over a fruit or berries in the dessert glasses, and serve at once: strawberry syllabub over sliced peaches, raspberry syllabub over fresh strawberries, or orange syllabub over blackberries or strawberries.

ℰ𝒳 Native New England Beverage Plants

There were actually no true beverage plants in New England. During the Revolutionary War, when colonists were cut off from their tea, they drank an infusion made from the dried leaves of native bush plant *Ceanothus americanus*. It was called New Jersey Tea, and we hear it hasn't been brewed since tea was again obtainable.

In Jamestown, on the other hand, they were able to make money by exporting sassafras bark to Europe and New England, where it was used as a preventive of seasickness. The pitching and heaving, rolling and corkscrewing, of a square-rigged ship on a stormy sea were not to be believed, and cures for seasickness were in great demand. We wonder whether the steadfast settling of the pioneers wasn't partly attributable to the dread of a return voyage home.

ℰ𝒳 Hot Spiced Tea

The English East India Company was granted a charter in 1599 and the first tea fleet set sail for China in 1600. They carried a cargo of dried English sage and exchanged it for Chinese tea at a rate of one pound of sage for four pounds of tea.

Tea and spices came to New England on the Mayflower along with a strong inclination to combine all things that came from the East. If cloves and cinnamon didn't actually go into the tea, they went into the cakes, bread and cookies that accompanied it in Mystic, as elsewhere. Mystic ships were in the tea trade, too.

On April 24, 1879 an item in *The Mystic Press* noted, "At Hiogo,

Japan, March 25th bark Sabine, William, for New York via Yokohama
to land tea at £1.5s/ton."

½ teaspoon whole cloves	1 orange, juice only
½ cinnamon stick	1 lemon, juice only
6 cups boiling water	½ cup sugar
1 tablespoon black tea	

Add cloves and cinnamon to boiling water. Add tea and remove from
heat. Cover and steep for 5 minutes. Stir in orange juice, lemon juice
and sugar, and serve very hot.
Makes 6 servings.

Cyder

"Cyder is an excellent drink made from the juice of apples, especially
of the more common table kinds," said Dr. J. S. Forsyth in *A Dictionary of Diet*.

Mystic's settlers came from England with an inborn love for apples
and also a working knowledge of how to turn them into cider and cider
concoctions.

Cider Cup

2 quarts sweet apple cider	⅓ cup Curaçao
Juice of 1 lemon	1 lemon, sliced thin
6 tablespoons sugar	Borage sprigs
⅔ cup brandy	

Mix first three ingredients and stir until sugar is dissolved. Add
brandy and Curaçao and chill. Serve over ice with a lemon slice and a
sprig of borage in each glass.
Makes about 12 servings.

CHAPTER XIII

~~~

Pickles and Relishes, Jam and Jelly

For a short time the early settlers were forced to eat in the manner of primitive man, mainly to nourish themselves. But in no time at all man's sharp sense of taste and smell, even a hardworking settler's, asserted itself. Food began to take on flavor, and savory whiffs came from hearth and oven.

Settlers had memories of the good food they had left behind them. Their instinct to make food more palatable accounted for lovely discoveries. We must admire the people who courageously bit into the first crane-berry, when all shiny red berries were believed to be poisonous. Barberries, beach plums, even elderberries had to be tasted for the first time by somebody. The Indians taught them about sap from sugar trees and meal from sunflower seeds, but it took considerable enterprise to eat the first puffball or chokecherry.

Later on, when a Mystic wife wanted a special ingredient or flavor for a certain dish, she had two alternatives. She could ask her husband to bring it home on his next voyage (which might mean as much as three or four years before she could serve it), or she could grow it in her garden. Both were long-range programs and both seem to have worked very well. Mystic herb gardens flourished, seeds and cuttings were shared and exchanged, and aromatic bunches of dried herbs lasted through the winters. Mystic wives had spices from India and saffron shreds, herbs in their gardens, and all the necessities of fine cookery. Sometimes they had to wait until the last ingredient arrived, "when their ship came in," before the splendid recipe could be tried.

ⴞⵆ Mustard Corn Relish

1 large white cabbage	1½ tablespoons flour
3 tablespoons salt	1 tablespoon celery seeds
7 large ears of corn	1 teaspoon mustard seeds
1½ cups sugar	1½ cups cider vinegar
½ cup dry mustard	1⅓ cups water

Trim and slice cabbage and chop coarsely. Spread it in a wide pan and sprinkle with 2 tablespoons of the salt. Set it aside for 1½ hours. Cook corn with remaining salt in a large kettle until tender, 7 to 10 minutes. Cut kernels off the ears into a large kettle. Stir sugar, mustard, flour, celery and mustard seeds in a small bowl. Boil vinegar and water for 3 to 4 minutes; stir very gradually into the dry ingredients. Continue to stir until smooth. Drain cabbage very well, add it to the corn and pour the mustard sauce over both. Heat the relish to just under boiling and pour it, while hot, into hot sterilized jars.
Makes 5 pints.

ⴞⵆ Mrs. B. F. Hoxie's Sweet Pickled Peaches

From Miss Malloy's *The Old Gem Cookbook*

7 pounds ripe peaches	1 quart vinegar
3 tablespoons whole cloves	7 cinnamon sticks
7 cups sugar	

Scald and peel the peaches and stick 1 or 2 cloves into each one. Boil the sugar and vinegar with the cinnamon sticks for 5 minutes. Add the peaches and boil gently until they are entirely tender. Take them out with a slotted spoon. Boil the syrup until it is reduced to half. Pour syrup over the peaches in 1 or 2 large pickling jars and cool. When cold, cover firmly and store in a cold place until needed. Serve with meats or poultry.

Makes about 6 pints.

✺ Pickled Plums

7 pounds plums	½ cup slivered or grated or-ange peel
3 pounds sugar	
1 ounce ground cinnamon	Wine vinegar (about 3 cups)
1 ounce ground cloves	¾ cup sugar per quart of juice

Select plums that are not too ripe. Prick their entire surface with the tines of a fork and arrange the plums and their juice in layers in crock or jar. Between layers sprinkle sugar, cinnamon, cloves and orange peel. Depending on the depth of the crock or jar, fill to just cover with vinegar. Cover closely and set aside for 24 hours.

Strain off the vinegary liquid and boil it over high heat for 10 minutes. Cool and pour back over the fruit. Cover and set aside again for 24 hours.

Strain off the liquid again and add sugar to it, in proportion of ¾ cup sugar to every quart of liquid drained from plums. Boil again for 10 minutes, cool, and pour into jars over the plums. Seal with waxed parchment paper and kitchen string, and store in a dry cool place. Very good with meats or on a relish tray. Good with pot cheese.

Makes about 6 pints.

✺ Pickled Beets

Use very small whole beets or large beets sliced. Remember that beets bleed; do not cut off root ends and leave stems as long as possible.

4 bunches of beets, washed under running water

2 cups vinegar, tarragon if possible

2 tablespoons sugar

1 teaspoon whole cloves

1 bay leaf

½ teaspoon salt

2 peppercorns

Boil beets in salted water until tender. Young beets will take 15 to 20 minutes, old beets may need 30 minutes. Pour them into a colander and run cold water over them until they are cool enough to handle. Trim and draw off skins. Slice thin over a bowl and place in a jar or jars with any juice obtained in slicing. Boil remaining ingredients for 10 minutes, pour over the beets and juice, and cool before chilling. These will keep in refrigerator.

Makes 3 to 4 pints, depending on size of beets.

Chowchow

Brought from India and China by the whalers, chowchow is similar to mixed pickles with all the Indian condiments added: mustard, tumeric, cloves, ginger, cayenne and black and white pepper.

1 cauliflower (2 pounds), or 2 smaller ones, separated into flowerets

3 green peppers, seeded and sliced thin

2 sweet red peppers, seeded and sliced thin

8 onions, sliced thick

2 cups corn kernels, yellow if possible

3 cups white vinegar

1½ cups boiling water

1½ cups sugar

Salt

3 white peppercorns

4 black peppercorns

1 tablespoon brown mustard seeds

1 tablespoon yellow mustard seeds

10 cloves

1 piece of fresh gingerroot (2 ounces), cut into 6 pieces, one for each pint jar

Boil cauliflower flowerets and sliced stem in salted water to cover for 5 minutes. Drain well and combine with peppers, onions and corn. Boil remaining ingredients until sugar is dissolved. Add vegetables and boil uncovered for 2 minutes after water returns to a boil. Pour into 6 hot sterilized pint jars, filling them to the top. Seal at once and cool. If vinegar does not cover vegetables completely, boil more water and vinegar and add it to the last jar.

Makes 6 pints.

Apple Chutney

This is a blended fresh chutney that must be eaten at once, or within a day.

8 sour green apples, peeled, cored and chopped

2 teaspoons salt

8 onions, chopped

2 green peppers, seeded and chopped

2 cups shredded coconut

2 lemons, juice and grated rind

Sprinkle apples with salt and 2 tablespoons water. Set them aside for 15 minutes; drain well. Place in a blender container with remaining ingredients and blend until smooth, or press through a sieve. Serve with meats or on a relish tray.

Makes about 4 pints.

Beet and Red-cabbage Chutney

1 red cabbage (2 pounds), shredded fine

2 pounds raw beets, peeled and diced fine

2 large onions, put through food grinder

3 teaspoons salt

2 cups sugar

3 juniper berries

2 teaspoons peppercorns

¼ cup mustard seeds

4 cups wine vinegar

Prepare the vegetables. Bring seasonings and spices to a boil in the vinegar. Add vegetables and simmer gently until beets are soft, 30 to 40 minutes. Pour into jars and seal. The chutney should not be cooled before it is bottled.

Makes about 4 pints.

ℰℛ Homemade Ketchup

Prepare for a day near the stove, or arrange to be spelled at intervals by members of the family. They might as well take a turn at stirrings since they will certainly take a turn at eating the ketchup later on.

12 quarts very ripe tomatoes
3 cups vinegar*
¼ cup brown mustard
½ cup salt
⅓ cup ground allspice

1 tablespoon ground cloves
1 teaspoon ground black pepper
1 teaspoon ground ginger
1 teaspoon paprika

Scald 6 quart or 12 pint bottles.

Trim stems and imperfections from tomatoes; quarter them over a kettle in order to catch all juice. Drop tomatoes into the kettle and cook them over low heat, stirring frequently, until soft; depending on the ripeness of the tomatoes, about 30 minutes. Press through a strainer to obtain 6 quarts tomato purée. Add all other ingredients and simmer in a heavy kettle for 3 to 4 hours, stirring frequently. Pour into bottles and cork with new corks heated in boiling water to soften.

Makes 12 pints.

ℰℛ Yellow Plum-tomato Jam

From the *Vineyard Gazette*—Theresa Morse

2 quarts yellow plum tomatoes
1 lemon, sliced paper-thin, the slices halved

3 teaspoons ground ginger
8 cups sugar
1 cup water

Wash tomatoes, but do not peel. Combine all ingredients. Cook until tomatoes have a clear look and syrup is as thick as honey. This can take from 40 minutes to 1½ hours. Stir frequently. Cool, pour into jars, and seal.

Makes about 4 pints.

* Use a flavored vinegar such as tarragon or basil, according to taste.

ॐ Recipe for Harold Disco's Block Island Blackberry Jam

From Jo Bingham Disco

The fruit is sweet
But thorns are sharp—
Wear old gloves.
Pick ripe till your heart's pleased,
Your eyes surfeited,
And the size of the pot calls halt;
Pick, too, the off-ripe—
For the tang and tart of the island
Should reach the palate;
Mash and drain if you wish
But dews and mist have preceded you
And the berries are sun-blown dry.

Prepare as usual for a jam session,
Drink a cold glass of spring water,
And go to work.

Take any basic recipe
But reduce the sugar;
Island berries are honeyed succulence;

Mint from doorstep garden
Brings its own spicy aura;
Small wild apples
Still green in August
Add delicate dimension;
Fresh lime, brought from the mainland,
Instills zest.

Work with love
And its flavor will enter the syrup;
Work with joy
And a sunny fragrance
Will seal itself in the jars.

Jar and seal as usual;
Label with year, and
"Season of Block Island blackberries."

Mystic Cranberry Sauce

2 pounds fresh cranberries	1 cup raisins, chopped
3 large oranges	4 cups sugar

Grind the cranberries, using the coarse blade of a food grinder, and catching all juice and ground pulp in a large kettle. Grate the orange rinds over the cranberries and add the scraped-out pulp and juice of the oranges. Add raisins and sugar. Set kettle over low heat and simmer,

stirring frequently, until thickened, about 1½ hours. Pour into jars, cool and chill. Serve with roast chicken or turkey.

Makes about 2 pints.

ᏋᎥᏌ Cranberry Relish

6 cups fresh cranberries	1½ cups chopped walnuts
1 cup cold water	2 large oranges
1 cup boiling water	4 cups sugar
1½ cups raisins	Grated rind of 1 lemon

Wash and pick over cranberries. Boil them with the cold water until the skins "pop" and berries are soft. Blend or strain them into a purée and add boiling water, raisins, walnuts and sugar. Peel the oranges and dice the pulp into the relish. Scrape the loose white peel off the inside of the orange rind with a knife; discard white peel and dice the rind into the relish. Stir in the lemon rind, cool the relish, and pour it into jars. Seal jars with melted parafin and store until needed.

Makes about 6 pints.

ᏋᎥᏌ Mint Jelly

Another "rule" from Mrs. Davis's collection of family recipes

1 cup tightly packed spearmint leaves and stems	Few drops of green food coloring
½ cup cider vinegar	½ bottle (6-ounce size) liquid pectin
1 cup water	
3½ cups sugar	

Wash spearmint and measure into 3-quart saucepan. Pound with a potato masher. Stir in vinegar, water, and sugar. Bring to a rapid boil over high heat and boil until sugar is dissolved. Strain out spearmint and add food coloring. Remove from stove and add pectin, cool, and pour into sterilized jars. Seal and store until time to serve your next roast of lamb.

Makes about 2 pints.

CHAPTER XIV

～～

Mystic Meals and Menus

THE larger part of the motivation behind the settlement of the New World was trade. The Pilgrim settlement of New England, however, was based on religious dissent; if they had found better soil and a gentler climate they might very easily have settled down to the pursuit of their religious freedom. As it was, they landed during a long and arduous winter, and when spring finally came they found rocks, undergrown forests and more rocks. They missed the open green countryside of England, the rolling meadows and orderly woods. Worst of all, the forests were sparsely populated by unpredictable Indians. They had visualized a new England and found themselves in a totally new world.

The Pilgrims had enormous courage, determination and fortitude. They had needed all of it to embark on the *Mayflower* to begin with, but they needed more. They had to survive, and survival meant intelligent, clear thinking and a shrewd appraisal of what their "Puritan Asylum" could be made to produce for them. Clearly they could subsist if they hugged the shore, but bare subsistence wasn't enough. To build and to prosper they had to turn to trade. New England had little to offer for cash that old England wanted.

The ingenuity and skill with which the settlers and their descendants built a flourishing maritime trade is history. The Marine Historical Association has given us tangible proof of that past and has preserved for us at Mystic a picture of the industrious, courageous and heroic people who earned the respect of the entire world.

With the building of ships and the growth of trade and whaling, New Englanders—and certainly Mysticians—were often in possession of treasures that Europeans could only acquire over medieval trade routes. Many a New England housewife hoarded a precious jar or two of ginger, had rum to flavor her apple pudding and possessed a dried vanilla bean, while many Europeans were unable to obtain them.

Cooking in and near the seaports began to achieve special favors and flavors. Mystic pies could be crimped with scrimshaw jaggers, they could contain tropical fruits and spices, and could be served with heavy farm cream. Fresh native berries found their way into breads and puddings, while fresh fish from the sea combined with fresh milk to make chowders.

A Mystic wife didn't wake up to wonder what she would cook for dinner; she awakened to say, "Today is fish day," or "Today is Monday so it must be hash day." If there was corned beef for dinner on Sunday there was inevitably corned-beef hash on Monday. Not only did she have the comfort of knowing what she was going to cook but she had a pretty good idea that everyone else in town would cook just about the same thing. On wash day, which meant no time to cook and no room on the stove, where wash boilers and irons were heating, dinner had to come out of the oven and there was always a baked pudding or beans. Then there was baking day, when the oven was used for baking bread and pies and dinner had to simmer on top of the stove. The griddle or the

deep-fat fryer were placed on the stove; everything else came out of a kettle, a skillet, a saucepan, or a roasting pan. There were no racks, but old roast-beef bones were laid across the pan to support the roast, and marbles or round washed pebbles went into the kettle to keep simmering food from burning. Washed cherry pits weighed down the empty pie pastry during baking.

Many of the old recipes for individual dishes were much as we know them today, but the rotation and meal arrangements were different. Breakfasts were hearty; it took a full day's hard labor to work them off. For a typical breakfast there was lots of hot colored water (water steeped with enough tea or coffee to turn it a pale tan), lovely hot breads simply saturated with fresh, creamy butter, followed by fried salt pork, bacon or ham, and salt beef. The breakfast ended with a nice hot pie and a heartening wedge of cheese. Nothing measures up to the fortifying qualities of hot pie and cheese early in the day.

Some modern people like hearty breakfasts, too, particularly if they are setting off on a long journey or embarking on a day of sailing, skiing, or some other physically demanding sport. For them we suggested these adaptations, with recipes for most of the dishes found in the various sections of the book:

Begin with stewed prunes, then serve Broiled Shad Roe with Bacon, Oatmeal Bread toast, and coffee or tea. Or try fresh apple slices before Baked Finnan Haddie with Griddle Scones, and end with American Apple Pie with hot beverage. Perhaps cranberry juice and Red Flannel Hash with Miniature Blueberry Muffins topped off with Green-Tomato Pie and coffee will please the teenagers and sports-bound father.

Lighter breakfasts, but still hearty enough for most people might feature vegetable juice, Blueberry Griddle Cakes with butter and syrup, adding Homemade Pork Sausage Meat for good measure. Or orange juice, Burnt-Sugar Pancakes, with tea and coffee. Sliced oranges or a half grapefruit, followed by Corn Flapjacks and Block Island Blackberry Jam with tea or coffee will make a visitor's weekend breakfast memorable.

The traditional New England dinner of present-day fame originated in tidewater settlements and whaling ports such as Mystic. It is still a happy combination of Indian and English cookery, admixed with the inventive genius of all the housewives and augmented by the treasures brought out of the sea, or over it.

There has been actually no major change in 350 years, only a natural development as new imports were added to the larder. Every dinner included something from the sea. Mystic wouldn't be Mystic without it. Start dinner with a chowder or stuff the turkey with oysters. Include cranberries in the bread or the stuffing, in jelly, relish, or as an appetizer juice. There should be corn and there must be apples, even if they only appear as fritters or hidden in the mincemeat. New England potatoes were white but when ships touched at southern ports, suddenly the sweet potato was added. Typically it was added, not substituted, for dinners included both white and sweet potatoes. No present-day dinner would be complete without a touch of maple sugar or syrup either for dessert or ham glaze, or on "stickies" (which are stickier in Mystic than anywhere else).

Given all these natural elements there is an almost indefinite number of combinations that can be made—

For example, these modern adaptations of Mystic menus:

Start off with a glass of spiced cranberry juice or lentil soup; serve a tangy mint jelly with a roast leg of lamb, fresh vegetables or roasted potatoes; and top off the dinner with a hot baked Indian pudding with soft ice cream on it. If a shore dinner pleases your palate, begin with steamed clams, followed by a clam juice with crackers, a broiled or boiled lobster with melted butter, a green salad and a blueberry pie with coffee to finish.

Sunday Supper

When Mystic men sailed the seas, they came home to their usual baked beans, but something from their voyages to the Orient or perhaps to Norway crept into the menus, before and after the beans. Today, after a day of sailing or an afternoon of physical activity of another sort, try one of these adapatations of the Mystic Sunday supper:

Chicken Curry Soup, then baked beans with Corn Bread and butter, honey and jam, and a hearty Apple Pie with Crumble Topping. Or try a Winter Soup with Pumpkin Bread, assorted relishes and finish with Vanilla Custard. Mystic Lobster Chowder with refrigerator rolls and relishes, followed by Baked Cranberry Pudding will make an elegant Sunday supper. Perhaps you will want to try making your own menus from these or other recipes in this book.

Mystic Sunday Dinner

There is a special kind of appetite which develops once a week, early in the afternoon on Sundays. It is probably the result of generations of good Mystic Sunday dinners to which the system has become accustomed. From Monday through Saturday a bowl of soup, a sandwich or a salad will do, but on Sunday there is a distinct craving for a roast with all the trimmings. The craving is subject to seasonal changes and fashions. Once it had to be roast chicken or capon and nothing else would do. There has also been a standing-rib-roast-of-beef era, and a roast-leg-of-lamb era, but the really good old-fashioned appetite still longs for roast capon, cranberry sauce, two vegetables, roast potatoes and all the before and after accompaniments.

Sunday dinner should come between church and the Sunday nap, and its preparation should be worked down to such a fine art that it need not absorb the entire morning.

ℰ✗ The Church Supper

Richardson Wright wrote in his introduction to *Stonington Cooks and Cookery*, "They [church suppers] served as competitions of individual culinary skills. The good sound eating of New England was advanced when chowder was pitted against chowder and pie against pie, the congregation assembled as a gustatory jury. Many a housewife's reputation was established and many others went home to try harder. What came out of all this was the perfection of plain and fancy New England cooking."

Church suppers, as Mystic and Stonington knew them, were not mild and devout affairs to gather the congregation together. They were actually the only large social gatherings the smaller settlements knew, and everyone participated with the utmost pleasure. Among the ladies there was a good deal of testing, perfecting and rivalry. Among the men there was considerable imbibation of imported rum and Madeira wine, as well as good homemade hard cider, all this mixed with a tactful taste of each housewife's contribution. Where young romance was concerned, great headway could be made by the suitor who ate all of his true love's biscuits or the one who overlooked a sodden pie crust.

When a wave of temperance hit the church supper, gentlemen were able to judge more fairly and ladies outdid themselves with ever shorter pie crusts and lighter biscuits.

ℰ✗ Church Supper Specialties

Some of the church supper specialties, for which recipes will be found in the appropriate sections are: Corn Chowder, hot or cold, Mystic Baked Beans, Steamed Boston Brown Bread, Chicken pie with Cheese Crust, Honey-glazed Baked Ham, Macaroni Pudding, Chicken Salad, Grandfather's Potato Salad, Cucumbers in Sour Cream, Open Peach Tart, Grandmother's Fruit Cake, Gingerbread, Ann Greenman's Leopard Cake, and Vanilla Sugar Horns.

The church supper recipes need not be limited to the church; they will make show-pieces for any cook to add to her repertoire.

A GLOSSARY OF
MYSTIFYING TERMS
≈

The cooking ladies of Mystic and New England spoke a cookery language all their own. Lots of it is still in use but some of it might just as well be clarified. There were such mystifying expressions as slumps, cobblers as against deep-dish pies, crumbles, brambles, bishops, johnny-cake, hoecake, flesh viands, and many more.

BISHOP: A warm spiced wine-and-fruit beverage.

BLOATED: Steeped in a marinade; marinated.

BRAMBLE: A large pielike pastry, not baked in a pie pan; served sliced.

CAULED: Heated to just under boiling point.

COBBLER: A deep-dish fruit pie with a heavy crumb or biscuit crust.

CRUMBLE: A crumbly cake or sugar-topped fruit dessert.

CRUNCH: A fruit dessert which, when turned out, is supposed to have a crunchy crust; or a cake with a baked-on crunchy crust.

CYDER: Cider of apples, old spelling.

DEEP-DISH PIE: Similar to a cobbler with a regular pie-crust top.

DRACHM: 60 grains or $\frac{1}{8}$ ounce, a dram.

FLESH: Old definition of meat of animals as well as fish.

GROG: A heated alcoholic beverage usually served in a handled mug. Rum is the usual ingredient on ships.

HOECAKE: Ashcake. A cornmeal pone originally baked on a hoe or shingle before the fire or in the ashes (usually while houses were being built).

INDIAN MEAL: Ground corn or cornmeal, sometimes coarsely ground.

INDIAN PUDDING: Cornmeal pudding.

JOHNNYCAKE: A fried cornmeal Indian cake which has other spellings and names: johnycake, journeycake, Shawnee cake, and many others. There is just as much disagreement about the recipe as the name.

JULEP: A tall frosted drink of bourbon whiskey poured over crushed ice, sugar and mint leaves. Decorated with a sprig of mint.

JUMBLE: Usually a drop cookie with a rough surface; also a mixture.

N.B. *Nota bene*, that Latin admonition to "Note Well." It is unfortunately no longer used in cookery books.

NOG (or NOGG): A beverage usually served on New Years Day. A mixture of milk and beaten eggs and usually some sort of liquor, sometimes sweetened.

PERRY: Fermented juice of pears, similar to cider, light in alcohol.

POSSETT (or POSSET): Sweetened and spiced beverage made of hot milk curdled with ale or wine.

PROVED: Tested.

PUNCH: An alcoholic or non-alcholic beverage. Wine and water flavored with lemon or spices; can be made of sweetened tea, fruit juices or carbonated waters. Liquors are also employed for certain kinds of punches.

RULE: Recipe.

SMALLAGE: An herb similar to parsley.

TRY, or TRY OUT: To render fat, producing lard or other fat for cooking.

VIANDS: Not meat at all but an article of any food or a special delicacy.

INDEX

~~~

Index to Contributors and
Sources of Information

~~~